Computer System, Organization and Architecture

Computer System, Organization and Architecture

Rajeev Ranjan

CENTRUM PRESS
NEW DELHI-110002 (INDIA)

CENTRUM PRESS
H.O.: 4360/4, Ansari Road, Daryaganj,
New Delhi-110002 (India)
Tel: 23278000, 23261597, 23255577, 23286875

B.O.: No. 1015, Ist Main Road, BSK IIIrd Stage,
IIIrd Phase, IIIrd Block, Bangalore-560085 (INDIA)
Tel: 080-41723429

Email: centrumpress@gmail.com
Visit us at: www.centrumpress.com

Computer System, Organization and Architecture

First Edition, 2011

PRINTED IN INDIA

Printed at Tarun Offset Printers, Delhi-110053

Contents

Preface *vii*

1. Introduction 1

2. Hardware and Software 23

3. Computer Networks 61

4. Central Processing Unit 120

5. Control Unit 169

6. Computer Memory 254

Bibliography 268
Index 270

Preface

Computer architecture or digital computer organization is the conceptual design and fundamental operational structure of a computer system. It's a blueprint and functional description of requirements and design implementations for the various parts of a computer, focusing largely on the way by which the central processing unit (CPU) performs internally and accesses The basic operational design of a computer system is called its architecture. John Von Neumann, a pioneer in computer design, is given credit for the architecture of most computers in use today. The 80 × 86 family uses the Von Neumann Architecture (VNA). A typical Von Neumann System has three major components: the central processing unit (or CPU), memory, and input/output (or I/O).

This book provides up-to-date coverage of fundamental concepts for the design of computers and their subsystems. It presents material with a serious but easy-to-understand writing style that makes it accessible to readers without sacrificing important topics. It is designed to teach computer organization/architecture to engineers and computer scientists.

Author

Preface

1

Introduction

HARDWARE AND SOFTWARE

SOFTWARE

System software is responsible for controlling, integrating, and managing the individual hardware components of a computer system so that other software and the users of the system see it as a functional unit without having to be concerned with the low-level details such as transferring data from memory to disk, or rendering text onto a display.

Generally, system software consists of an operating system and some fundamental utilities such as disk formatters, file managers, display managers, text editors, user authentication (login) and management tools, and networking and device control software. Application software, on the other hand, is used to accomplish specific tasks other than just running the computer system.

Application software may consist of a single programme, such as an image viewer; a small collection of programme (often called a software package) that work closely together to accomplish a task, such as a spreadsheet or text processing system; a larger collection (often called a software suite) of related but independent programmes and packages that have a common user interface or shared data format, such as Microsoft Office, which consists of closely integrated word processor, spreadsheet, database, etc.; or a software system, such as a database management system, which is a collection of fundamental programmes that may provide some service to a variety of other independent applications.

Software is created with programming languages and related utilities, which may come in several of the above forms: single programmes like script interpreters, packages containing a compiler, linker, and other tools; and large suites (often called Integrated Development Environments) that include editors, debuggers, and other tools for multiple languages.

Technique

There is one last technique in the arsenal of the software optimizer that may be used to make most machines run at tip top speed. It can also lead to severe code bloat and may make for almost unreadable code, so should be considered the last refuge of the truly desperate. However, it's performance characteristics are in many cases unmatched by any other approach, so we cover it here. It is called software pipelining, or sometimes loop staggering or loop inversion, because the inner loop does the operation in backwards order from the starting algorithm. It can be applied in varying amounts, resulting in varying levels of code bloat.

Software Modelling

Software pipelining at its core seeks to model a calculation as if it was actually implemented in hardware as a single instruction with a multistage pipeline. Well some of the same factors that make this technique useful in hardware also lead to high performance in software. In particular, it leads to a high degree of parallelism, which works well with modern superscalar cores. In addition, in implementation it usually does a good job of hiding latencies for any particular step in the process.

When done properly, an algorithm can be made to perform as if each of the instructions that make it up has a single cycle latency. You will likely be able to take advantage of maximum dispatch bandwidth available most cycles, so multiple things can be done concurrently.

Even more fun, you can do multiple steps concurrently even if one step normally would depend on the result of the step before it before it can start. We will take as our working example the conversion of 16 bit integers to floating point values. On PowerPC, there is no direct conversion for ints to floats in hardware. Everything is done in software.

We will use virtual cycle 6 as an example (red) to see what happens once we get to the point when the pipeline is full of data. Notice that in this virtual CPU cycle, we have to do 6 different things. The six things are essentially our starting algorithm, except executed in reverse order. None of the data used by any of these instructions relies on the results from the other instructions in that row, so they can all be done in parallel, subject to the limitations of the parallelism of the machine.

Happily, they use a lot of different execution units, so we may imagine that many of them are in fact executed in parallel – the PowerPC can dispatch and retire two or three instructions per cycle. For example, we might imagine that both the stfs and fsub (underlined) can enter execution in the same cycle because one is performed by the LSU and the other by the FPU. In addition, though there is a ton of code here, register pressure is actually quite light because the registers are tied to the pipeline stages.

When the virtual pipeline is full of data, every virtual CPU cycle uses every register that we declare. So we don't have any data sitting stagnant in registers waiting for the right part of the loop to roll around. Code like this is highly likely to saturate the capacity of the CPU for getting work done. This is promising!

COMPUTER HARDWARE

Main Components of Computer System:

- *Motherboard*: A motherboard is the central or primary circuit board making up a computer system or other complex electronic system
- *Storage*: The terms storage or memory refer to those parts of a computer that retain data for some period of time, possibly even after the computer is turned off

- *Input/output devices:* Or I/O, refers to the interfaces that different functional units of a system use to communicate among each other, or to the signals sent through those interfaces

Hardware is a comprehensive term for all of the physical parts of a computer, as distinguished from the data it contains or operates on, and the software that provides instructions for the hardware to accomplish tasks. The boundary between hardware and software is slightly blurry-firmware is software that is "built-in" to the hardware, but such firmware is usually the province of computer programmers and computer engineers in any case and not an issue that computer users need to concern themselves with.

A typical computer (Personal Computer, PC) contains in a desktop or tower case the following parts:

- Motherboard which holds the CPU, main memory and other parts, and has slots for expansion cards
- Power supply-a case that holds a transformer, voltage control and fan
- Storage controllers, of IDE, SCSI or other type, that control hard disk, floppy disk, CD-ROM and other drives; the controllers sit directly on the motherboard (on-board) or on expansion cards
- Graphics controller that produces the output for the monitor
- The hard disk, floppy disk and other drives for mass storage
- Interface controllers (parallel, serial, USB, Firewire) to connect the computer to external peripheral devices such as printers or scanners

COMPUTER TYPES

A computer is one of the most brilliant inventions of mankind. Thanks to the computer technology, we were able to achieve an efficient storage and processing of data; we could rest our brains by employing computer memory capacities for storage of the information. Owing to computers, we have been able speed up daily work, carry out critical transactions and achieve accuracy and precision in work output. The computers of the earlier years were of the size of a large room and were required to consume huge amounts of electric power. However, with the advancing technology, computers have shrunk to the size of a small watch.

Depending on the processing powers and sizes of computers, they have been classified under various types. Let us look at the classification of computers. Based on the operational principle of computers, they are categorized as analog computers and hybrid computers.

ANALOG COMPUTERS

These are almost extinct today. These are different from a digital computer because an analog computer can perform several mathematical operations simultaneously. It uses continuous variables for mathematical operations and utilizes mechanical or electrical energy.

HYBRID COMPUTERS

These computers are a combination of both digital and analog computers. In this type of computers, the digital segments perform process control by conversion of analog signals to digital ones.

MAINFRAME COMPUTERS

Large organizations use mainframes for highly critical applications such as bulk data processing and ERP. Most of the mainframe computers have the capacities to host multiple operating systems and operate as a number of virtual machines and can thus substitute for several small servers.

MICROCOMPUTERS

A computer with a microprocessor and its central processing unit is known as a microcomputer. They do not occupy space as much as mainframes. When supplemented with a keyboard and a mouse, microcomputers can be called as personal computers. A monitor, a keyboard and other similar input output devices, computer memory in the form of RAM and a power supply unit come packaged in a microcomputer. These computers can fit on desks or tables and serve as the best choices for single-user tasks. Personal computers come in a variety of forms such as desktops, laptops and personal digital assistants. Let us look at each of these types of computers.

DESKTOPS

A desktop is intended to be used on a single location. The spare parts of a desktop computer are readily available at relative lower costs. Power consumption is not as critical as that in laptops. Desktops are widely popular for daily use in workplaces and households.

LAPTOPS

Similar in operation to desktops, laptop computers are miniaturized and optimized for mobile use. Laptops run on a single battery or an external adapter that charges the computer batteries. They are enabled with an inbuilt keyboard, touch pad acting as a mouse and a liquid crystal display. Its portability and capacity to operate on battery power have served as a boon for mobile users.

PERSONAL DIGITAL ASSISTANTS (PDAS)

It is a handheld computer and popularly known as a palmtop. It has a touch screen and a memory card for storage of data. PDAs can also be effectively used as portable audio players, web browsers and smart phones. Most of them can access the Internet by means of Bluetooth or Wi-Fi communication.

MINICOMPUTERS

In terms of size and processing capacity, minicomputers lie in between mainframes and microcomputers. Minicomputers are also called mid-range systems or workstations. The term began to be popularly used in the 1960s to refer to relatively smaller third generation computers. They took up the space that would be needed for a refrigerator or two and used transistor and core memory technologies. The 12-bit PDP-8 minicomputer of the Digital Equipment Corporation was the first successful minicomputer.

SUPERCOMPUTERS

The highly calculation-intensive tasks can be effectively performed by means of supercomputers. Quantum physics, mechanics, weather forecasting, molecular theory are best studied by means of supercomputers. Their ability of parallel processing and their well-designed memory hierarchy give the supercomputers, large transaction processing powers.

WEARABLE COMPUTERS

A record-setting step in the evolution of computers was the creation of wearable computers. These computers can be worn on the body and are often used in the study of behaviour modeling and human health. Military and health professionals have incorporated wearable computers into their daily routine, as a part of such studies.

When the users' hands and sensory organs are engaged in other activities, wearable computers are of great help in tracking human actions. Wearable computers are consistently in operation as they do not have to be turned on and off and are constantly interacting with the user.

These were some of the different types of computers available today. Looking at the rate of the advancement in technology, we can definitely look forward to many more types of computers in the near future.

PARTS OF COMPUTER

INTRODUCTION

Look inside any computer and you will see items of hardware. There is the motherboard, processors, disks drives, power supply and the memory chips. Many of these items are interchangeable which mean that the computer can be easily upgraded with additional items of hardware, which just plug into the main system.

DESCRIPTION

Opening the computer exposes both it and you to a myriad of hazards. From nasty cuts from very sharp edges on the sheet metal and circuit cards, to potentially lethal high voltage inside the power supply and its power switch, there are numerous ways to hurt or kill yourself. Over 300 volts can be found inside the power supply of most computers. Most colour monitors have areas of over 20,000 volts inside, *even when they are turned off* and unplugged. Other computer peripherals such as printers, scanners, etc. can also have hazardous areas inside them.

Even with all the dangers to you, it is far more likely you will hurt the computer, than it will hurt you. Improperly handling or installing a card in the computer can cause damage to it or other components. Misalignment of a card in its socket can cause the card or motherboard, or both, to expire the instant power is applied.

Simply mishandling an internal component can cause problems. Fingerprints on connectors can cause intermittent trouble, simply touching certain cards, after walking across the floor can transfer enough static electricity to ruin or prematurely age the component. Static electricity, even so low that you can't feel it, can wreck havoc with today's large-scale microelectronics.

All computer boards should be left in their anti-static bags until just before you install them in the computer. You should insure your body is connected to a good ground through a Megohm resistance. Use a professional wrist type grounding-strap, not a homemade device. *Improper grounding of you could cause a lethal shock hazard.*

In 20 years plus, in the computer business I have seen thousands of computer problems created by the improper handling and installation of circuit boards, hard drives, CD-ROMs, modems, and other devices. Many *computer professionals* don't even fully understand the proper care and handling of the parts inside a computer, and by their ignorance, mishandle a part that should run for over ten years and reduce its life span to less than one year.

Inside the computer,It may look like a complicated mess of wires, and chips, but really it's quite simple.

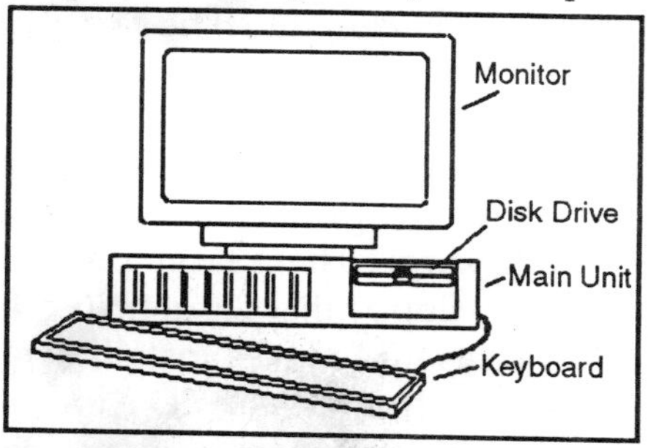

COMPUTER HARDWARE PARTS

Disks Drives

Disk drives provide a means of storing work, or data. *Floppy disks* are transportable from PC to PC and come in two sizes, 31/2"and 51/4"diameter. Floppy disks provide a means of storing work. You can *write* information onto the disk and *read* information from the disk. Floppy disks are used by inserting them into a disk drive.

A light on the disk drive indicates when the disk is being accessed. Removing or inserting a disk while the drive light is illuminated may cause damage to the disk and is likely to result in the loss of data stored on the disk.

Hard Disks

Hard disks (or fixed disks) work on the same principle as

floppy disks but are fixed inside the PC in a sealed unit. They can store a great deal more information than floppy disks and range in capacity from 10Mb to several hundred Mb. Access times (*i.e.* the time taken to read and write information) for hard disks are much faster than for floppy disks. Manufacturers often quote access times as well as capacities for hard disks. Information is stored on disk in the form of *files*. A file might be a programme or data such as a word processor document. Files can be grouped together on disk in *directories*. Hard disks are contained in an air-sealed unit and are thus less liable to physical problems than floppies. However the consequences of any disk failure are much higher than for floppies so some form of backup must be carried out regularly.

CD ROM Drives

Today, many software programmes come n CD instead of floppy dosks. The programmes for newer software applications are quite karge. These large programmes, which may take as many as 20 floppy disks, can fit just fine on a single CD, which reduces costs and makes installation much easier.

To distinguish them from music CD's the computer CD's are called CD-ROMS. This stands for Compact Disk-Read Only Memory.That is, a consumer is unable to erase or record information or programmes onto a CD. If you want to advantage of recording, deleting and re-recording, then you use a a rewritable disk,(CR-RW).

Ports and Expansion Slots

Located at the rear of the PC are various sockets or ports. These allow the keyboard and monitor to be connected. Most PCs include a *parallel* port (usually used for printers) and two *serial* ports (usually used for communications with other computer systems or connecting mice and plotters).

Also included inside the system box are *expansion slots*. These allow extra hardware to be added to the PC using printed circuit boards, or *cards*, plugged into the expansion slots. The slots are connected to the CPU via the *bus*. The bus is a set of wires which transfers data. Think of it as a freeway.

Motherboards

If the CPU is the brain of the computer, the motherboard and its components are the major systems this brain uses to control the rest of the computer. It is possibly the most important part of the computer. Having a good understanding of how the motherboard and its contained subsystems work is probably the most critical part of getting a good understanding of how PCs work. Here you can see the connection from the power supply to the motherboard. The power supply serves two functions. First of all it draws power from the outlet (usually 120V AC) and translates it into voltages the computer can use (usually 12V DC). It also runs the main cooling fan which prevents the computer from overheating which can be detrimental to the integrity of your data.

The motherboard is the foundation of any PC. All the critical subsystems, including the CPU, the system chipset, the memory, the system I/O, the expansion bus, and other critical components run directly off the motherboard. Likewise, the interconnections among these components are built into the motherboard itself. It manages all transactions of data between the CPU and the peripherals. It houses the CPU and its second level cache, the chipset, the BIOS, the main memory, the I/O chips, the port for the keyboard, the serial I/O, the parallel I/O, the disks, and the plug-in cards.

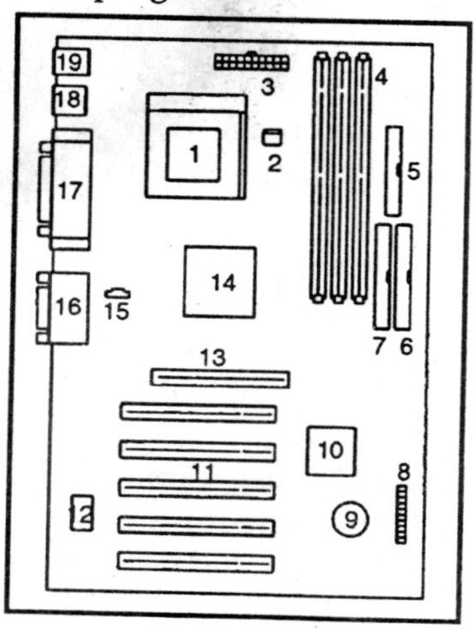

Components of a Motherboard

- CPU Socket (for processor)
- CPU fan connector
- ATX power supply connector (for plug from power supply in computer case)
- Memory Slots (for memory modules-new mainboards use DDR modules, previous generation uses SDRAM modules)
- Floppy Drive Connector (for data cable to floppy drive)
- Primary IDE Connector (data cable for hard drive, cd-drive-up to two devices)
- Secondary IDE Connector (data cable for hard drive, cd-drive-up to two devices)
- Panel for connecting power switch, reset switch, hard drive light, etc.
- CMOS Battery (keeps current BIOS Setup information intact)
- Chipset (controls specific functions)
- PCI Slots (for plugin cards such as modems, network cards, pci video cards, sound cards, etc.)
- BIOS chip
- AGP Slot (for Accelerated Graphics Port video card, today's standard)
- Chipset (controls specific functions)
- Connector for CDROM audio cable (for sound already built onto main board)
- On-board Audio Jacks (line in, line out, microphone jacks)
- Parallel Port and Serial Ports (parallel printer port plus one or two serial ports which are hidden from view)
- USB Ports (new mainboards use USB 2.0, older use USB 1.1)
- Keyboard and Mouse Connectors (PS2 connectors, one for keyboard, one for mouse)

Many mainstream PC's today, especially lower priced ones, have the AGP Video controller, the Audio controller,

Modem and NIC (Network Interface Card) built onto the mainboard rather than on separate plug-in cards. On-board video uses a portion of the memory provided by the plug-in memory modules which is typically reserved for the rest of the system.

This type of video does not perform well when used for high-end graphics such as games. It is possible that, even though the video chip is built on board, the manufacturer may have supplied an AGP slot so you can install your own Video card. Today's video cards contain at least 32mb of their own memory, and may go up to as high as 256mb. The on-board video would first need to be disabled in the BIOS/CMOS setup routine before installing the card. If the modem, sound, or network interface fail, or you want to upgrade them, they can usually be disabled in the BIOS settings also, allowing for installation of a plug-in replacement card.

Connections

Ports

- *Parallel*: This port is commonly used to connect a printer.
- *Serial*: This port is typically used to connect an external modem.
- *Universal Serial Bus (USB)*: Quickly becoming the most popular external connection, USB ports offer power and versatility and are incredibly easy to use.
- *Firewire (IEEE 1394)*: FireWire is a very popular method of connecting digital-video devices, such as camcorders or digital recorders, to your computer.

Internet/Network

- *Modem:* This is the standard method of connecting to the Internet..
- *Local Area Network LAN Card*: This is used by many computers, particularly those in an Ethernet office network, to connected to each other.
- *Cable Modem:* Some people now use the cable-

television system in their home to connect to the Internet.

- Digital Subscriber Line DSL Modem. This is a high-speed connection that works over a standard telephone line.
- *Very high bit rate DSL (VDSL)*: A newer variation of DSL, VDSL requires that your phone line have fibre optic cables.

The Main Unit

The main unit contains the Central Processing Unit (CPU) and various supporting Integrated Circuits (or *chips*) all of which are fixed to a printed circuit board (PCB) called the *motherboard*. The main unit also houses disk drives, expansion slots and the power supply.

The CPU

The CPU (Central Processing Unit) or processor is the 'brain' of any computer system. In the PC it is contained on a single Integrated Circuit or 'chip'. The CPU processes all instructions and data. The CPU is driven by an internal clock. Simply speaking, every time the clock pulses the CPU processes one instruction. Thus, the faster the clock the quicker the CPU processes its instructions. Clock speed is measured in MegaHertz (MHz). All the real computing work is done by the CPU.

Memory

All PCs are fitted with a certain amount of workspace memory called *Random Access Memory* (RAM). This memory is used for storing running software and data which the software requires, as well as the*operating system*. The contents of RAM are lost when the PC is switched off. This in known as volitile because it is tempory in nature.For example, if you are running word processing software then the software and the document you are working on are stored in RAM. To save the document, after making any changes you wish to keep, it is necessary to copy the document from RAM onto *disk*.

RAM

Chips can be individually installed directly on th motherboard or in the banks of several chips on a small board that plugs into the motherboard.The most common types of boards that hold memory chips are called SIMMS (single inline memory modules), DIMMS (duel inline memory modules), andRIMMS (memory modules manufctured by Rambus, Inc.)

By contrast, another kind of memory holds its data permanently, even when the power is turned off. This type of memory is called non-volitile and is called ROM (read only memory).

ROM (Read-only Memory)

They contains the commands the computer needs to activate itself. Instructions in ROM let the computer start when the power is turned on, and, unlike RAM, its contents are retained even when the power is off. A Sound Card is an expansion card that lets a computer produce sound. Examples of practical uses for sound capabilities include games, music applications, and interactive educational software.

The Expansion Card is a circuit board that slides into an expansion slot. It is used to add peripherals, such as a sound card or modem, to the PC. An Expansion Slot is an opening on the motherboard into which a board or card can be inserting, expanding the capability of the computer. The Power Supply is the vehicle through which electricity is regulated and sent to the various components of a computer.

BIOS or CMOS setup

The motherboard contains a special chip called the BIOS, which is short for Basic Input/Output System. Burnt onto this chip are software instructions on how to load basic computer hardware. Many PCs have what is called a flash BIOS, allowing the user to update the BIOS if necessary. The BIOS also includes a sort of diagnostic routine known as the POST (Power On Self Test). This test ensures that the computer meets the necessary requirements to boot up correctly. If the computer doesn't pass the POST you will hear a pattern of beeps that indicate the problem encountered. CMOS (Complementary Metal Oxide Semiconductor) is a chip on the motherboard which stores system information and computer settings such as date, time, hard drive settings, boot sequence, parallel port settings, on-board audio and video, etc. This information can be accessed and changed through the BIOS/ CMOS setup programme which is available as the computer begins to boot up. As the computer boots, there will typically be some text on the screen such as "Press Del to enter Setup". Depending on the manufacturer, the key required to enter the BIOS setup may be F1, F2, Del, or Esc.

Unlike earlier generations of PC's, the user is no longer required to go into the BIOS Setup and enter new information such as the number of cylinders, heads, sectors, etc. when changing IDE hard drives, for instance. These and some other settings are now detected automatically. If the CMOS battery dies, any changes made in the the BIOS Setup will be lost. After replacing the battery, the user will need to re-enter the Setup programme and make the changes again.

Driver

After the computer boots up, the operating system begins the process of loading into memory. Unlike the information burnt into the BIOS and CMOS chips, Windows must detect the hardware and load device specific files into memory that allow the operating system to understand and communicate with the hardware devices. As part of the Windows operating system, Microsoft includes a great many device drivers (for the more popular devices and peripherals). These load automatically as the hardware is detected. However, you may have a particular modem or sound card that isn't included in Windows database. While the operating system may detect the device's presence, it can't assign a driver file to it, since their isn't one in it's database. This is where you come in.

You will need to locate the correct driver for the version of Windows you are using. If you have a disk that came with the device you'll need to use it to install the driver, provided it was created for your version of Windows. A driver written for Windows '98 won't work with XP, so you'll have to get on the internet and find a current one. A good site to look for the driver is DriverGuide.com, but you'll need to know something about the device such as the manufacturer, model number, etc. to get the proper driver.

COMPUTER PERFORMANCE

IMPROVING COMPUTER PERFORMANCE

Many computer problems can be solved with free or low-cost products or just by using a few common sense tips to improve performance and keep your PC running for a long time. Computers often freeze or crash when one needs them the most; in the middle of an important presentation, a term paper that's due the next day, or while updating our financial software. Many computer problems can be solved with free or low-cost products or just by using a few common sense tips to improve performance and keep your PC running for a long time.

- *Virus Scan Programme*: The most essential thing to have is a virus scan that is run weekly. Most new computers come with a virus scan already installed. If the computer you are using doesn't have a virus scan there are free scans available online, but one really should be installed on your computer if you spend any time at all online. Spend the time learning how to use your virus scanner. Find out how it's updated-most update automatically-and use the options to set it up to run automatically at a set time every week. Most computer problems can be prevented just by having a virus scanner installed.
- *Run the Scandisk programme*: At least every two months you should run a programme called Scandisk. It is automatically on your computer. Scandisk actually scans your files and even your hard drive and can let you know of any problems it discovers.

To run Scandisk, first make sure everything running in the background on your PC is turned off. To do this press

"Ctrl-Alt-Delete" and your close programme box will appear. Highlight each item EXCEPT "explorer" and "systray". Click on "End Task" to close the programme. Then go to your start button and choose "Programmes". Choose "Accessories" at the top of the list. Move your cursor down to "SystemTools" and Choose "Scandisk". A box will appear giving your choices of what you want your computer to scan. You can have it scan your files only or your entire hard drive. Scanning your hard drive will take longer.

- *Run the Defragmenter programme*: Another programme that you should run about every two months is called Disk Defragmenter. Defrag will arrange your files better so your PC can access them faster. It's best to run this programme after the Scandisk programme is finished.

To run Disk Defragmenter go back to the "System Tools" and choose "Disk Defragmenter". It's best to run this programme overnight as it takes a long time. You should not be using these programmes while using other programmes on your computer. If the Scandisk or Defrag programme keeps starting over you may need to run the programmes in Safe Mode, a special diagnostic mode. Read the manual for your PC to find out how to put your PC into Safe Mode.

- *Use a Firewall programme*: For anyone on a DSL or cable connection a personal firewall keeps viruses, hijackers and hackers from your computer. Since you are constantly connected to the internet by using these connections there is a constant threat that others may try to access your computer. There are free firewall programmes available for download.
- *Run a Spyware programme*: Anyother important rogramme is a spyware search programme. When you download something from the internet sometimes other software is included. This software is called "spyware" and it can do many things to harm your computer, including letting someone from another website see what websites you surf in order to send you advertising. Other spyware tries to steal

your passwords or other personal information. You should run a spyware checker at least once a month or at any time you are experiencing problems with your connection or computer speed.

- *Run a hi-jacker search programme*: Another important programme to have is a hi-jacker search programme. A hi-jacker changes your homepage to a different search engine page and can also block links to common search pages. They are trying to force you to use their homepage. Some of the hi-jacker's homepages are not pages you would like your children to see. You should use a hi-jacker search programme at least once a month or whenever you are having a problem with your homepage.
- *Clear your temporary files*: Sometimes your PC's virtual memory will become full. When this happens your computer may run slow, give you error messages or freeze during a programme. This happens because everything you do on your PC-every picture on every webpage, every document you type, every photo you change-is saved somewhere on your PC, even after you have left that page and closed the document. In order to erase this memory you need to do the following steps:
  - Open your internet browser. Go to "Tools", "Internet Options".
  - A box will pop open. It should be open to the "General" tab.
  - In the centre of the box is a section marked "Temporary Internet Files".
  - Click on "Delete Cookies" and "Delete Files" one at a time. This will delete the temporary files that are clogging the PC's memory.
- *Change your history options*: Another way to clean out your computer's memory is to change how many days it saves visited pages. You will find a "history" box in your internet options. It asks how many days you wish to keep pages in history. This is the part of

the computer that saves all pages you've visited for as many days as you wish. By saving these pages for a smaller number of days you can clear up more of your PC's memory.

- *Clean out old files*: Periodically going through the files in My Documents or other folders you have set up and deleting or archiving them on a CD can also help your computer's memory and performance. Do you really need to keep a saved copy of last semester's English term paper? If not, delete it. You can also go through the programmes on your PC from the control panel and delete those you no longer use. Don't delete any of the shared files, though, if it asks, because that can cause more problems.
- *Reboot the PC occasionally*: The last thing that is very important to do but seems simple is just to turn your computer off periodically. Your PC needs to be restarted in order to reset itself after new programmes or equipment is installed. It also erases the virtual memory from the last session and goes through a self-diagnostic to look for any problems. It sounds like a simple solution, but most problems can be fixed simply by restarting your PC.

COMPUTER'S PERFORMANCE

Get Organized

It's likely that more time is wasted in business trying to hunt down a file or e-mail than anything else. There are several reasons for this, and each has a simple fix. First is poor folder structure. If you can't make out your wallpaper image because you have so many files on your desktop, you've got a problem. It's time to put those files in their proper folders.

Think about how you would organize these files if they were paper. You might structure them by project, project type, date, client or process of completion, for example. Don't be afraid to nest your folders as deep as they need to be to make things easier to find. Also, if you find old files that you don't expect to use anytime soon, burn them onto a disc and delete them from your hard drive.

This will save hard drive space and ultimately improve the performance of your computer. A simple trick if you have a bunch of folders or files and you want a particular folder to always appear at the top is to start the folder name with an underscore. For example, _Projects would appear before Invoices. Another trick is to improve the metadata for quicker searching in the future. Both Mac OSX and Windows Vista offer useful systemwide search, which you can improve by right-clicking on any file, then clicking on Properties (for Windows) or Get Info (for Macs).

Here, you'll want to add useful tags that you might search by later, such as an individual's name, client name, project phase and so on. One final organization trick is to use Smart Folders (Macs) or Search Folders (PCs). You create a smart folder identifying the criteria of the files you want included. This may mean your folder contains files opened within the past five days, files of a certain file type, files modified by a specific user, and so on. The criteria can be filtered by themselves or combined to offer targeted results.

Back it Up

Beyond dumping old files, back up your system in case you accidentally delete something or face a more serious catastrophe. Macs and PCs both have backup software built in. For PCs, it's called the Backup and Restore Centre; for Macs, it's called Time Machine. For both of these to work, you'll need to buy an external hard drive so you'll have someplace to store the data. For most personal computers, a 500GB to 1TB drive should offer plenty of room, and can be had for about $100.

Slow Computer

A slow computer can make you want to pull your hair out. The easiest way to speed it up is to reduce the number of applications running simultaneously. Applications running in the background sap power, so turn on your radio instead of running your music player; close your calendar app if you're not using it. The next step is to defragment your hard drive. (This is a Windows-only step since Mac OSX operates differently and doesn't need defragging.) Go to Accessories, then System Tools, click Disk Defragmenter, and click Defragment Now. This takes little bits of data scattered all over your computer's hard drive and reorganizes them so your computer can find them faster.

Widgets

If you really need to look at a calendar, use Widgets (for Macs) or Gadgets (for PCs). Widgets are small, typically single-purpose applications that provide useful information at a glance. So instead of firing up your Web browser to find stock quotes, your Google AdSense balance and news headlines, use Widgets. Mac OSX even offers a quick tool built in to the Safari browser that allows you create a Widget by clicking on the Open in Dashboard button (next to Forward and Back buttons), then selecting the part of the Web page you want to track. For example, clip part of a page on eBay to track bidding, and you'll never have to open your browser to keep an eye on things

2

Hardware and Software

INPUT/OUTPUT DEVICES

INPUT DEVICES

A keyboard and mouse are the standard way to interact with the computer. Other devices include joysticks and game pads used primarily for games. A hardware device that sends information into the CPU. Without any input devices a computer would simply be a display device and not allow users to interact with it, much like a TV.

Types of Input Devices

Digital Camera

A type of camera that stores the pictures or video it takes in electronic format instead of to film. There are several features that make digital cameras a popular choice when compared to film cameras.

First, the feature often enjoyed the most is the LCD display on the digital camera. This display allows users to view photos or video after the picture or video has been taken, which means if you take a picture and don't like the results, you can delete it; or if you do like the picture, you can easily show it to other people.

Another nice feature with digital cameras is the ability to take dozens, sometimes hundreds of different pictures. To the right is a picture of the Casio QV-R62, a 6.0 Mega Pixel digital camera used to help illustrate what a digital camera may look like.

Digital cameras have quickly become the camera solution for most users today as the quality of picture they take has greatly improved and as the price has decreased. Many users however are hesitant in buying a digital camera because of the inability of getting their pictures developed.

However, there are several solutions in getting your digital pictures developed. For example, there are numerous Internet companies capable of developing your pictures and send you your pictures in the mail. In addition, many of the places that develop your standard cameras film now have the ability to develop digital pictures if you bring them your camera, memory stick, and/or pictures on CD.

- A listing of services that can be used to store, share, and print your personal digital pictures can be found on document CH000978.
- See document CH001149 for additional information about opening and moving pictures from your digital camera to your computer.

Joystick

A peripheral input device that looks similar to a control device you would find on an arcade game at your local arcades. A computer joystick allows an individual to easily navigate an object in a game such as navigating a plane in a flight simulator. The image to the right of this text is an image of the Logitech Freedom 2.4 joystick and is an example of what you would expect most computer joysticks to look like.

Keyboard

One of the main input devices used on a computer, a PC's keyboard looks very similar to the keyboards of electric typewriters, with some additional keys. Below is a graphic of the Saitek Gamers' keyboard with indicators pointing to each of the major portions of the keyboard.

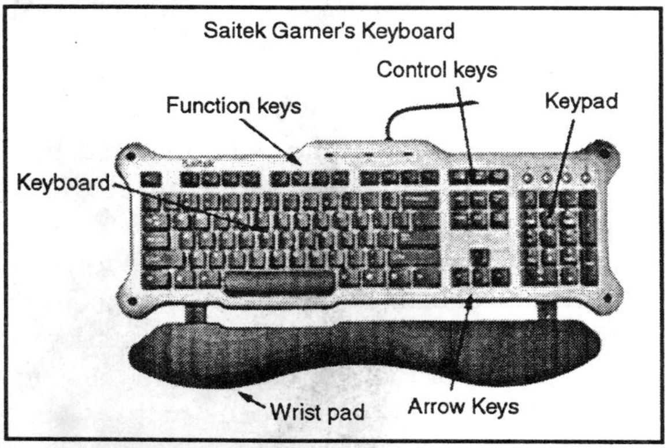

Finally, today most users use the QWERTY style keyboards. Below is a graphic illustration of where each of the keys are on a U.S. QWERTY style keyboard

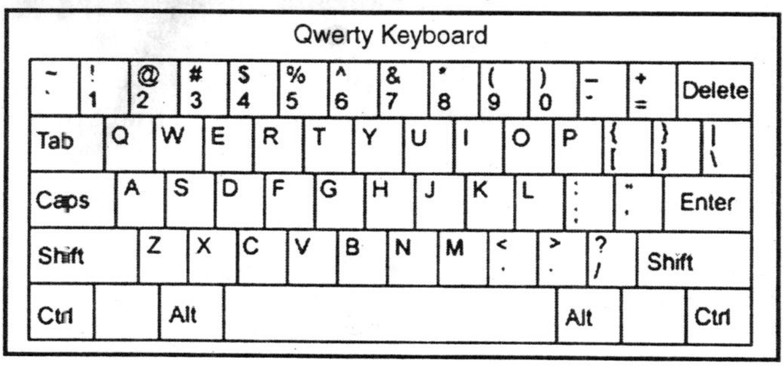

Microphone

Sometimes abbreviated as mic, a microphone is a hardware peripheral that allows computer users to input audio into their computers. To the right is a visual example of a USB headset from Logitech with a microphone. A popular solution for computer gaming.

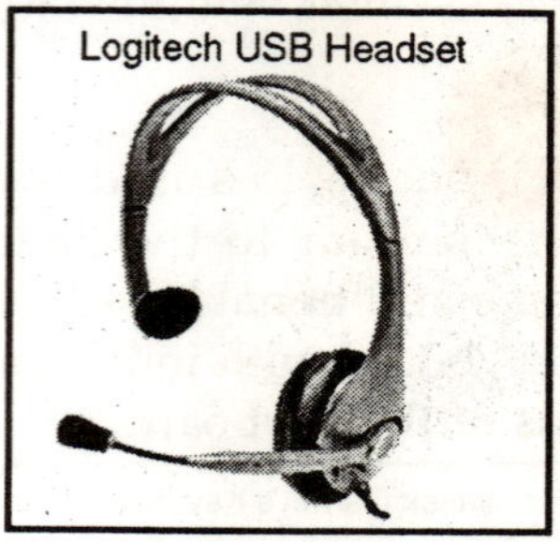

Mouse

A hardware input device that was invented by Douglas Engelbart, who at the time was working at the Stanford Research Institute, which was a think tank sponsored by Stanford University. The mouse allows an individual to control a pointer in a graphical user interface (GUI). Utilizing a mouse a user has the ability to perform various functions such as opening a programme or file and does not require the user to memorize commands, like those used in a text-based command line environment such as MS-DOS. To the right is a picture of a Microsoft IntelliMouse and is an example of what a computer mouse may look like. The Mouse was originally referred to as an X-Y Position Indicator for a Display System. Xerox later applied the mouse to its revolutionary Alto computer system in 1973. However, because of Alto's unfortunate success, it was first widely used in the Apple Lisa computer.

Types of Computer Mouse

- Cordless
- Glidepoint
- J mouse
- Footmouse
- IntelliMouse
- Joystick

- Mechanical
- Touchpad
- TrackPoint
- Optical
- Trackball
- Wheel mouse

Interface with a Computer

- Blue tooth
- PS/2 Port
- USB
- Infrared
- Serial Port

Scanner

Hardware input device that allows a user to take an image and/or text and convert it into a digital file, allowing the computer to read and/or display the scanned object. A scanner commonly connected to a computer USB, Firewire, Parallel or SCSI port.

Web Cam

A camera connected to a computer or server that allows anyone connected to the Internet to view still pictures or motion video of a user. The majority of webcam web sites are still pictures that are frequently refreshed every few seconds, minutes, hours, or days. However, there are some sites and personal pages that can supply streaming video for users with broadband.

Logitech
QuickCam Express
Model: 961183

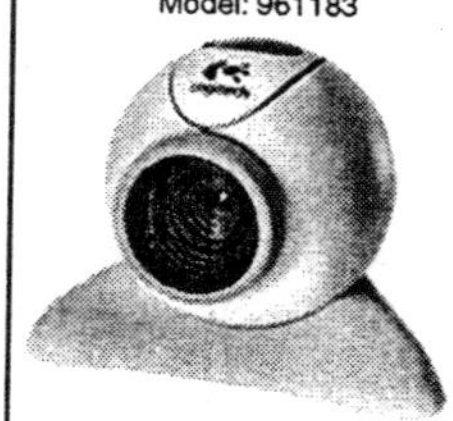

The image to the right is a picture of the Logitech Quick Cam Express and an example of what a webcam may look like. Today, most webcams are connected to the USB or Firewire port on a computer.

- There are millions of webcams around the world that allow you to view other people, places, and even events. If you're interested in looking at webcams, click here to open a search for webcams.
- If you're looking to chat with other webcam users live a great site with millions of other webcam users is Stickam.
- Parents with children should be aware of the potential dangers of children and webcams. Additional information about protecting children from harmful material on the Internet can be found on document CH000526.

OUTPUT DEVICES

The monitor (the screen) is how the computer sends information back to you, whether it be surfing the web or writing a memo. A printer is also an output device.

Storage Devices

Hard disk drives are an internal, higher capacity drive which also stores the operating system which runs when you power on the computer. "Floppy" disk drives allow you to save work on small disks and take the data with you.

Memory

When you use a programme, the computer loads a portion of the programme from the hard drive to the much faster memory (RAM). When you "save" your work or quit the programme, the data gets written back to the hard drive.

Microprocessors

PCs primarily use microprocessors (sometimes called the chip) manufactured by Intel. The older Intel versions include the 386, 486 and now the Pentium line. Macintoshes use PowerPC processors by Motorola.

Megahertz (MHz) is the internal processor speed in which computer instructions are performed. The MHz speed does not always indicate the power of the microprocessor. Newer processors can execute more instructions at the same or slower MHz. For example, an Intel 486 @100MHz is*less powerful* than a Pentium 75 MHz (but the MHz is "faster").

HARDWARE ACCESSORIES

MODEMS

Modems allow you to communicate with other computers using a phone line. Modem speeds are in bits per second (14.4, 28.8 and 56 thousand bits per second are standard).

CD-ROM DRIVES

A CD-ROM drive is a high capacity storage device which lets you read data from the disk, but not write data back. The speed of the drive (how fast the CD platter spins) is measured in multiples from the first generation drives. New drives are up to 24X (or 24 times the first drives), but while the CD spins faster, it is not really 24 times faster in actual output.

PRINTERS

There are different types of printers (laser, ink jet, dot matrix) with differing quality of output. They are measured in dpi (dots per inch) and ppm (pages per minute), the higher the better.

SCANNERS

Scanners "digitize" printed material (like photos and graphics) and save it to a graphic file format (like.GIF or.JPG) for display on the computer.

OPERATING SYSTEM SOFTWARE

Operating system software provides a "user interface" for users to manage files, start programmes, customise computer settings, and other tasks. The operating system also provides the fundamental core computer functionality for programmers.

Intel based PCs use Microsoft Windows version 3.1 (older) or Windows 95 as the operating system. Macintoshes use the Macintosh operating system.

SOFTWARE APPLICATIONS

Application software uses the operating system software and provides the real functionality of a computer.

Applications include:

- Word Processing (MS Word, WordPerfect, Ami...)
- Spreadsheets (Lotus 123, MS Excel...)
- Database (DBase, Fox Pro, Oracle...)
- Presentation (MS PowerPoint, Persuasion...)
- Internet Browsers (Netscape Navigator, MS Internet Explorer)
- Games

SOFTWARE

OVERVIEW

Various types of computer software are used to simplify the operations and applications of computer programmes. Computer software enables the computer system to perform in accordance with the given tasks. Computer software involves all types of software related applications. Electronic media content is also explained by the computer software.

EXPLANATION

Computer software, a general term used for computer programmes and data. Principally it makes up the operating system of the computer, and this computer software can either be created or purchased. Computers have vast and varied capabilities because of the many different kinds of available computer software.

Computer software is held in the storage of computers for a very specific purpose and performs the function of the programme it implements, either by directly providing instructions to the computer hardware or by serving as an input to another piece of software. Computer software is described as the information processed by the systems.

Computer software can be classified into two types:

- *Systems software*: Includes basic input-output systems, device drivers etc. In most cases this software comes along in the box when the computer is purchased.
- *Applications software*: Examples of this type of software includes office suites and video games, and may be purchased separately from the computer. Computer users can also create their own computer software, including spreadsheet templates, word processor macros etc.

Once you have installed the software by following the correct instructions, the computer is then able to operate the software.

The computer will pass the instructions from the application software, through the system software and on to the hardware. Each instruction carries out an operation on the computer.

There is such a wide variety of computer software, I think we could successfully list pages and pages. Here is an example of a few types of different software: animated models software, communication software, desktop publishing software, ERP software, help desk software, PDF conversion software, simulation software etc. Basically there is a software on the market for nearly every human need.

Different specifications to consider when selecting your computer software:

- Firstly decipher your needs and then ensure the software fulfils all your requirements.
- Ensure the software is compatible with your computer.
- Ensure you purchase an adequate number of licenses from your supplier as prescribed.

Remember that the function of computer software is to perform a specific task you need completed! There is even dating software out there to start your own dating service, or join americansingles.com which is a dating system setup already and many members to choose from.

With the innovative technology of low vision devices, it is possible for people to regain visual independence from low vision conditions. If you are having computer software problems, call an IT help line for help getting your computer working correctly.

CLASSIFICATION

Different types of computer software are available in the global computer market. Programming software, system software and application software are the three main types of computer software used in computer networking. System software is the most commonly used variety of computer software. System software offers a protective shield to all software applications. It also provides support to the physical components of computers.

System software coordinates all external devices of computer system like printer, keyboard, displays etc. Programmers use the programming software to develop the programming languages necessary to run computer software. Compliers, interpreters, linkers and text editors are some of the basic tools used in programming software.

Application software is used for commercial purpose. The application software is widely used in educational, business and medical fields. Computer games are the most popular forms of application software. Industrial automation, databases, business software and medical software prove to be of great help in the respective fields. Educational software is widely used in educational institutes across the globe.

Accounting Software

It is critical for any business (small, medium or large) wishing to be successful in industry to have accurate accounting systems in place. Systems which diagnose and record financial transactions of an organization, such as acquisitions and sales or cost information within the organization. With this comes the installation of appropriate accounting software.

Accounting software is a class of computer programmes that perform accounting operations. The accounting software is to aid the business in developing accounting solutions that allow for accelerated and more reliable processing of their accounting information.

They may vary from simple to more complicated:

- Single-entry systems which automate check writing and record keeping.
- Double-entry systems, this includes a wider variety of functions in accounts receivable, general ledger, and accounts payable.

Some of the tasks to out look for that may be offered in various packages, is that of invoice creation, calculating sales tax, tracking of employee hours and payment. You should even be able to create tax reports to send to your accountant. Expand your accounting knowledge by taking a bookkeeping course to maximize your time and efficiency. In today's high tech society there are plenty of quality accounting software providers you can choose from.

It is not always the best idea to purchase the most expensive accounting software, as programmes vary in what they offer, so maybe it is best to sit down after you have drawn up a list of what you need, and study the different packages available and purchase that best suited to your needs. Also try and research into the support and maintenance assistance that is available on offer for accounting software packages.

Track employee time and attendance with Spectrum TimeClock, web based time clock software.

Advantages of using accounting software packages:

- Back office and other functions are taken care of allowing you to focus on the primary purpose of your business-the reason you started the business.
- It improves the efficiency of your business, allowing more time.

To manage your accounts sufficiently also enables managers to determine product profitability and to investigate inefficiencies. They come to scrutinize information in a different way which is more relevant to the needs of the business.

Ecommerce Software

Ecommerce is the business of buying and selling things online. It allows a store owner to setup shop, run and maintain their online store with absolute minimum effort. There is a variety of ecommerce software available in order to make this efficient for both store owner and buyer.

Before ecommerce software the ecommerce business used to keep track of things on disks, or even hand written in books which is time consuming and not as accurate. Ecommerce software is however considered to be much more reliable. Basically you can't have ecommerce without the software, or successfully anyway. Before purchasing just any ecommerce software, research what your needs are, what is available and that your needs are met. Consider issues such as electrical failure, computer viruses, hackers on the net, and that the maintenance on the ecommerce software is kept up to date on a regular basis.

The selling for a company is only half of their battle. Current ecommerce software packages enables you the store owner to build a site where buyers can view your goods, add or delete items from their selection, and most important are able to review their final selection prior to buying.

Necessary requirements are:

- Storefront appearance
- Proper records kept of purchases made, customer details, shipping details
- Can handle currencies and tax levels
- Buyer e-mailed with purchase confirmation
- Software has a good customer base

An ecommerce store is handled via a very easy-to-use browser. There are different options to keep in mind for the buyer, *e.g.* should it include VAT and postage costs, accept all major credit cards (as people are buying online globally), search by keyword or brand, browse by a category or subcategory. The process for order facilities can include: printing off order summaries and invoices, being able to modify orders online and delivery dates, finding orders by status, date, surname or ID.

One of the most important features is the sites security, does it have a password protected admin area, firewall and daily backup, credit card orders address verification, CV credit card signature strip check as well as anti-spam and anti-virus options.

CD Burning Software

A new innovation since the development of tape recording is CD burning. A compact disc (CD) is a small disc on which audio signals, video signals, or other data can be recorded in digital form. CD burning is the production of information recorded as a succession of discrete, rather than as continuously varying parameters. There is a variety of software available for doing this including free cd burning software on the market.

The question still remains, why do people want to burn cd's and it is simple, because you would like to create mixed CD's from your current cd collection or maybe from your MP3 music collection. CD burning software purchased in the shops can be incredibly expensive and free CD burning software is often just as good.

So browse on the internet for the many sites available offering this free CD burning software, rather than wasting your money. With today's technology free CD burning software gives you an error free burn in the fastest possible time.

Some features included in free cd burning software:

- Audio recording
- Overburn feature
- Burn-proof technology to prevent CD coasters
- Creates multi-session CD's
- Creates bootable CD's

- Enables you to design your very own CD inserts and covers
- Supports all popular CD standards
- Rip audio CD's
- Burns audio CD without gaps between tracks

The above are only some of the features that can be included so when wanting to burn your CD's carefully review what is available. With free CD burning software you can burn from either CD-R, CD-RW and depending on the component set of the software the CD burner may support the creation of data CD's and audio CD's. Some may even support the burning of a CD-R/RW.

To purchase this free CD burning software all you need to do is prepare this search function in your regular browser, and once you have found one that suits your needs, click on the download button. It is that simple.

Video Editing Software

We all love to capture that special moment, holiday or memory. Some of us have spent thousands on video cameras and have stacks of videos lying around, unedited and boring. However all you need is the right video editing software to change them into awe inspiring videos.

Luckily with today's computers we can kiss goodbye all those expensive and specialized equipment and say hello to the new video editing software. With this introduction editing one's videos has become easier to do, and there is a variety to choose from, basic programmes to compile the video and add simple transitions, or why not a sophisticated programme with advanced effects, sound and editing tools. There is something for everyone. The possibilities as well as the choices are endless.

Qualities to look for when seeking video editing software:

- *Ease of use*: Easy software is a key to video editing success.
- *Feature set*: They may vary in quality and quantity; but those with large feature sets are often more difficult to use than software with smaller feature

sets. Purchase those with the features that closely match your needs.

- *Installation and setup*: Ensure the video editing software is easy to install, otherwise you may not even use it.
- *Help and Tech support*: this is not a bonus but in actual fact a necessity.

There is also a variety of types of video files that need editing for *e.g.* AVI, MPG. etc. So ensure you are aware what it is you will be editing. Some video editing software do include features to edit a combination. Operations that can be included in the video editing software are: deleting the frame, delete selection, crop, resize, rotate, mirror, flip, trim, text overlay, adjusting audio volume. In addition to those just mentioned some may even include powerful video enhancement and alternation. Some even include a scene content detection which automatically breaks your home movie up into scenes. Every time the camera is started and then stopped again, this is considered a scene.

Some of the more specific features of video editing software include:

- Allowing you to arrange video clips exactly as you would arrange pictures on the page of your photo album, each pic representing a separate video clip. Some allow you to display your video clips using a timeline.
- The potential to split one scene into two separate scenes.
- Video signals or animation effects that indicate that one scene has ended and another is about to begin.
- Allows you to remove the beginning or end of a sound track.

Inventory Software

Inventory is a listing of the assets of any organization, but specifically referring to it's stock. Organizations need to keep records of stocks of raw materials, semi-finished, and finished but unsold goods to help determine profitability and efficiency levels. Annual financial records need to take account of inventory costs.

In times of inflation a particular problem is how to value inventory when the value of some assets rises above the cost paid for them, but with inventory software this is done for you. If we take a look back to the past, the calculating of inventory was originally done by hand, which proved to be extremely tedious and possibly inaccurate.

Now with the introduction of inventory software it tracks the inventory of goods for sale or used in manufacturing of products for sale, saving both time and inaccurate losses. Some of the current inventory software that has been introduced is a flexible solution for inventory accounting, check depositing, sales purchase tracing and tracking. They are also implemented with high-class and quick edit functions enabling optimal formatted content to print, to export or to send out as an e-mail.

Off the shelf inventory software are easy to use bar-code based tracking solutions. They maintain a perpetual inventory so that when items are received inventory levels go up and when items are issued inventory levels go down. Uses for off the shelf inventory control includes anything that can be bar-coded such as supply rooms, food stock in shops, industrial supplies and chemicals etc.

Stand alone inventory software is available for a variety of tasks and are able to manage inventory in multiple locations, manage consignment inventory along with the company owned inventory, track and maintain the history of serial numbers, lots and batches of items and all inventory movement. Putting in place a sufficient inventory software system may be a hard task but definitely calls for success once everything is in place.

Educational Software

Educational software may be considered the relationship between formal education> and economic and social development. Research has indicated that the investment in education is necessary to effect changes in social and economic life. Educational software has thus become an essential component in today's fast moving world. Educational software has become fun, and an incredibly rich way for children to learn, no matter what their weakness, there is something to choose from:

- Phonics
- Vocabulary
- Reading Comprehension
- Spelling
- Grammar
- Writing
- Math logic
- Multiplication
- Geometry
- Mastering numeration

The above are only a very small example of what is out there, and majority of educational software can be purchased on different levels aiding children specifically in that with which they need assistance. When purchasing educational software, study the package and see by whom it is developed etc. A lot of the time it is teachers, or people in the education system designing it and thus making it all the more suitable. Today even schools are using the educational software in classrooms to aid learning.

Majority of educational software builds the skills of the learner systematically due to them being designed by education experts and thereby assures success through the beneficial use of reward, reinforcement and review. They are useful teaching tools in all fields of learning due to the balance of auditory and visual activities.

The results of children using educational software is as follows:

- Children enjoy learning more
- It creates confidence in the learner
- It improves on weaknesses
- Level of understanding in the learner increases
- Children who may battle with multiplication tables, now grasp the concept, children who had difficulty in reading, now read effectively etc...

For the future in our world, labour productivity can be increased by implementing the correct education, as this is the fundamental building block. Primary education is required before effective literacy is achieved and this is what majority of the children's educational software is aimed at. Educational software is all a form of development.

Medical Billing Software

In most countries throughout the world health care is voluntary, however the billings related to one's healthcare can sometimes prove to be an absolute nightmare for both the patient and the institute.

In today's society most company's etc, are moving towards a paper free society, so why not do away with patient files and invest in suitable medical billing software that takes care of everything from beginning to end.

If you want your medical practice efficiently run, here are some reasons why it would be a good idea to invest in medical billing software:

- It manages medical aid authorization referrals.
- You will be able to store medical billing information for nearly all medical aid insurance.
- Mail electronic claims for error-checking that minimizes rejections thus by hurrying up payments.
- It allows you to verify the specific patients status with their healthcare plan electronically and payments are done quicker.
- Automated accounting, will keep trace of every penny going in or out.
- Printing of reports is easy-daily reports, month or year end journals and summaries can be printed.

Medical billing software leads to efficiency which in turn leads to satisfaction, smoother operation and greater profitability, reaching most people's target at the end of the day. There are phenomenal medical billing software packages available on the market place, eliminating volumes of paperwork and the chance for administrative error. Today they are not only automated but also offers customizability.

Included in the medical billing software is:

- Scheduling of patient appointments.
- Patient details, including their allergies, past medical history, diagnosis and treatments, remarks about the patient and a patient summary.

In conclusion the technology of medical billing software assists with the functions to accurately complete claim forms, thereby timeously billing insurance companies in accordance with each insurance company's policies and procedures. Obstacles are thus removed, eliminating weaknesses and increasing your revenues and at the same time giving you more time.

Mortgage Software

A mortgage is a legal contract between a mortgagor (borrower) and mortgagee (lender) secured by the assets (most commonly land or buildings) owned by the mortgagee. A mortgage is unlike a hire-purchase agreement in that the mortgaged property belongs to the borrower. Mortgages of various kinds are typically extended by building societies, banks and insurance companies to businesses and individual house buyers. Mortgage software is available to both the mortgagor and mortgagee focusing on each sector's individual needs. Mortgage software for the mortgagee is advisory software and usually includes some of the following features:

- Enabling calculations of mortgage payment and total costs of mortgage.
- Enabling comparison of different interest rates and mortgage amounts.
- Enables a view of a detailed breakdown of mortgage over time the with mortgage schedule.
- And very important it teaches you how to pay off your mortgage early and save yourself some money.
- With constant changes in interest rates, it enables you to view your repayment accurately with the handy mortgage grid.

This mortgage software assists you in working out complicated sums, with the inflation that is occurred over time and what you can afford. Mortgage software also has its benefits within the workplace.

Two extremely important considerations are:

- People without mortgage experience can be sufficiently trained on most mortgage billing software. With this minimization of having to employ specially skilled people in mortgage it gives flexibility and a huge advantage on cost.
- Mortgage billing software automates every step of your mortgage loan workflow.

However like most software out there, ensure you can receive 24 hour help/support, to quickly solve any problem that may occur.

The mortgage industry business is huge but it doesn't matter if you are a bank, traditional retail or wholesale lender, correspondent lender, sub-prime lender, builder subsidiary, state housing lender, there is something for everyone. Majority of mortgage software is easy to use software and parallels the entire loan process.

Designing Software

Designing implies a special regard for the requirement of appearance and improvement of marketability by imparting an attractive appearance with current fashions, within the margins of variation imposed by the requirements of use and economy. The importance of consumer appeal in design is shown by the recent expansion of home design software.

Home design software can assist if you are having a problem visualizing what you so desire in your home. It is a compelling tool used in the design planning and building of the ultimate home. Home design software also goes beyond what you see in planning books, by customizing your home design to match your needs!

Before purchasing your home design software research the different products available and their feature capabilities. Today a lot of these programmes come with step by step instructions, wizards, drag and drop down menus with furniture (It allows you to position interior objects such as beds, chairs and tables, appliances and more within your floor plan creating a virtual feel for the size, layout and function of each room), home fixtures, plants to add to plans, decks and patios and helpful videos.

Most of them also include both a 2-D and 3-D view. Some of the home design software successfully allows you to visualize your plan on an actual colour photo. These software programmes can help you create a brand new home or home improvement remodeling to your existing home to your wishes. After you have planned your dream house most home design software will offer you a 3-D walk through you house. You can now view how your design looks before implementing.

And remember changes are easy to make however you feel necessary. If you are happy with what you see it is also possible to print off colour images. Some home design software is so advanced it goes as far as calculating beams and footings etc. As in the case with purchasing all software ensures you have a support/help centre that can assist with any glitches. I think an appealing feature of home design software is that it is fun to utilize, allowing for a gratifying designing adventure.

Bar Code Software

A bar code is an identification system that is be read by a computer. Though there are several variations they all consist of printed patterns of lines and spaces, which record information such as price and batch number as a binary code. A computer-based cash register or point of sale system are able to read bar codes optically.

There are a variety of reasons why one would require bar code software in a business:

- *Bar code production software*: Generating the actual bar codes
- *Bar code data collection software*: Collecting data from bar code readers, magnetic strip readers etc... The type of data collection software you need depends primarily on your bar code scanner output, of which there are several types.

- *Database and inventory control software*: Storing data collected from bar codes. Generally the most important part of any bar code framework is the collection of data in a database. The whole point of the introduction of bar codes is to remove slow or error given entries

Basically you can determine which product to purchase just by knowing your needs. Bar code software without much difficulty produces good quality graphic images of bar codes that can usually be imported or pasted directly into a programme *e.g.* Microsoft word or publisher, Adobe, Quark etc. It can get quite involved so its always best to research exactly what you need.

Several types of output:

- Keyboard Wedge output or USB output
- RS232 output (includes some RFID scanners)
- TCP/IP output (includes some RFID scanners)

If you are not too clued up on the technicalities of things, there are bar code software packages available that are fast, simple to install and requires not much background experience. Bar code software can be manufactured for first time databases straight from the keyboard, portable bar code scanners, current Microsoft access databases etc... The express check in or check out proficiency maintains quick and trouble-free processing of asset issues, receipts, returns or moves.

Once can assess current and past records for any items and at any time derived from location, department, employee, status or any other criteria. As in the case of all software, bar code software is licensed per computer. In other words if you will be printing from various computers in house you will have to buy multiple licenses for each computer.

Control Software

The internet is a global network that connects users together with software and protocols. The internet offers users a number of services including electronic mail, and the ability to access information even in remote areas. There are a number of high level services but unfortunately the reality of the situation is, you do find online internet predators such as pedophiles, stalkers and sex offenders.

Another problem encountered with computers is children tend to spend hours surfing or playing games, thus neglecting other areas of their life. It is said that a child's psychological growth is determined by how their parents relate to them and situations. Hopefully with parental control software the recent studies showing that children are becoming more introverted by constantly being in front of their computer, can now somewhat be curbed.

Most parental control software can include any or all of the below features specifically for when a child is online:

- *Internet conversation logging*: Usually both sides of the conversation.
- Integrated scheduler enabling parents to easily but invisibly monitor their children when absent from the home.
- *Window activity logging*: Captures all information that was viewed by your child.
- Printed document logging, logs information on documents sent to the printer spool.
- Some have a VCR style playback function that detains features of what your child has been doing.
- Enables you to block websites you would prefer your child not to visit.

With parental control software you can now gain control of your child's access on the computer. You can control when they use the computer, the amount of time they spend on the computer by automatically logging your child out at a specific times, say for instance at bed time or during study times and can easily divide computer time among siblings to prevent ongoing fights.

Another advantage of most parental control software is that it remains invisible to the user. Before buying research the products available on the market, and purchase the parental control software best suited to your needs. Some are easier to install and to use, others more difficult, so obviously purchase that best suited to your computer knowledge.

Real Estate Software

Real estate brokers market real property on behalf of the owner. A career in real estate may involve long, irregular hours but if the correct systems are in place it can be rewarding with huge amounts of success.

With most things in life organization is of the utmost importance, and with the introduction of real estate software this can now be practiced within the industry. If you are in the industry you will now be able to sufficiently escalate the work you produce and minimize other time consuming constraints. There are some real estate software programmes that allow you to manage a number of properties all at the same time. These programmes allow the user to accomplish their appraisal in a logical set out manner, and with absolute accuracy in their figures.

If you're in the market to purchase a home or homes- Access Investment Property has a large database of investment properties to choose from. With houses and developments located all across the globe, there's no better place to turn to. If you're looking for east coast property, check out south Jersey real estate for the home of your dreams.

Do you keep losing real estate deals due to incompetent real estate agents? Here at Weichert we pride ourselves in giving our clients prompt and curteous service. Our clients are our #1 priority, so if there's a home for sale that you want, we'll do everything in our power to make sure you get it! If you're looking for a southern California realtor to help you find your dream home, the Real Estate Store is waiting to work for you!

The concept behind real estate software is to make the entire process for both the seller of the house and your business as smooth as possible, from beginning to end. Some of the software goes as far as creating a virtual website for each loan transaction on which you are working.

It is a safe point containing your name with access to document communication, messaging, calendars, contact details, task tracking etc... The seller of the house can log in at any given time with his log on information to view the status information of the transaction. At the end of each day you can print your management reports of all current transactions and their status.

When face to face with a client or over the phone, you have easy access to all information, no teetering through pages and pages. Within your database you can store descriptions of your properties with a matching image, all contact details, expiry dates and notifications of contracts and payment deadlines.

It even has a calculation method where any kind of calculation can be done, including mortgage calculations etc... To avoid embarrassment of forgetting something important it contains scheduling tasks that constantly remind you. There is user friendly real estate software available on the market, so research those that will best suit your individual needs.

Embroidery Software

Embroidery is a general term used to describe ornamental stitch work applied to any kind of fabric using any kind of thread. It is an extremely ancient and widespread craft, yet still popular today. And with the commencement of embroidery software has become a lot more convenient and easier to administer. The most important step is selecting the correct embroidery software for your needs, and ensuring it is user friendly.

It doesn't have to be difficult purchasing this software and some important things that need to be considered when selecting your embroidery software is as follows: ensure the software you select has a wide range of stitch types from fancy design to combining effects and first-class stitch quality, make sure the software you purchase is compatible with both your computer and sewing machine (remember applications are constantly being upgraded, it might be a good idea to purchase Microsoft certified products), select an embroidery software programme with efficient technical support with either e-mail or phone support for any problems that may occur and software that offers upgrades or expansion modules can be purchased later on as you progress.

Everyone has different ideas and styles so it may be a good idea to purchase embroidery software that allows individualized techniques and editing of your designs, easily attainable methods to find and manage your designs once saved. There is such advancements in design editing and lettering power to expect, and always new innovations being lead on to the market.

Embroidery software is developed by skilled digitizers and artists, bringing you a wide variety of stock designs to choose from. It is such an easy way to create masterful looking embroidery designs in no time. Embroidery has been used in the past and will continue to be used in t he future for secular purposes for designs on costumes, curtains, book covers etc.

Retail Software

Retail trading is the sale of goods in relatively small quantities which can be fast-selling foodstuffs, toiletries, clothing or consumer durables. Most retailing is done via shops or stores and includes the vast numbers of retail chains. Current trends in retailing is the optimization of profits and fewer losses, which means it is of the utmost importance to have the correct and necessary retail software.

Therefore depending on the size of the retail store, different retail software packages are designed to suit different sized stores.

Regardless of which retail software you purchase there are a number of common features to look out for:

- *Point of sale products*: Ensure they are easy to learn and use, up to date with up to date retail tools, including bar codes and credit card readers, adaptable and flexible.
- *Customer database*: Accurate in storing your customer's details such as names and a history of previous buying.
- *Inventory control and Kiosk*: This is to avoid creating disappointment in your customer by being under stocked at any stage, or overstocked which can be damaging to the company. Some retail software

programmes can print sales, inventory, low-stock or over-stock reports to keep you up to date. Some retail software even comes with features that will remind you when you need to re-order certain stock.

- *Convenience features*: With keeping to your goal of increased sales, convenience features are an added bonus for *e.g.* totally touch screen suited.
- *Security features*: Needs to be incorporated at each and every level, using passwords to avoid unauthorized staff making certain transactions, including the date, time and name of sales person working at specific check out location.
- *Back office functions*: Linked to the back office making their functions easier and more accurate by transporting all necessary information.

If you are able to implement the right retail software you should constantly be able to view a thorough picture of your business and ensure you are continuously on top of things. Thus by keeping you up to date of popular products in your store, and maybe those that are not selling so great with your customers, allowing you to make profitable changes. Stay neck and tie with your competitors and up with the times, lose cash registers and join the computer revolution with retail software, it has been determined that it does save money.

Photo Editing Software

Today an immense range of photographic materials, equipment and skills has made the photographic industry a highly articulate industry. With the introduction of digital cameras, people have hundred and thousands of un-edited or un-usable photos.

It might be a good idea to invest in good photo editing software, and get those pics out there. With photo editing software you can keep you photo looking natural, yet it includes so many functions that one can do.

See below a few examples:

- Auto trim
- Border remove
- Colour resolution
- Contour

- Contrast
- Crop
- Dilate
- Dot remove
- DPI resolution
- Edge detector
- Emboss
- Flip
- Gamma correct
- Gradient
- Hue
- Impressionist
- Invert
- Invert text
- Line remove
- Line segment
- Median
- Mirror
- Mosaic
- Multiply
- Pixelate
- Posterize
- Resample
- Resize
- Ripple
- Rotate
- Sharpen
- Shear
- Smooth
- Solarize
- Stretch intensity
- Swirl
- Unsharp mask
- Wave
- Zoom blur
- Zoom wave

And the above is just a little sample, it might be a good idea to familiarize yourself with all the photo editing terminology before you get started. Photo editing software enables suitable editing, processing or conversion to each photo image that is processed.

Some of the above functions assist you in accomplishing the following:

- Red-eye reduction
- Increasing the brightness by using an added flash
- Throw away parts of the photo that you don't want

Today when purchasing a digital camera, it mostly does come with photo editing software which is sufficient enough. However if you would like to get a little more advanced there is a variety of software available on the market to choose from. There is programmes for beginners, and seriously advanced photo editing software.

Some software programmes include a browser menu for obtaining and characterizing photos, while others are purely for intensifying and editing digital images. Photo editing software also aids one in arranging, sorting and logging all photo images. Some software has features which will allow you to execute an exercise on more than one image at a time, or to rename bunches of images. So no matter what your task is before you-e-mailing your photo, correcting poor photos or the printing of your photos, photo editing is a great tool. So why not make your own perfect prints in the comfort of your home.

Loan Software

A loan is a sum of money borrowed by one individual or organization from another. Borrowers may pay interest in addition to repaying the capital sum borrowed. Loan servicing software assists in streamlining how you keep track of all money going in and out in order to:

- Increase revenues
- Reduce expenses
- Clarify portfolio management
- Boost customer satisfaction
- Escalate management control

Loan servicing software allows lenders to do their own loan servicing and loan accounting with cost effective methods. It would not be wise to get left behind in today's fast paced and competitive environment, and loan servicing software connects you to keep up with the progression. Powerful software packages can be obtained on the market, with constant upgrades that can be conducted.

Most software companies also offer a collector's software package that can be used in conjunction with the loan software packages. Majority will have a wizard teaching you the ins and outs of the functions, otherwise they might send in an instructor to you show you the ropes or your new package. Some packages come as a standard system, but if you have more complex needs, loan servicing software packages can be custom designed. These packages will handle your most demanding financial information requirements.

As in the case of you purchasing any software for your computer, ensure it is compatible with your system, meets the needs you are wanting, versatile, and offers a thorough support system either online or by phone. There are versions of loan servicing software available that will meet the needs of lenders of all types and sizes in industry including banks, private finance companies, credit unions and individual lending organizations, and includes vast capabilities that will enable you to print loan documents in-house for all your loan types and remain profitable.

If you are looking for hard money lenders and hard money loans check out the Avatar Financial Group for low rates in all 50 states. Find military loans and computer financing at the military loan company. Instant approval for our online loans and you can apply any time, day or night. Now you won't have to worry about your financial problems anymore when you're in a bind.

Music Software

Music software can assist you in the making of music. The western world has always regarded music as being the unique creation of an individual composer, and now with music software, it makes it so much easier. Music software packages allow you to work creatively, and with nearly over 5000 types of music software to choose from – audio sequences, lyric writing tools to guitar software, there is something available for everyone's interest.

With music software you are able to form music from scratch, re-arrange music files oruse a composing function to develop brilliant formatting options. The most important step is to decipher what it is you would like to get out of your music software, and purchase it relatively.

Whether you are into writing and creating your own music, or no matter which instrument there is absolutely something for everybody. The entry of your notes can be made directly from your computer with most packages, and you can create them in the exact way that you would like to view them. You can print your music or view it on the screen as your notes play, you can sing or play your instrument/s as it goes along etc. Find sheet music download for new ideas to implement into your own music.

Each music software package will have its own range of tools that need to be used. With most of the software packages you are also able to play back your music at any given stage. And of course as with most software ensure there is a sufficient support system. With the introduction of music software it is considered the bridging gap between technology and musical talent. If you purchase the right software you literally have your own music production studio to record your songs, and even to complete your editing.

You can compose your own songs that you will be recording, and once you have completed composing and recording you can then add in professional sounding effects. There are those music software programmes that will allow you to produce opulently layered musical compositions by recording drums, guitars, keyboards, bass guitars or what ever you so wish for.

It's a safer and much more popular method of recording with music software using digital audio files on the PC as vinyl is easily scratched, and cassettes are easily ruined. The introduction of music software into the music industry is a great advantage as anybody can mix music and voice overs to create professional sounding tracks.

Trucking Software

Trucking has become quite a necessity in the business world today. Modern trucks may be either straight or articulated; in the latter, one or more trailers are connected to the power unit by standardized couplings. Many specialized trucks have been evolved *e.g.* refrigerated vehicles for bulk distribution of food etc... With trucks becoming such a part of business and the economy, it has been necessary to introduce trucking software.

If you purchase the correct trucking software it should present you with an appropriate and effortless to use multi purpose software solution. It should be able to build in all your employee records and be a complete solution in assisting you to run a profit making company. Trucking software should also help sustain and record all the information to enable getting through each business day. The complete transportation management process can be addressed by using trucking software which furnishes a business with comprehensive and integrated forms of functions and services. When selecting your trucking software ensure all your needs are met, the basic criteria to check for is dispatching, billing, accounting, payroll, settlements, maintenance, safety, brokerage and satellite tracking.

Imagine being able to keep track of all these features. Of course there are different trucking software systems to meet different needs and expenses. Some come as standard packages but as in the case with most software others can be customised to suite your individual needs. Don't overlook the standard systems as some come fully featured, with a fleet management system that gives both small to medium sized carriers exceptional functionality.

Another couple of options to look out for are user friendly systems, that have server compliant databases to maintain your system. Also ensure the support system of the trucking software you choose is adequate and extensive. If you purchase the right trucking software for your company it can be a powerful tool, extremely dependable, in maintaining the functions of your day to day trucking business.

Landscape Software

Landscaping involves the design and development of land by human beings for use and enjoyment. It is concerned with the beauty of natural surroundings as well as practical ways to use land and the objects on it. If you would like to turn your garden into a masterwork invest in landscape software to assist you in creating your dream garden.

If you are having trouble planning your garden, don't automatically turn to a garden architect, landscape software will help you remain in control of any construction or redesign that needs to take place to your land. You can experiment with different functions available on your software until you get the final finish you have been fantasizing about, and have fun at the same time.

Landscape software will assist you step by step as follows:

- It will aid you in exploring your options.
- You can change your mind as often as you like while in the planning phase.
- Experiment with the actual accessories before you purchase them.
- You can create a perfect and precise shopping list with landscape software by using its available tools.
- With some landscape software packages you are able to merge in an actual photo of your home and landscape in order to accurately plan.
- It will assist you in viewing your garden design from different perspectives.
- With some landscape software you can view your garden as it develops, see how the trees and plants will look in the years to come. Some packages include a landscape estimator to assist you in pricing out what your final costs will be.
- And to be on the safe side before you invest your money in those final costs some packages will give you an accurate view of final plans.
- With all these advantages of keeping you in control of your land before commencement of construction is fully engaged, I think landscape software is worth a try. There are enough user friendly products on the market to allow you to feel comfortable with what you are doing.

All landscape software packages are different but most will contain some or all of the above mentioned features. So experiment to your hearts content with your garden with only a few mouse clicks. You can load a photo of your garden into your software package and form full-colour printable images as you go.

Some will allow you a 3D walk through your entire garden, appearing as virtually real as possible. You can record how your garden looks in all the different seasons, and track the changes. Delete those you don't like in your garden, or add in things you so wish for. Some landscape software packages go as far as allowing you to plot the slope elevation of your design.

Research the different software packages available and be careful not to purchase something a landscape architect would use as it might be a little too complicated for you to work with. Even the easier packages usually have a database of hundreds of product images to choose from.

Day Care Software

Day care can be split into different sectors: namely for children and the elderly but can go as far as dog day care centres, where they are all respectively looked after. Different day care software can be purchased for the different types, however they are all run along the same lines. If you want to make a success of your institute it is of the utmost importance to keep track of what is going on, and the right day care software can help you.

It is considered as in most business sectors that the crucial area for automatation is with the managing of the accounts. Day care software should have the proficiency of tracking all money going in and out to maintain profitability. Day care centres have a huge responsibility and need to keep track of who they have in there centres, waiting lists, special needs, history etc... They also need to manage year-end records of payments and fees. With the right day care software this can be done in a hassle free way.

As discussed day care software packages are all different and you need to research which one most specifically meets your needs. Different functions need to be put in place to meet the needs of different payment methods etc. Some people prefer to pay monthly and others quarterly, some prefer debit orders and others credit cards, so ensure it has accurate methods of enabling these needs.

When it comes to child day care centres, children are present for different amounts of hours in the day (depending on their parents schedule) and are obviously billed different rates, up to date day care software takes care of all this. Day care software goes as far as managing the centre's check book, produces financial statements, payroll, etc... Day care software keeps you up to date with who is present in your centre, regardless of whether its child day care or day care for the elderly. You can track meals, allergies, next of kin contact details and very important is the history of the child/adult.

There are things to look out for in purchasing day care software, like most software the availability of support and help systems. If you stumble upon a hurdle it is nice to know you can receive instantaneous help. A thorough and easy to use database is important, where necessary information can be found at the click of a button. A built in back up system is also a good idea, as it is information that needs to be stored safely and securely.

Stock Trading Software

The stock exchange is the market in which securities are bought and sold. Most capital cities have stock exchanges with some of the largest being in New York, Paris, Frankfurt, Tokyo and London. And with stock trading software anyone can take part in stock trading and from any where in the world. You are able to raise long-term capital if you so wish, by issuing securities to investors and can again sell them when you wish.

Stock trading software is freely available and can be purchased for day traders, short term and long term traders. You also don't need to be a computer whiz to make use of this software as most stock trading software is user friendly. With the right stock trading software you can make thousands by buying and selling stocks.

Stock trading software has been created to assist as follows:

- Spot channel breakouts
- Control your money
- Limit your inclination towards fear and greed
- Produce high prospect buy/sell signals
- Disclose trading drifts for just about any time period

Stock trading software does the research for you preventing you from making the frequent blunders of buying prematurely if the stock price tends to drop, as well as buying too late *i.e.* when prices are at the top of the cycle.

Stock prices are continuously updated, giving the entry price and the stop price. When a stock is a certain distance above or below its moving average, it will eventually move back to the average. The norm is that stocks generally change back to the average.

This phenomenon is known as "reversion to the mean". With most stock market software there are filters available that down load tens of thousands of stock each day in lists. It is best to try stock trading software that offers a free trial, to see how user friendly it is. Some will offer a hundred per cent money back guarantee if you are not happy. Also look into the support system the software offers in case any problems occur.

Astrology Software

Astrology is a pseudo-science which attempts to make predictions about worldly events and people's day to day lives through interpreting the supposed influences of the position and motion of celestial bodies, principally the sun, moon and planets.

Today there is astrology software to aid people interested in doing this. Astrology software is vast (although not a hard and fast rule, obviously depending on the astrology software you purchase) and comes in three types of programmes:

1. Calculations
2. Interpretation or report writing
3. Research

Astrology software packages are able to create precise and enlightening interpretations and thereafter provide a function for you to print these astrological reports. The majority of astrology software is user friendly, powerful and can calculate and integrate astrological charts with high astronomical accuracy and professional quality. There are a variety of options to choose from-house systems, zodiacal reference etc...

Before purchasing your astrology software, you will have to define your needs in order to see what you want it for and what you would like to achieve. The top priority is to ensure you purchase a well-crafted programme. Ensure you understand the product descriptions, feature lines, screen shots and read the professional reviews. Majority of astrology software will give a detailed astrological report, including interpretation help for each symbol present on the chart.

Astrological computations such as birth charts, chart comparisons and prediction methods can all be carried out through the relative calculation software programmes. After completing all your tasks it is then possible to print out all your chart wheels, tables, maps and graphs that you have created.

Reports can be created for interpreting or report writing, that describes birth charts, compatibility, vocation or any other astrological topic you may think of.

We can then divide research software into an additional two categories:

1. Research features are usually automatically built into major chart calculation software programmes.
2. Dedicated research programmes which include chart databases, containing hundreds or thousands of famous people's birth data, as well as other methods of researching charts.

There are different price ranges of variations of astrology software that can be purchased for all of the above types, also ranging in advancement, so it is very dependable as to what level you are at. Majority of astrology software is designed to run under DOS or windows, so always ensure it is compatible with your PC.

Childcare Software

Child care software is a computerized schedule management system and will aid any centre in keeping track of everything-from each student enrolled (including emergency contact details, authorized guardians for pickup, permission forms, siblings etc), current and historical billing. A schedule can be entered for children and goes as far as scheduling in the holidays or temporary schedule changes.

It keeps track of day to day attendance sheets, each child care software programme having its own unique system of doing this. It is often difficult to recall each and every child present in the centre but child care software will make it easier for storing the following information: medical information, tracking and charging of extra hours, immunization tracking, door access control. It also controls enrollment of new children, adding in new applicants, placing some on a waiting list or removing children that have left the centre.

Child care software in appropriate centres also aids with the financial side of things by keeping track of billing structures, all the important information you may need about payments and billings are stored. Some can even automatically post all late fees. It can also produce financial summaries, specifically at month end. Automatic printing of client receipts on payment.

3

Computer Networks

LAN'S AND WAN'S

NETWORKING

Networking is the term that describes the processes involved in designing, implementing, upgrading, managing and otherwise working with networks and network technologies. Networks are used for an incredible array of different purposes. In fact, the definitions above are so simple for the specific reason that networks can be used so broadly, and can allow such a wide variety of tasks to be accomplished. While most people learning about networking focus on the interconnection of PCs and other "true" computers, you use various types of networks every day.

Each time you pick up a phone, use a credit card at a store, get cash from an ATM machine, or even plug in an electrical appliance, you are using some type of network. In fact, the definition can even be expanded beyond the world of technology altogether: I'm sure you've heard the term "networking" used to describe the process of finding an employer or employee by talking to friends and associates. In this case too, the idea is that independent units are connected together to share information and cooperate.

The widespread networking of personal computers is a relatively new phenomenon. For the first decade or so of their existence, PCs were very much "islands unto themselves", and were rarely connected together. In the early 1990s, PC networking began to grow in popularity as businesses realised the advantages that networking could provide. By the late 1990s, networking in homes with two or more PCs started to really take off as well. This interconnection of small devices represents, in a way, a return to the "good old days" of mainframe computers. Before computers were small and personal, they were large and centralized machines that were shared by many users operating remote terminals. While having all of the computer power in one place had many disadvantages, one benefit was that all users were connected because they shared the central computer.

Individualized PCs took away that advantage, in favour of the benefits of independence. Networking attempts to move computing into the middle ground, providing PC users with the best of both worlds: the independence and flexibility of personal computers, and the connectivity and resource sharing of mainframes. in fact, networking is today considered so vital that it's hard to conceive of an organization with two or more computers that would not want to connect them together!

TYPES OF NETWORK

The word "networking" strikes fear into legions of otherwise intrepid job hunters. It conjures up one of three images: calling everyone in your address book to see whether anyone knows anyone who may know anyone who may give you an informational interview, attending club meetings with other job hunters or having your friends come up with ideas and contacts instead of advising you to get out there and network. But there is no need to fear because there are many different types of networking techniques you can use to help with your job search and references.

Obviously number three doesn't always work. But the other two aren't so appealing either. Who enjoys calling total strangers and asking them to meet with you when there's nothing in it for them? If they're successful in what they do – and why else would you want to meet with them? – they're likely to be busy doing it.

- *Strong-Contact Networks*: Structured explicitly to pass business referrals among members, they allow only one member per profession. Strong-contact networks are particularly good for developing in-depth relationships because you see the same members week after week and pass referrals as a part of each meeting.

- *Casual-contact Networks*: Bring businesspeople together in a less-structured context than strong-contact networks, but for many they are a primary source of referrals; membership is not limited by profession. These groups are good for developing breadth in your network, but deep, long-lasting relationships can be formed as well.
- *Service Organizations*: Associations that exist to provide and support humanitarian efforts and good works in the community and larger venues. They also bring people together in settings that facilitate referral and knowledge networking. Like casual-contact groups, they help you add breadth and diversity to your network.
- *Professional Associations:* Established to exchange information and ideas among those in a given industry, as well as to promote and support that industry. These networks often include direct competitors, but they also provide contacts in related, non-competing businesses as well.
- Social/business Organizations Combine social activities with business networking and can provide a variety of networking opportunities; many tend to resemble singles bars.
- *Women's Networking groups*: Still important networking organizations, but are slowly disappearing as women enter the business mainstream, especially as professionals, entrepreneurs, and small-business owners.
- Online Networks—A new phenomenon covering a wide range of interests.

COMPUTER NETWORKS

A computer network is two or more computers connected

together using a telecommunication system for the purpose of communication and sharing resources". Ask any computer network expert to simplify this definition to you and you will start a debate on how it should not be just two computers but three. Simply put a network is a means of communication between computers. Within a given network, computers can send files, e-mails and other correspondence to each other. Even things like instant messaging, is set up within a computer's network. There are two basic types of computer Networks. Lan and Wan.

LAN

LAN or Local Area Network is the most common kind of network set up. There are two ways to connect a LAN network. The simplest and easiest way is the peer-to-peer connection network. This is when two or more computers are directly connected to each other. For example if there were four computers in the network, computer 1 would be connected to computer 2, computer 2 would be connected to computer 3 and computer 3 would be connected to computer 4.

This means each computer is dependent on the other. And if there were a network problem with any one computer, all of them would be affected. The other type if the client server connection. This is the type of connection where all the computers in a given network are connected to one central computer. This is a more complicated network but one that is much more efficient that peer-to-peer.

A local area network, or LAN, is a network of connected computers in a room, building, or set of buildings. Local area networks have been around since the beginning of computer use. A LAN is defined as a user network whereby data is sent at high rates between people located relatively close to each other. LANs do not usually make use of leased communication lines, but only means of communication that are provided by the installer of the network.

The Internet is a wide area network, or WAN, which is distinct from a LAN. In contrast to the term *Internet,* local area networks are often called *intranets,* though sometimes this term refers to a cluster of LANs associated with a particular company or organization but not connected to the larger Internet. A local area network uses a hub or router to connect computers together.

The means of communication is the omnipresent Ethernet cable or wireless wi-fi technology. These technologies offer data transfer rates running between 10 to 10000 Mbit/s. Larger, more important LANs have redundant lines or other backup protocols. In networked computers, the most popular communication protocol is TCP/IP. Smaller LANs may be temporary and used between friends to play computer games over the network.

Over a network, users can share files, view files, make changes to data on other computers if permitted, play movies or music on multiple computers at once, chat with instant messaging, send e-mails to each other, play games, and so on. All the advantages of the Internet apply, although they only include others on the LAN, and the data transfer rates are high.

Perhaps the most frequently employed use of a LAN is to connect users to the Internet with only one connected router. In modern times, we use broadband cable or DSL modems to connect to the Internet, and it would be clumsy to have a modem associated with every computer, so we simply plug the modem into a router and link the router to computers with Ethernet cables. Configuring a LAN can be intimidating at first, but contemporary operating systems have programmes that do most of the necessary configurations automatically, so setting up a local area network is pretty easy. A local area network (LAN) supplies networking capability to a group of computers in close proximity to each other such as in an office building, a school, or a home. A LAN is useful for sharing resources like files, printers, games or other applications. A LAN in turn often connects to other LANs, and to the Internet or other WAN.

Most local area networks are built with relatively inexpensive hardware such as Ethernet cables, network adapters, and hubs. Wireless LAN and other more advanced LAN hardware options also exist.

Examples

The most common type of local area network is an Ethernet LAN. The smallest home LAN can have exactly two computers; a large LAN can accommodate many thousands of computers. Many LANs are divided into logical groups called subnets. An Internet Protocol (IP) "Class A" LAN can in theory accommodate more than 16 million devices organized into subnets.

High Performance Network

The HPN is used for the exchange of large amounts of operational data. Two Force10 E600 Routers, interconnected via 4-way 10-Gigabit Ethernet aggregated links, provide connectivity between the High Performance Computing Facility (HPCF) and the Data-Handling System (DHS). The HPCF network nodes are connected via 10-Gigabit Ethernet and all DHS nodes via Gigabit Ethernet aggregated links.

General Purpose Network

The GPN is used for all other traffic. It has at its core two Foundry BigIron RX-16 routers and at the edge seven Foundry Super-X switches. The core routers are interconnected via 4-way 10-Gigabit Ethernet aggregated links and have multiple Gigabit Ethernet uplinks to the edge routers. The core also includes two further Super-X switches that are dual-attached to the RX-16s via 10-Gigabit Ethernet.

The GPN provides connectivity to:

- The HPCF, the DHS and additional servers via Gigabit Ethernet ports in the core.
- The user desktops and laptops via Gigabit Ethernet ports on the edge switches.
- The firewalls (for the Wide Area Network and the Demilitarized Zone (DMZ) via Gigabit Ethernet ports in the core. The DMZ includes ECaccess, web servers, the mail gateway and DNS (Domain Name Servers).

The Hardware

Both the Force10 E600 chassis are populated with 24 10-

Gigabit-Ethernet and 144 Gigabit Ethernet ports. For resiliency there are four power supplies, two CPU modules and nine switching fabric modules. Both the RX-16 chassis are populated with 8 10-Gigabit Ethernet ports and 144 Gigabit Ethernet ports. For resiliency there are seven power supplies, two CPU modules and four switching fabric modules. The Super-X chassis each contain up to 156 Gigabit Ethernet ports and dual power-supplies.

WAN

Definition

The wide area network, often referred to as a WAN, is a communications network that makes use of existing technology to connect local computer networks into a larger working network that may cover both national and international locations. This is in contrast to both the local area network and the metropolitan area network, which provides communication within a restricted geographic area. Here is how the wide area network functions, and why it is so important to communications today.

The concept of linking one computer network with another is often desirable, especially for businesses that operate a number of facilities. Beginning with the local area network and going up to the wide area network, this is most easily accomplished by using existing telephony technology. Essentially, fibre optics are used to create the link between networks located in different facilities.

Often, this means using standard phone lines, referred to as POTS, or employing PSTN (public switched telephone network) technology. During the 1990s, a third option, that of ISDN (integrated services digital network) solutions for creation a wide area network gained a great deal of popularity, mainly because the concept made it more cost effective to extend the network beyond national boundaries.

With coverage in a broad area, a wide area network allows companies to make use of common resources in order to operate. For example, many retail drugstores make use of a wide area network as part of their support to customers who fill prescriptions with one of their stores. Once in the common customer database for the pharmacy, the client is free to fill a prescription at any of the company's locations, even while vacationing in another state.

Companies also make good use of the wide area network as well. Internal functions such as sales, production and development, marketing and accounting can also be shared with authorized locations through this sort of broad area network application. The concept of a wide area network as a means of taking individual location based computer networks and using them to create a unified computer network for the entire corporation means that employees can work from just about anywhere. Should one facility be damaged or rendered inaccessible due to natural disaster, employees simply move to another location where they can access the unified network, and keep on working.

Overview

WAN or Wide Area Network is when several LANs or independent computers are connected to a single, wider network. The Internet is the perfect example of WAN. E-mails, Chat Rooms and IMs all connect to the WAN of the Internet. WAN is much more complex and requires connecting devices or hubs from all over the world. The term Wide Area Network (WAN) usually refers to a network which covers a large geographical area, and use communications circuits to connect the intermediate nodes.

A major factor impacting WAN design and performance is a requirement that they lease communications circuits from telephone companies or other communications carriers. Transmission rates are typically 2 Mbps, 34 Mbps, 45 Mbps, 155 Mbps, 625 Mbps (or sometimes considerably more). Numerous WANs have been constructed, including public packet networks, large corporate networks, military networks, banking networks, stock brokerage networks, and airline reservation networks.

Some WANs are very extensive, spanning the globe, but most do not provide true global coverage. Organizations supporting WANs using the Internet Protocol are known as Network Service Providers (NSPs). These form the core of the Internet. Wide Area Networks, or WANs, connect a geographically diverse group of computers within a state, country, or even across several states or countries. WANs typically are connected by telephone lines, other types of communication lines, or radio waves.

Quite often, smaller local area networks (LANs) are linked together to form a WAN. This is accomplished via dedicated private lines, leased from telecommunications firms like Sprint and ATandT, or by Switched Multi-Megabit Data Services (SMDS) technology, developed in 1995 to eliminate the need for a leased line. WAN technology has been refined over a period of several decades. It first emerged in the mid-twentieth century with the advent of networks like ARPAnet. Developed in 1969 by the Department of Defence, ARPAnet and several other networks eventually evolved into the Internet, the largest WAN in the world.

The packet switching technology most commonly used with WANs surfaced in the 1960s, and standard packet switching protocol, known as X.25, was developed in 1976. To increase network speed, packet switching allows for the parceling of data into smaller chunks, known as packets, prior to transmission. These packets can travel independently via alternate routes, and they are reassembled once they reach their target.

Although X.25 remained the most popular WAN packet switching protocol for years, other packet switching protocols used with increasing frequency by WAN developers and administrators include the Internet standard, Transmission Control Protocol/Internet Protocol (TCP/IP), and Frame Relay, used most often by WANs connected via high speed T-1 and T-3 lines.

WANs are used for a variety of purposes. A corporation with offices in several locations may use a WAN to form an intranet. Quite often, the individual offices will use their own LANs for things like internal messaging, data processing functions, and hardware and software sharing. When these

LANs are joined together to form a WAN, similar data sharing and messaging capabilities become possible across a much broader geographic area.

Businesses wanting to link up with their suppliers or distributors may create a WAN as a means of establishing an extranet. For example, an extranet could provide a sales representative with electronic access to information in about the time it might take to deliver a product, or the availability of a product.

Some WANs bring together various types of communications, such as data, video, and voice. Some organizations, including companies, universities, research centres, hospitals, and libraries, use WANs to connect to the Internet. By connecting the NSP WANs together using links at Internet Packet Interchanges (sometimes called "peering points") a global communication infrastructure is formed.

NSPs do not generally handle individual customer accounts (except for the major corporate customers), but instead deal with intermediate organizations whom they can charge for high capacity communications.

They generally have an agreement to exchange certain volumes of data at a certain "quality of service" with other NSPs.

So practically any NSP can reach any other NSP, but may require the use of one or more other NSP networks to reach the required destination. NSPs vary in terms of the transit delay, transmission rate, and connectivity offered.

The characteristics of the transmission facilities lead to an emphasis on efficiency of communications techniques in the design of WANs.

Controlling the volume of traffic and avoiding excessive delays is important. Since the topologies of WANs are likely to be more complex than those of LANs, routing algorithms also receive more emphasis.

Many WANs also implement sophisticated monitoring procedures to account for which users consume the network resources. This is, in some cases, used to generate billing information to charge individual users.

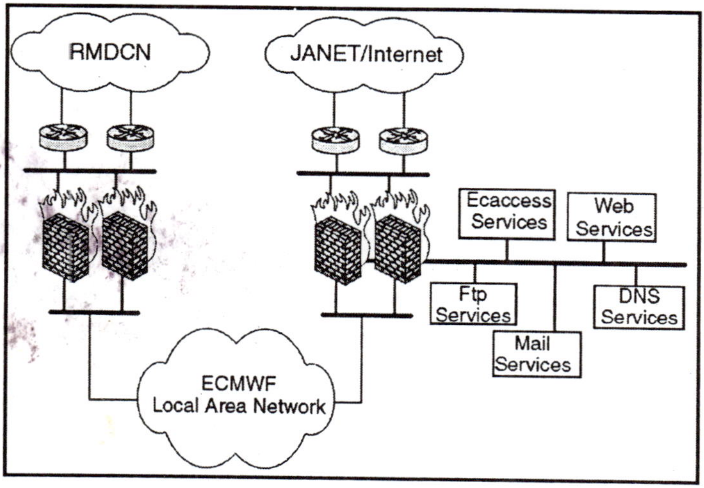

The size of a network is limited due to size and distance constraints. However networks may be connected over a high-speed communications link (called a WAN link) to link them together and thus becomes a WAN. WAN links are usually:

- Dial up connection
- Dedicated connection-It is a permanent full time connection. When a dedicated connection is used, the cable is leased rather than a part of the cable bandwidth and the user has exclusive use.
- Switched network-Several users share the same line or the bandwidth of the line.

  There are two types of switched networks:

  1. *Circuit switching*: This is a temporary connection between two points such as dial-up or ISDN.
  2. *Packet switching*: This is a connection between multiple points. It breaks data down into small packets to be sent across the network. A virtual circuit can improve performance by establishing a set path for data transmission. This will shave some overhead of a packet switching network. A variant of packet switching is called cell-switching where the data is broken into small cells with a fixed length.

Connection Technologies

- X.25-This is a set of protocols developed by the CCITT/ITU which specifies how to connect computer devices over an internet work. These protocols use a great deal of error checking for use over unreliable telephone lines. They establish a virtual communication circuit. It uses a store and forward method which can cause about a half second delay in data reception when two way communications are used. Their speed is about 64Kbps. Normally X.25 is used on packed switching PDNs (Public Data Networks). A line must be leased from the LAN to a PDN to connect to an X.25 network. A PAD (packet assembler/disassembler) or an X.25 interface is used on a computer to connect to the X.25 network. CCITT is an abbreviation for International Telegraph and Telephone Consultative Committee. The ITU is the International Telecommunication Union.
- Frame Relay-devices at both sides of the connection handle Error checking. Frame relay uses frames of varying length and it operates at the data link layer of the OSI model. A permanent virtual circuit (PVC) is established between two points on the network. Frame relay speed is between 56Kbps and 1.544Mbps. Frame relay networks provide a high-speed connection up to 1.544Mbps using variable-length packet switching over digital fibre-optic media. Frame relay does not store data and has less error checking than X.25.
- Switched Multi-megabit Data Service (SMDS)-Uses fixed length cell switching and runs at speeds of 1.533 to 45Mbps. It provides no error checking and assumes devices at both ends provide error checking.
- Telephone connections
  - Dial up
  - *Leased lines*: These are dedicated analog lines or digital lines. Dedicated digital lines are called digital data service (DDS) lines. A modem is

used to connect to analog lines, and a Channel Service Unit/Data Service Unit or Digital Service Unit(CSU/DSU) is used to connect to digital lines. The DSU connects to the LAN and the CSU connects to the line.

- *T Carrier lines*: Multiplexors are used to allow several channels on one line. The T1 line is basic T Carrier service. The available channels may be used separately for data or voice transmissions or they may be combined for more transmission bandwidth.
- T1 and T3 lines are the most common lines in use today. T1 and T2 lines can use standard copper wire. T3 and T4 lines require fibre-optic cable or other high-speed media. These lines may be leased partially called fractional T1 or fractional T3, which means a customer, can lease a certain number of channels on the line. A CSU/ DSU and a bridge or router is required to connect to a T1 line.
- Integrated Services Digital Network (ISDN)- Comes in two types and converts analog signals to digital for transmission. It is a dial up service
  a. Basic Rate ISDN (BRI)-Two 64Kbps B-channels with one 16Kbps D channel. The D-channel is used tor call control and setup.
  b. Primary Rate ISDN (PRI)-23 B-channels and one D channel. A device resembling a modem (called an ISDN modem) is used to connect to ISDN. The computer and telephone line are plugged into it.
- *Switched-56*: A switched line similar to a leased line where customers pay for the time they use the line. Speed is 56Kbps. It is not dedicated and will not work to connect a WAN.

- *Asynchronous Transfer Mode (ATM)*: May be used over a variety of media with both baseband and broadband systems. It is used for audio, video, and data. It uses fixed length data packets of 53 8 bit bytes called cell switching. 5 bytes contain header information. The cell contains path information that the packet is to use. It uses hardware devices to perform the switching of the data. Speeds from 155Mbps to 622 Mbps are achieved. Error checking is done at the receiving device, not by ATM. A permanent virtual connection or circuit (PVC) is established. It may also use a switched virtual circuit (SVC). *Service classes*:

- Constant bit rate for data.
- Variable bit rate for audio or video.
- Connection less for data.
- Connection oriented for data.

ATM can be embedded in other protocols such as ATM-25, T1, T3, OC-1, OC-3, OC-12, and OC-48.

Some ATM technologies include:

- ATM-25-25Mbps speed.
- STS-3-155Mbps on fibre or category 5 cable.
- STS-12-620 Mbps on fibre cable for campus wide network.
- STS-48-2.2 Gbps on fibre cable on a MAN.
- STS-192-8.8 Gbps on fibre cable on intercity long distance. Phone companies normally use this.

Synchronous Optical Network (SONET)-A physical layer standard that defines voice, data, and video delivery methods over fibre optic media. It defines data rates in terms of optical carrier (OC) levels.

The transmission rate of OC-1 is 51.8 Mbps. Each level runs at a multiple of the first. The OC-5 data rate is 5 times 51.8 Mbps which is 259 Mbps.

SONET also defines synchronous transport signals (STS) for copper media which use the same speed scale of OC levels. STS-3 runs at the same speed of OC-3. Mesh or ring topology is used to support SONET. SONET uses multiplexing. The ITU has incorporated SONET into their Synchronous Digital Hierarchy (SDH) recommendations.

WAN Technology Comparisons

Terms

- *Circuit switching*: Physical switched connection.
- *Message switching*: A store and forward mechanism where messages are treated as individual units.
- *Packet switching*: Messages are broken down into smaller packets with individual destination information. Independent routing is used which allows the packets to use any route between the source send destination. Much RAM and processing power is required to support this switching type.
- *Data gram packet switching*: Uses independent paths.
- *Virtual circuit packet switching*: This is used for audio and video streaming. A set path is established between the source and destination and a connection-oriented service is made.

NETWORKING TOPOLOGIES

DEFINITION

Network topology refers to the way that your computer network is arranged. The network can have a physical or a logical topology. The physical topology describes the layout of computers and where the workstations are positioned. The logical network topology describes how the information flows through the network.

Choosing your physical topology is important because if it is not chosen correctly, this could cause your network to not operate properly. There are several terms that describe the type of physical topology that a network can have. The most common topologies are bus, ring, star, and mesh. In a bus topology, all of the computers are attached to a single cable using terminators.

The terminators work to absorb the energy from the signals in the network. The bus topology is easy to install, but it is not reliable because a single default can bring down your network.

In a ring topology, each computer is connected directly to two other computers on the network. As with a bus topology, a single fault can disrupt a ring network. This type of network does have advantages, however, and does not require a network server. In a star topology, each computer is connected using its own separate cable. This set up is more reliable than a bus topology because its design makes it fault tolerant and susceptible to errors. The information on the network is transmitted from one system to another and the data flows in one single direction. The topology is expensive to maintain and is not reliable because removing one computer can disrupt your entire network.

In a mesh topology, a path is present from one computer to another computer in the network. The mesh topology is usually used in internet structure. The mesh topology can be complicated to construct because it has multiple connection between locations. For every computer that you have you will need at least one and a half connections for each one. This contributes to the expensive structure.

In choosing a network topology, understand that each one has its advantages and disadvantages. Research each one and see which one fits within your budget and which one fits your network layout. Also consider the amount of maintenance required in each topology. When setting up a network at home, consider a network topology that is simple and easy to maintain. You will also want a topology that is inexpensive to set up. If you are choosing a topology for a business, you will want to consider a topology that is reliable and resistant to errors. Your customers will need a network that is free of downtime; therefore, be sure that your topology is one that withstands disruption.

TYPES OF NETWORKING TOPOLOGIES

Bus Topology

A bus topology is a method of transmission on networks that uses a common vehicle for transmissions and thus it is categorized as shared communication. Imagine a bus picking up various people from one stop and dropping of people as it travels and then picking a few more. That is what happens in a bus network exactly. A bus network uses a multi-drop transmission medium, all node on the network share a common bus and thus share communication. This allows only one device to transmit at a time. A distributed access protocol determines which station is to transmit. Data frames contain source and destination addresses, where each station monitors the bus and copies frames addressed to itself.

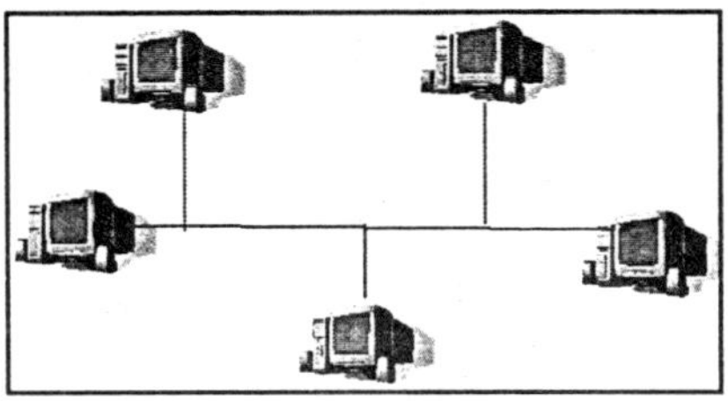

A bus topology connects each computer (nodes) to a single segment trunk (a communication line, typically coax cable, that is referred to as the 'bus'. The signal travels from one end of the bus to the other. A terminator is required at each to absorb the signal so as it does not reflect back across the bus. A media access method called CSMA/MA is used to handle the collision that occur when two signals placed on the wire at the same time. The bus topology is passive. In other words, the computers on the bus simply 'listen' for a signal; they are not responsible for moving the signal along.

However in a Bus topology only one device is allowed to transmit at a given point of time. The DAP or the Distribute Access Protocol has the information about which station has to transmit the data. The data that is being transmitted have frames that will have the source name and the network address.

Function of Bus Topology

The bus topology connects each computer on the network into something called the segment trunk. A bus is usually referred to a cable that connects end to end and this is used to transmit the signals from one end to the other end. At every end a terminator is placed so that it understands in which direction the data is traveling and also the terminator is used to absorb the signals. If the terminator does not absorb the signal then the same signal is reflected back to the bus confusing the whole data flow. The bus is considered to be a passive network because the computers are largely dependant on the signal that is being transmitted.

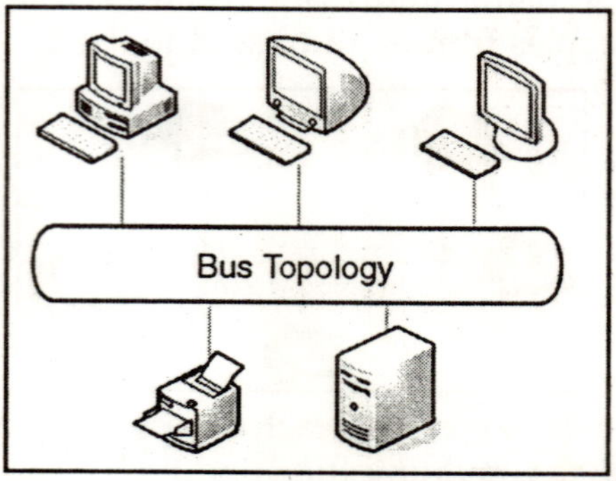

Advantages

The advantage of the Bus network is that if one computer fails in the network the others are still not affected and they continue to work. Bus network is very simple and easy to set up. If there is an urgent need to set up a network and perhaps be used on a short term basis then the Bus network is the best possibility. Bus networks use the least amount of cable to set up making it cost effective.

Limitations

In the bus network you will need a network connection in order to determine if the data is being transferred between two nodes. If the data transfer rate is high then the Bus network does not perform very well because the data travels in a stream and cannot be overloaded. The bus network is a bit challenging when you have to troubleshoot the problems. Bus networks are not suitable as large networks as there are limitations to the number of nodes you can set up for one single cable. As the number of computers increase in the network the data transfer rate goes down accordingly and noticeably.

Conclusion

The bus networks in spite of its limitations is considered to be the easiest and the fastest network that can be set up compared to the other kinds of network. In bus networks there is a collision handling system which ensures that data travels without errors and data is delivered correctly. There is a bus master on the network which ensures that data is flowing in the right direction and order. All the computers on the bus network however listen for the signals and they do not hold the responsibility to move the signal forward.

The signal carries forward on its own. So if one computer is not receiving any signals the signal still carries forward without stopping at the computer that has failed. These days bus networks are less common due to the advancement of networks and there are much lesser complicated networks that are easy to operate and efficient. However even these newer technologies derive their basics from older technologies like the Bus Topology.

Ring Topology

Definition

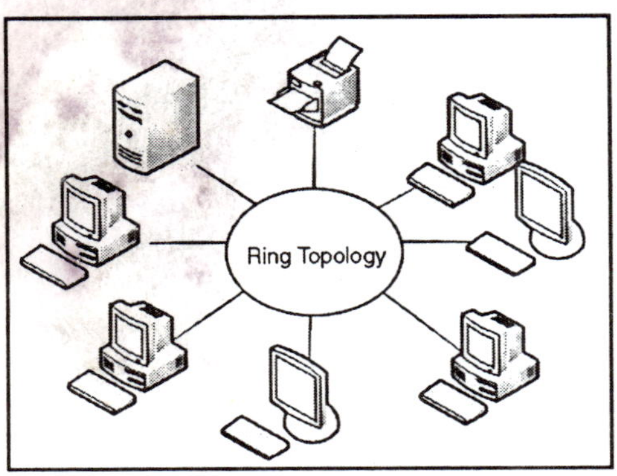

A ring topology is a network topology or circuit arrangement in which each network device is attached along the same signal path to two other devices, forming a path in the shape of a ring. Each device in the network that is also referred to as node handles every message that flows through the ring. Each node in the ring has a unique address. Since in a ring topology there is only one pathway between any two nodes, ring networks are generally disrupted by the failure of a single link.

The redundant topologies are used to eliminate network downtime caused by a single point of failure. All networks need redundancy for enhanced reliability. Network reliability is achieved through reliable equipment and network designs that are tolerant to failures and faults. The FDDI networks overcome the disruption in the network by sending data on a clockwise and a counterclockwise ring. In case there is a break in data flow,the data is wrapped back onto the complementary ring before it reaches the end of the cable thereby maintaining a path to every node within the complementary ring.

Ring network connects computers in a circle of point-to-point connections, with no central server, such as a series of desktop computers in an office.

Each node handles its own applications and also shares resources over the entire network. If one node becomes inoperative, the other nodes are still able to maintain contact with one another. Such a network is best for decentralized systems in which no priorities are required

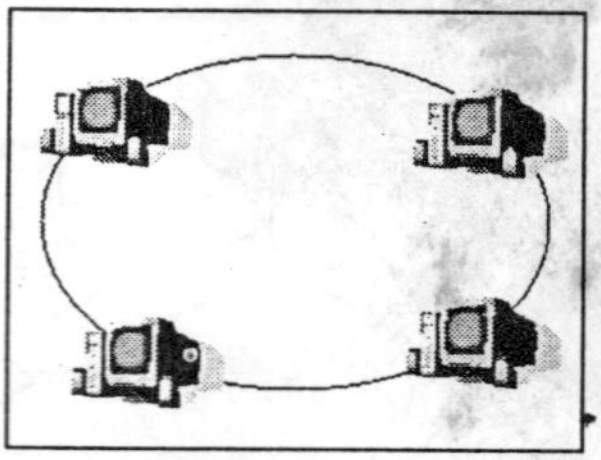

Under the network, a signal is transferred sequentially via a "token" fro one station to the next. When a station wants to transmit, it "grabs" the token, attaches data and an address to it, and then sends it around the ring.

The token travels along the ring until it reaches the destination address. The receiving computer acknowledges receipt with a return message to the sender. The sender then releases the token for the token for use by another computer. Each station on the ring has equal access but only one station can talk at a time. To allow an orderly access to the ring, a single electronic token passes from one computer to the next around the ring as seen in (token ring). A computer can only transmit dat

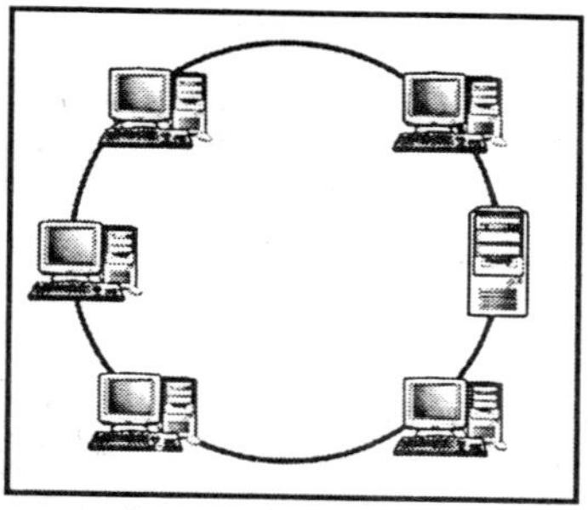

In a true ring topology, if a single computer or section of cable fails, there is an interruption in the signal. The entire network becomes inaccessible. Network disruption can also occur when computers are added or removed from the network, making it an impractical network design in environments where there is constant change to the network.

Ring networks are most commonly wired in a star configuration. In a Token Ring network, a multistation access unit (MSAU) is equivalent to a hub or switch on an Ethernet network. The MSAU performs the token circulation internally. To create the complete ring, the ring in (RI) port on each MSAU is connected to the ring out (RO) port on another MSAU. The last MSAU in the ring is then connected to the first, to complete the ring.

Token Ring Topology

Unlike Ethernet, Token Ring uses a ring topology whereby the data is sent from one machine to the next and so on around the ring until it ends up back where it started. It also uses a token passing protocol which means that a machine can only use the network when it has control of the Token, this ensures that there are no collisions because only one machine can use the network at any given time.

Figure below shows the basic of a Token Ring Topology. Although 16Mbps is the standard ring speed these days (and

Fast Token Ring is being developed) we will consider a 4Mbps Token Ring in this tutorial to explain the basic concepts.

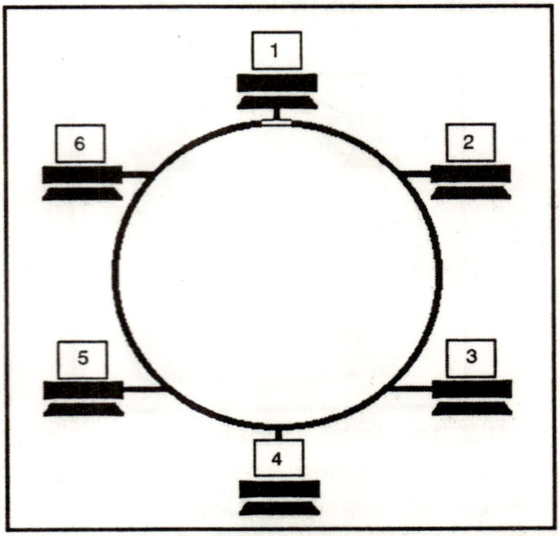

At the start, a free Token is circulating on the ring, this is a data frame which to all intents and purposes is an empty vessel for transporting data. To use the network, a machine first has to capture the free Token and replace the data with its own message. In the example above, machine 1 wants to send some data to machine 4, so it first has to capture the free Token. It then writes its data and the recipient's address onto the Token.

The packet of data is then sent to machine 2 who reads the address, realises it is not its own, so passes it on to machine 3. Machine 3 does the same and passes the Token on to machine 4. This time it is the correct address and so number 4 reads the message. It cannot, however, release a free Token on to the ring, it must first send the message back to number 1 with an acknowledgement to say that it has received the data (represented by the purple flashing screen).

The receipt is then sent to machine 5 who checks the address, realises that it is not its own and so forwards it on to the next machine in the ring, number 6. Machine 6 does the same and forwards the data to number 1, who sent the original message. Machine 1 recognizes the address, reads the acknowledgement from number 4 (represented by the purple flashing screen) and then releases the free Token back on to the ring ready for the next machine to use.

Token Ring Self Maintenance

When a Token Ring network starts up, the machines all take part in a negotiation to decide who will control the ring, or become the 'Active Monitor' to give it its proper title. This is won by the machine with the highest MAC address who is participating in the contention procedure, and all other machines become 'Standby Monitors'.

The job of the Active Monitor is to make sure that none of the machines are causing problems on the network, and to re-establish the ring after a break or an error has occurred. The Active Monitor performs Ring Polling every seven seconds and ring purges when there appears to be a problem.

The ring polling allows all machines on the network to find out who is participating in the ring and to learn the address of their Nearest Active Upstream Neighbour (NAUN). Ring purges reset the ring after an interruption or loss of data is reported. Each machine knows the address of its Nearest Active Upstream Neighbour.

This is an important function in a Token Ring as it updates the information required to re-establish itself when machines enter or leave the ring. When a machine enters the ring it performs a lobe test to verify that its own connection is working properly, if it passes, it sends a voltage to the hub which operates a relay to insert it into the ring.

If a problem occurs anywhere on the ring, the machine that is immediately after the fault will cease to receive signals. If this situation continues for a short period of time it initiates a recovery procedure which assumes that its NAUN is at fault, the outcome of this procedure either removes its neighbour from the ring or it removes itself.

Token Ring Operation Using a Hub

A Token Ring hub simply changes the topology from a physical ring to a star wired ring. The Token still circulates around the network and is still controlled in the same manner, however, using a hub or a switch greatly improves reliability because the hub can automatically bypass any ports that are disconnected or have a cabling fault.

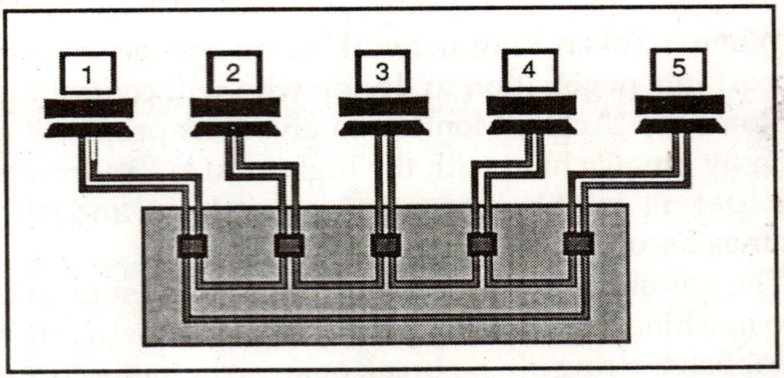

Further advancements have been made in recent years with regard to Token Ring technology, such as early Token release and Token Ring switching but as this site is primarily concerned with cabling issues we will not go into any more detail here.

Star Topology

Star topology is the most commonly used physical technology in Ethernets LANS, when installed, the star topology resembles spokes I n a bicycle wheel. The star topology is made up of a central connection point that is a device such as a hub, switch, or router, where all the cabling segments meet. Each host in the network is connected to the central devices with its own cables although a physical star topology costs more to implement than the physical bus topology , the advantage of star topology make it worth the additional cost.

Because each host it connected to the central device with its own cable, when that cable has a problem, only that host is affected, the rest of the network remains operational this benefit is extremely important and is why virtually every newly designed Ethernet a central connection point might be desirable for security or restricted access, but this is also a main disadvantage of a star topology.if the central device fails, the whole network become disconnected.when a star network is expanded to include an additional networking device that is connected for the main networking device, it is called an extended star topology.

Description

A star topology is designed with each node (file server, workstations, and peripherals) connected directly to a central network hub or concentrator. Data on a star network passes through the hub or concentrator before continuing to its destination. The hub or concentrator manages and controls all functions of the network. It also acts as a repeater for the data flow. This configuration is common with twisted pair cable; however, it can also be used with coaxial cable or fibre optic cable. Many businesses and home networks use the star topology. A star network features a central connection point called a "hub" that may be an actual hub or a switch as shown below:

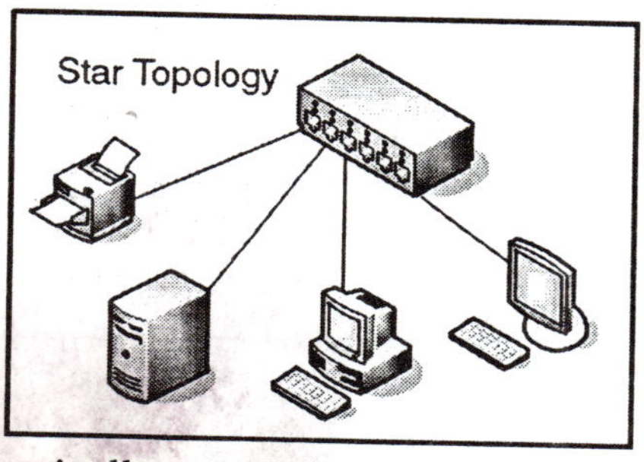

Devices typically connect to the hub with Unshielded Twisted Pair (UTP) Ethernet cables also known as RJ45 cables. Compared to the bus topology, a star network generally requires more cable, but a failure in any star network cable will only take down one computer's network access and not the entire LAN.

Star topology has the following advantages:

- Easy to manage
- Easy to locate problems (cable/workstations)
- Easier to expand than a bus or ring topology
- Easy to Install and Wire
- No disruptions to the network then connecting or removing devices.
- Easy to detect faults and to remove parts.

Star topology has following disadvantages:

- It is susceptible to a single point of failure be it the server or hub/switch
- With Increased devices and traffic can make the network slow
- Requires more Cable Length.
- If the hub or concentrator fails, nodes attached are disabled.
- More expensive than linear bus topologies because of the cost of the concentrators.

Tree Topology

Among all the Network Topologies we can derive that the Tree Topology is a combination of the bus and the Star Topology. The tree like structure allows you to have many servers on the network and you can branch out the network in many ways.

This is particularly helpful for colleges, universities and schools so that each of the branches can identify the relevant systems in their own network and yet connect to the big network in some way.

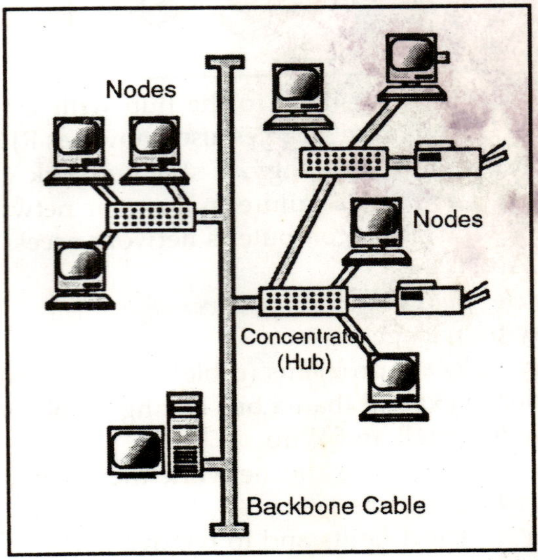

A Tree Structure suits best when the network is widely spread and vastly divided into many branches. Like any other topologies, the Tree Topology has its advantages and disadvantages. A Tree Network may not suit small networks and it may be a waste of cable to use it for small networks. Tree Topology has some limitations and the configuration should suit those limitations.

Benefits

A Tree Topology is supported by many network vendors ad even hardware vendors. A point to point connection is possible with Tree Networks. All the computers have access to the larger and their immediate networks. Best topology for branched out networks.

Limitations

In a Network Topology the length of the network depends on the type of cable that is being used. The Tree Topology network is entirely dependant on the trunk which is the main backbone of the network. If that has to fail then the entire network would fail. Since the Tree Topology network is big it is difficult to configure and can get complicated after a certain point.

The Tree Topology follows a hierarchical pattern where each level is connected to the next higher level in a symmetrical pattern. Each level in the hierarchy follows a certain pattern in connecting the nodes. Like the top most level might have only one node or two nodes and the following level in the hierarchy might have few more nodes which work on the point to point connectivity and the third level also has asymmetrical node to node pattern and each of these levels are connected to the root level in the hierarchy. A Tree Structured network is very similar to this and that is why it is called the Tree Topology.

Features

There will be at least three levels of hierarchy in the Tree Network Topology and they all work based on the root node.

The Tree Topology has two kinds of topology integral in it, the star and the linear way of connecting to nodes. The Tree Topology functions by taking into account the total number of nodes present in the network. It does not matter how many nodes are there on each level. Nodes can be added to any level of the hierarchy and there are no limitations a far as the total number of nodes do not exceed. The higher levels in the hierarchy are expected to perform more functions than the lower levels in the network.

Advantages of a Tree Topology

- Point-to-point wiring for individual segments.
- Supported by several hardware and software venders.

Disadvantages of a Tree Topology

- Overall length of each segment is limited by the type of cabling used.
- If the backbone line breaks, the entire segment goes down.
- More difficult to configure and wire than other topologies.

Mesh Topology

A type of network setup where each of the computers and network devices are interconnected with one another, allowing for most transmissions to be distributed, even if one of the connections go down. This type of topology is not commonly used for most computer networks as it is difficult and expensive to have redundant connection to every computer. However, this type of topology is commonly used for wireless networks. The *mesh* topology incorporates a unique network design in which each computer on the network connects to every other, creating a point-to-point connection between every device on the network.

The purpose of the mesh design is to provide a high level of redundancy. If one network cable fails, the data always has an alternative path to get to its destination.

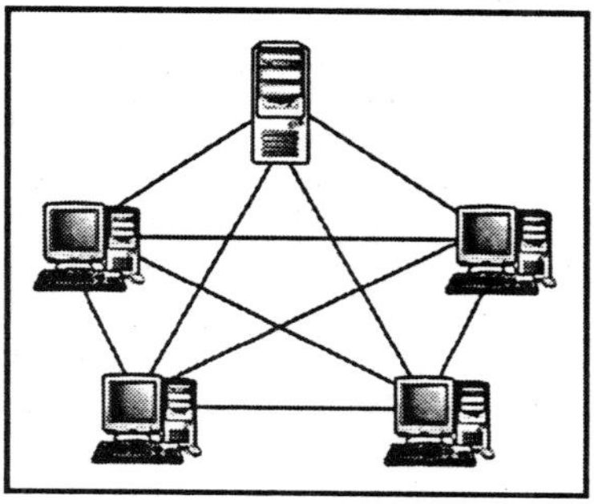

As seen in the above figure, the wiring for a mesh network can be very complicated. Further, the cabling costs associated with the mesh topology can be high, and troubleshooting a failed cable can be tricky. Because of this, the mesh topology is rarely used. A variation on a true mesh topology is the hybrid mesh. It creates a redundant point-to-point network connection between only specific network devices.

Wireless Mesh Networks

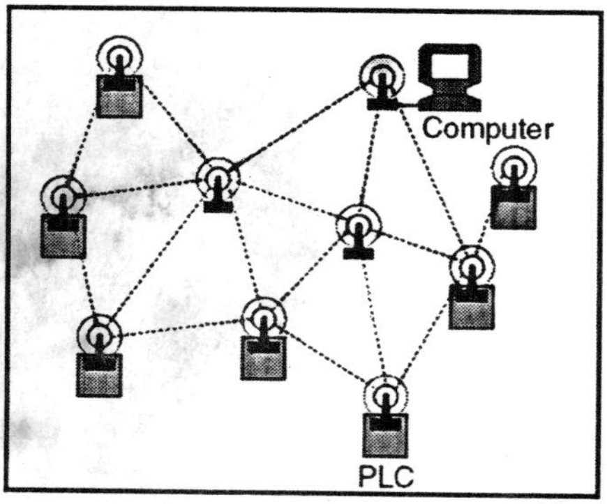

Wireless Mesh Networks work based on the radio frequencies and was originally developed by the army to be able to communicate. The reliability factor is high in any kind of Mesh Network. There are three types of wireless Mesh Topologies.

- Fixed Wireless Connections
- Peer to Peer or Adhoc Networks
- Node to Node

Fixed Mesh Networks

The fixed Mesh Networks will work only in the specified location and they are not mobile networks. They are meant to be used in a limited surrounding with boundaries. The location of nodes in affixed Mesh Network is all pre determined and they are not interchangeable. The fixed Mesh Network does not work on line of sight like the other types of Mesh Networks. The total number of hops in a fixed Mesh Network is usually fixed and also short. There may not be many nodes as this kind of Mesh Networks exist within an office or building. More often than not the data travels ion a specific direction.

Peer to Peer Mobile Networks

In a peer to peer mobile network the individual devices connect to each other using the Mesh Network. The peer does not require connecting to the main node and they can still communicate from one device to another device by taking the shortest possible data transfer route. However many experts believe that in the peer to peer Mesh Networks the problems with scalability in terms of time taken for data transfer is questionable. The device has to know to transmit the data in the most optimal path and the entire data transfer or depends on this single factor. If the device is incapable then the whole purpose of using it in a peer to peer connection is lost.

INTERNET

The Internet is a global network of computers. Every computer that is connected to the Internet is considered a part of that network. This means even your home computer. It's all a matter of degrees, you connect to your ISP's network, then your ISP connects to a larger network and so on. At the top of the tree is the high-capacity backbones, all of these interconnect at 'Network Access Points' 'NAPs' at important regions around the world.

The entire Internet is based on agreements between these backbone providers who set in place all the fibre optics lines and other technical aspects of the Internet. The first high speed backbone was created by the 'National Science Foundation' in 1987. The Internet was first created by the Advanced Research Projects Agency (ARPA) of the U.S. government in 1960's, and was first known as the ARPANet. At this stage the Internet's first computers were at academic and government institutions.

They were mainly used for accessing files and to send e-mail. From 1983 onwards the Internet as we know it today started to form with the introduction of the communication protocol TCP/IP to ARPANet. Since 1983 the Internet has accommodated alot of changes and continues to keep developing. The last two decades has seen the Internet accommodate such things as network LANs and ATM and frame switched services. The Internet continues to evolve with it becoming available on mobile phones and pagers and possibly on televisions in the future. The actual term "Internet" was finally defined in 1995 by FNC (The Federal Networking Council). The resolution created by the The Federal Networking Council (FNC) agrees that the following language reflects our definition of the term "Internet". "Internet" refers to the global information system that,

EVOLUTION

The underpinnings of the Internet are formed by the global interconnection of hundreds of thousands of otherwise independent computers, communications entities and information systems. What makes this interconnection possible is the use of a set of communication standards, procedures and formats in common among the networks and the various devices and computational facilities connected to them. The procedures by which computers communicate with each other are called "protocols."

While this infrastructure is steadily evolving to include new capabilities, the protocols initially used by the Internet are called the "TCP/IP" protocols, named after the two protocols that formed the principal basis for Internet operation. On top of this infrastructure is an emerging set of architectural concepts and data structures for heterogeneous information systems that renders the Internet a truly global information system.

In essence, the Internet is an architecture, although many people confuse it with its implementation. When the Internet is looked at as an architecture, it manifests two different abstractions. One abstraction deals with communications connectivity, packet delivery and a variety of end-end communication services. The other abstraction deals with the Internet as an information system, independent of its underlying communications infrastructure, which allows creation, storage and access to a wide range of information resources, including digital objects and related services at various levels of abstraction.

Interconnecting computers is an inherently digital problem. Computers process and exchange digital information, meaning that they use a discrete mathematical "binary" or "two-valued" language of 1s and 0s. For communication purposes, such information is mapped into continuous electrical or optical waveforms. The use of digital signaling allows accurate regeneration and reliable recovery of the underlying bits.

We use the terms "computer," "computer resources" and "computation" to mean not only traditional computers, but also devices that can be controlled digitally over a network, information resources such as mobile programmes and other computational capabilities. The telephone network started out with operators who manually connected telephones to each other through "patch panels" that accepted patch cords from each telephone line and electrically connected them to one another through the panel, which operated, in effect, like a switch. The result was called circuit switching, since at its conclusion, an electrical circuit was made between the calling telephone and the called telephone. Conventional circuit switching, which was developed to handle telephone calls, is inappropriate for connecting computers because it makes limited use of the telecommunication facilities and takes too long to set up connections. Although reliable enough for voice communication, the circuit-switched voice network had difficulty delivering digital information without errors. For digital communications, packet switching is a better choice, because it is far better suited to the typically "burst" communication style of computers. Computers that communicate typically send out brief but intense bursts of data, then remain silent for a while before sending out the next burst. These bursts are communicated as packets, which are very much like electronic postcards.

The postcards, in reality packets, are relayed from computer to computer until they reach their destination. The special computers that perform this forwarding function are called variously "packet switches" or "routers" and form the equivalent of many bucket brigades spanning continents and oceans, moving buckets of electronic postcards from one computer to another. Together these routers and the communication links between them form the underpinnings of the Internet.

Without packet switching, the Internet would not exist, as we now know it. Going back to the postcard analogy, postcards can get lost. They can be delivered out of order, and they can be delayed by varying amounts. The same is true of Internet packets, which, on the Internet, can even be duplicated. The Internet Protocol is the postcard layer of the Internet. The next higher layer of protocol, TCP, takes care of re-sending the "postcards" to recover packets that might have been lost, and putting packets back in order if they have become disordered in transit.

Of course, packet switching is about a billion times faster than the postal service or a bucket brigade would be. It also has to operate over many different communications systems, or substrata. The authors designed the basic architecture to be so simple and undemanding that it could work with most communication services.

Many organizations, including commercial ones, carried out research using the TCP/IP protocols in the 1970s. Email was steadily used over the nascent Internet during that time and to the present. It was not until 1994 that the general public began to be aware of the Internet by way of the World Wide

Web application, particularly after Netscape Communications was formed and released its browser and associated server software.

Thus, the evolution of the Internet was based on two technologies and a research dream. The technologies were packet switching and computer technology, which, in turn, drew upon the underlying technologies of digital communications and semiconductors. The research dream was to share information and computational resources. But that is simply the technical side of the story. Equally important in many ways were the other dimensions that enabled the Internet to come into existence and flourish. This aspect of the story starts with cooperation and far-sightedness in the U.S. Government, which is often derided for lack of foresight but is a real hero in this story. It leads on to the enthusiasm of private sector interests to build upon the government funded developments to expand the Internet and make it available to the general public.

Perhaps most important, it is fueled by the development of the personal computer industry and significant changes in the telecommunications industry in the 1980s, not the least of which was the decision to open the long distance market to competition. The role of workstations, the Unix operating system and local area networking (especially the Ethernet) are themes contributing to the spread of Internet technology in the 1980s into the research and academic community from which the Internet industry eventually emerged.

Many individuals have been involved in the development and evolution of the Internet covering a span of almost four decades if one goes back to the early writings on the subject of computer networking by Kleinrock, Licklider, Baran, Roberts, and Davies. The ARPANET, described below, was the first wide-area computer network.

The NSFNET, which followed more than a decade later under the leadership of Erich Bloch, Gordon Bell, Bill Wulf and Steve Wolff, brought computer networking into the mainstream of the research and education communities. It is not our intent here to attempt to attribute credit to all those whose contributions were central to this story, although we mention a few of the key players

ROLE OF DARPA

Modern computer networking technologies emerged in the early 1970s. In 1969, The U.S. Defence Advanced Research Projects Agency (variously called ARPA and DARPA), an agency within the Department of Defence, commissioned a wide-area computer network called the ARPANET. This network made use of the new packet switching concepts for interconnecting computers and initially linked computers at universities and other research institutions in the United States and in selected NATO countries.

At that time, the ARPANET was essentially the only realistic wide-area computer network in existence, with a base of several dozen organizations, perhaps twice that number of computers and numerous researchers at those sites. The programme was led at DARPA by Larry Roberts.

The packet switches were built by Bolt Beranek and Newman (BBN), a DARPA contractor. Others directly involved in the ARPANET activity included the authors, Len Kleinrock, Frank Heart, Howard Frank, Steve Crocker, Jon Postel and many many others in the ARPA research community.

Back then, the methods of internetworking (that is interconnecting computer networks) were primitive or non-existent. Two organizations could interwork technically by agreeing to use common equipment, but not every organization was interested in this approach. Absent that, there was jury-rigging, special case development and not much else. Each of these networks stood on its own with essentially no interaction between them – a far cry from today's Internet.

In the early 1970s, ARPA began to explore two alternative applications of packet switching technology based on the use of synchronous satellites (SATNET) and ground-based packet radio (PRNET). The decision by Kahn to link these two networks and the ARPANET as separate and independent networks resulted in the creation of the Internet programme and the subsequent collaboration with Cerf.

These two systems differed in significant ways from the ARPANET so as to take advantage of the broadcast and wireless aspects of radio communications. The strategy that had been adopted for SATNET originally was to embed the SATNET software into an ARPANET packet switch, and interwork the two networks through memory-to-memory transfers within the packet switch.

This approach, in place at the time, was to make SATNET an "embedded" network within the ARPANET; users of the network would not even need to know of its existence. The technical team at Bolt Beranek and Newman (BBN), having built the ARPANET switches and now building the SATNET software, could easily produce the necessary patches to glue the programmes together in the same machine. Indeed, this is what they were under contract with DARPA to provide.

By embedding each new network into the ARPANET, a seamless internetworked capability was possible, but with no realistic possibility of unleashing the entrepreneurial networking spirit that has manifest itself in modern day Internet developments. A new approach was in order. The Packet Radio (PRNET) programme had not yet gotten underway so there was ample opportunity to change the approach there. In addition, up until then, the SATNET programme was only an equipment development activity. No commitments had been obtained for the use of actual satellites or ground stations to access them. Indeed, since there was no domestic satellite industry in the U.S. then, the only two viable alternatives were the use of Intelsat or U.S. military satellites. The time for a change in strategy, if it was to be made, was then.

ARCHITECTURE

The authors created architecture for interconnecting independent networks that could then be federated into a seamless whole without changing any of the underlying networks. This was the genesis of the Internet, as we know it today. In order to work properly, the architecture required a global addressing mechanism (or Internet address) to enable computers on any network to reference and communicate with computers on any other network in the federation. Internet addresses fill essentially the same role as telephone numbers do in telephone networks.

The design of the Internet assumed first that the individual networks could not be changed to accommodate new architectural requirements; but this was largely a pragmatic assumption to facilitate progress. The networks also had varying degrees of reliability and speed. Host computers would have to be able to put disordered packets back into the correct order and discard duplicate packets that had been generated along the way.

This was a major change from the virtual circuit-like service provided by ARPANET and by then contemporary commercial data networking services such as Tymnet and Telenet. In these networks, the underlying network took responsibility for keeping all information in order and for re-sending any data that might have been lost. The Internet design made the computers responsible for tending to these network problems. A key architectural construct was the introduction of gateways (now called routers) between the networks to handle the disparities such as different data rates, packet sizes, error conditions, and interface specifications. The gateways would also check the destination Internet addresses of each packet to determine the gateway to which it should be forwarded. These functions would be combined with certain end-end functions to produce the reliable communication from source to destination. A draft paper by the authors describing this approach was given at a meeting of the International Network Working Group in 1973 in Sussex, England and the final paper was subsequently published by the Institute for Electrical and Electronics Engineers, the leading professional society for the electrical engineering profession, in its Transactions on Communications in May, 1974.

DARPA contracted with Cerf's group at Stanford to carry out the initial detailed design of the TCP software and, shortly thereafter, with BBN and University College London to build independent implementations of the TCP protocol (as it was then called – it was later split into TCP and IP) for different machines. BBN also had a contract to build a prototype version of the gateway.

These three sites collaborated in the development and testing of the initial protocols on different machines. Cerf, then a professor at Stanford, provided the day-to-day leadership in the initial TCP software design and testing. BBN deployed the gateways between the ARPANET and the PRNET and also with SATNET. During this period, under Kahn's overall leadership at DARPA, the initial feasibility of the Internet Architecture was demonstrated.

The TCP/IP protocol suite was developed and refined over a period of four more years and, in 1980, it was adopted as a standard by the U.S. Department of Defence. On January 1, 1983 the ARPANET converted to TCP/IP as its standard host protocol. Gateways (or routers) were used to pass packets to and from host computers on "local area networks." Refinement and extension of these protocols and many others associated with them continues to this day by way of the Internet Engineering Task Force.

RUNNING OF INTERNET

Domain Name System

The Internet evolved as an experimental system during the 1970s and early 1980s. It then flourished after the TCP/IP protocols were made mandatory on the ARPANET and other networks in January 1983; these protocols thus became the standard for many other networks as well. Indeed, the Internet grew so rapidly that the existing mechanisms for associating the names of host computers (*e.g.* UCLA, USC-ISI) to Internet addresses (known as IP addresses) were about to be stretched beyond acceptable engineering limits.

Most of the applications in the Internet referred to the target computers by name. These names had to be translated into Internet addresses before the lower level protocols could be activated to support the application. For a time, a group at SRI International in Menlo Park, CA, called the Network Information Centre (NIC), maintained a simple, machine-readable list of names and associated Internet addresses which was made available on the net.

Hosts on the Internet would simply copy this list, usually daily, so as to maintain a local copy of the table. This list was called the "host.txt" file (since it was simply a text file). The list served the function in the Internet that directory services (*e.g.* 411 or 703-555-1212) do in the US telephone system-the translation of a name into an address. As the Internet grew, it became harder and harder for the NIC to keep the list current. Anticipating that this problem would only get worse as the network expanded, researchers at USC Information Sciences Institute launched an effort to design a more distributed way of providing this same information. The end result was the Domain Name System (DNS) which allowed hundreds of thousands of "name servers" to maintain small portions of a global database of information associating IP addresses with the names of computers on the Internet. The naming structure was hierarchical in character. For example, all host computers associated with educational institutions would have names like "stanford.edu" or "ucla.edu".

Specific hosts would have names like "cs.ucla.edu" to refer to a computer in the computer science department of UCLA, for example. A special set of computers called "root servers" maintained information about the names and addresses of other servers that contained more detailed name/ address associations.

The designers of the DNS also developed seven generic "top level" domains, as follows:

- *Education*: EDU
- *Government*: GOV
- *Military*: MIL
- *International*: INT
- *Network*: NET
- *Organization*: ORG
- *Commercial*: COM

Under this system, for example, the host name "UCLA" became "UCLA.EDU" because it was operated by an educational institution, while the host computer for "BBN" became "BBN.COM" because it was a commercial organization. Top-level domain names also were created for every country: United Kingdom names would end in ".UK," while the ending ".FR" was created for the names of France.

The Domain Name System (DNS) was and continues to be a major element of the Internet architecture, which contributes to its scalability. It also contributes to controversy over trademarks and general rules for the creation and use of domain names, creation of new top-level domains and the like. At the same time, other resolution schemes exist as well.

One of the authors (Kahn) has been involved in the development of a different kind of standard identification and resolution scheme that, for example, is being used as the base technology by book publishers to identify books on the Internet by adapting various identification schemes for use in the Internet environment.

For example, International Standard Book Numbers (ISBNs) can be used as part of the identifiers. The identifiers then resolve to state information about the referenced books, such as location information (*e.g.* multiple sites) on the Internet that is used to access the books or to order them.

These developments are taking place in parallel with the more traditional means of managing Internet resources. They offer an alternative to the existing Domain Name System with enhanced functionality. The growth of Web servers and users of the Web has been remarkable, but some people are confused about the relationship between the World Wide Web and the Internet. The Internet is the global information system that includes communication capabilities and many high level applications.

The Web is one such application. The existing connectivity of the Internet made it possible for users and servers all over the world to participate in this activity. Electronic mail is another important application. As of today, over 60 million computers take part in the Internet and about 3.6 million web sites were estimated to be accessible on the net. Virtually every user of the net has access to electronic mail and web browsing capability. E-mail remains a critically important application for most users of the Internet, and these two functions largely dominate the use of the Internet for most users.

INTERNET STANDARDS PROCESS

Internet standards were once the output of research activity sponsored by DARPA. The principal investigators on the internetting research effort essentially determined what technical features of the TCP/IP protocols would become common. The initial work in this area started with the joint effort of the two authors, continued in Cerf's group at Stanford, and soon thereafter was joined by engineers and scientists at BBN and University College London.

This informal arrangement has changed with time and details can be found elsewhere. At present, the standards efforts for Internet are carried out primarily under the auspices of the Internet Society (ISOC). The Internet Engineering Task Force (IETF) operates under the leadership of its Internet Engineering Steering Group (IESG), which is populated by appointees approved by the Internet Architecture Board (IAB) which is, itself, now part of the Internet Society.

The IETF comprises over one hundred working groups categorized and managed by Area Directors specializing in specific categories. There are other bodies with considerable interest in Internet standards or in standards that must interwork with the Internet. Examples include the International Telecommunications Union Telecommunications standards group (ITU-T), the International Institute of Electrical and Electronic Engineers (IEEE) local area network standards group (IEEE 801), the Organization for International Standardization (ISO), the American National Standards Institute (ANSI), the World Wide Web Consortium (W3C), and many others. As Internet access and services are provided by existing media such as telephone, cable and broadcast, interactions with standards bodies and legal structures formed to deal with these media will become an increasingly complex matter. The intertwining of interests is simultaneously fascinating and complicated, and has increased the need for thoughtful cooperation among many interested parties.

MANAGING THE INTERNET

Perhaps the least understood aspect of the Internet is its management. In recent years, this subject has become the subject of intense commercial and international interest, involving multiple governments and commercial organizations, and recently congressional hearings. At issue is how the Internet will be managed in the future, and, in the process, what oversight mechanisms will insure that the public interest is adequately served.

In the 1970s, managing the Internet was easy. Since few people knew about the Internet, decisions about almost everything of real policy concern were made in the offices of DARPA. It became clear in the late 1970s, however, that more community involvement in the decision-making processes was essential. In 1979, DARPA formed the Internet Configuration Control Board (ICCB) to insure that knowledgeable members of the technical community discussed critical issues, educated people outside of DARPA about the issues, and helped others to implement the TCP/IP protocols and gateway functions.

At the time, there were no companies that offered turnkey solutions to getting on the Internet. It would be another five years or so before companies like Cisco Systems were formed, and while there were no PCs yet, the only workstations available were specially built and their software was not generally configured for use with external networks; they were certainly considered expensive at the time.

In 1983, the small group of roughly twelve ICCB members was reconstituted (with some substitutions) as the Internet Activities Board (IAB), and about ten "Task Forces" were established under it to address issues in specific technical areas. The attendees at Internet Working Group meetings were invited to become members of as many of the task forces as they wished.

The management of the Domain Name System offers a kind of microcosm of issues now frequently associated with overall management of the Internet's operation and evolution. Someone had to take responsibility for overseeing the system's general operation. In particular, top-level domain names had to be selected, along with persons or organizations to manage each of them. Rules for the allocation of Internet addresses had to be established.

DARPA had previously asked the late Jon Postel of the USC Information Sciences Institute to take on numerous functions related to administration of names, addresses and protocol related matters. With time, Postel assumed further responsibilities in this general area on his own, and DARPA, which was supporting the effort, gave its tacit approval. This activity was generally referred to as the Internet Assigned Numbers Authority (IANA). In time, Postel became the arbitrator of all controversial matters concerning names and addresses until his untimely death in October 1998.

It is helpful to consider separately the problem of managing the domain name space and the Internet address space. These two vital elements of the Internet architecture have rather different characteristics that colour the management problems they generate. Domain names have semantics that numbers may not imply; and thus a means of determining who can use what names is needed. As a result, speculators on Internet names often claim large numbers of them without intent to use them other than to resell them later. Alternate resolution mechanisms, if widely adopted, could significantly change the landscape here.

The rapid growth of the Internet has triggered the design of a new and larger address space (the so-called IP version 6 address space); today's Internet uses IP version 4. However, little momentum has yet developed to deploy IPv6 widely. Despite concerns to the contrary, the IPv4 address space will not be depleted for some time. Further, the use of Dynamic Host Configuration Protocol (DHCP) to dynamically assign IP addresses has also cut down on demand for dedicated IP addresses.

Nevertheless, there is growing recognition in the Internet technical community that expansion of the address space is needed, as is the development of transition schemes that allow interoperation between IPv4 and IPv6 while migrating to IPv6. In 1998, the Internet Corporation for Assigned Names and

Numbers (ICANN) was formed as a private sector, non-profit, organization to oversee the orderly progression in use of Internet names and numbers, as well as certain protocol related matters that required oversight. The birth of this organization, which was selected by the Department of Commerce for this function, has been difficult, embodying as it does many of the inherent conflicts in resolving discrepancies in this arena. However, there is a clear need for an oversight mechanism for Internet domain names and numbers, separate from their day-to-day management. Many questions about Internet management remain. They may also prove difficult to resolve quickly. Of specific concern is what role the government and indeed governments around the world need to play in its continuing operation and evolution.

ADVANTAGES OF INTERNET

There are many advantages of using the Internet, such as.

Global Audience

Content published on the World Wide Web is immediately available to a global audience of users. This makes the World Wide Web a very cost-effective medium to publish information. Reaching more than 190 countries.

Operates 24 hours and 365 days

You don't need to wait until resources are available to conduct business. From a consumer's perspective as well as a provider's business can be consummated at any time. The fact that the Internet is operational at all times makes it the most efficient business machine to date.

Relatively Inexpensive

It is relatively inexpensive to publish information on the Internet. At a fraction of the cost to publish information by traditional methods, various organizations and individuals can now distribute information to millions of users. It costs only a few thousand dollars to establish an Internet presence and publish content on the Internet.

Product Advertising

You can use the World Wide Web to advertise various products. Before purchasing a product, customers will be able to look up various product specification sheets and find out additional information. You can use the multimedia capabilities of the World Wide Web to make available not only various product specification sheets but also audio files, images, and even video clips of products in action.

The beauty of the Web is that it allows customers to explore products in as much detail as they desire. If the client just wants a general overview, he or she can look at the advertising information. For those wanting more in depth information, you can provide white papers and product descriptions for download. The Web allows a business to provide timely information, you can simply place the information on the Web page and it is available immediately for your customers.

Distribute Product Catalogs

The World Wide Web is a very effective medium for distributing product catalogs. In the old days, putting together a product catalog used to be very costly in terms of time and money needed to publish and distribute it. The World Wide Web changes all this by allowing content developers to put together a sales catalog and make it available to millions of users immediately.

Furthermore, unlike printed product catalogs that are usually updated around once a month, product catalogs on the World Wide Web can be updated as needed to respond to various changing market conditions.

Online Surveys

Traditional methods of performing surveys are often relatively slow and expensive compared to online surveys conducted on the Internet. For example, in order to fill out various needs of customers or what they would like to see in a future product, it's often necessary to compile a list of address and mail a questionnaire to many customers.

The success of such an attempt is not always guaranteed and can be very costly in terms of mailing the questionnaires and entering responses to a databases and analyzing it. On the other hand, you can use the World Wide Web to automate the whole process. For example, you can set up a CGI script to conduct online surveys. Results of such a survey can be automatically updated to a database. This database can then be used to keep a pulse on various opinions and needs of customers.

Announcements

With the World Wide Web, you can distribute various announcements to millions of users in a timely manner. Because there is virtually no time lag from the time it takes to publish information to making the information available to users, the Web is an ideal medium to publicize announcements.

As more people discover the virtues of the Web and get connected to the Internet, the Web will become the medium of choice for many organizations and individuals to publicize various announcements.

Provide Technical Support

You can also use Web site to provide technical support to users. Because Web pages can be updated immediately with new information, various technical support literature can be immediately modified in light of new findings and developments. This can be accomplished without having to distribute changes to all users affected by any changes using traditional mediums of information distribution, which are often quite costly compared to the World Wide Web.

Create Online Discussion Forums

By using applications such as WebBoard, it's possible to set up online discussion forums on the Web.

Obtain Customer Feedback

The interactive nature of the World Wide Web is ideal for

obtaining customer feedback. You can easily set up a CGI script to obtain customer feedback about a product or service. Because customer feedback submitted by customers can be read immediately, it's possible to respond to various customer concerns in a timely manner, increasing customer satisfaction and quality of customer service.

Immediate Distribution of Information

When information is added to a Web site, it's immediately available for browsing by millions of Internet users. The World Wide Web is an ideal medium of information distribution because it takes away the time lag associated with publishing content and actually making it available to users

Easy Integration with Internal Information Systems

Internet information systems deployed on the Internet can be easily integrated with internal information systems managed with office productivity applications such as Microsoft Office.

Powerful Content Publishing Tools

A new breed of Internet aware applications will start emerging in software stores by the time you read this. These applications will enable users to develop content for the World Wide Web by simply saving as an HTML file. In addition to software developers making existing applications Internet aware, various new, powerful, and easy-to use Internet content publishing applications are also being developed. These applications will make the task of publishing content on the Internet even easier. Most of these applications are developed for Windows users.

Multimedia

The capability to incorporate multimedia into Web pages is a major advantage of using World Wide Web to publish information. For example, many Web sites use sounds and video clips to make the content easier and more interesting to browse.

Formatting Capabilities

Content published on the World Wide Web can be richly formatted by using various HTML tags and graphic formats. The capability to do this is a major reason for the success of the World Wide Web. In addition to using HTML tags and various multimedia formats in Web pages, various interactive controls can also be added to a web page. This capability allows Web site content developers to create "active" Web sites. For example, before a user sends some information to a Web server for processing, a VBScript or JavaScript subroutine can be used to verify information typed in by the user. Various formatting capabilities, along with technologies such as Java and VBScript, make the World Wide Web a richly interactive medium that you can use to distribute information to millions of users.

DISADVANTAGES OF INTERNET

Many fear the Internet because of its disadvantages. They claim to not use the Internet because they are afraid of the possible consequences or are simply not interested. People who have yet connected to the Internet claim they are not missing anything. Today's technological society must realise, it is up to them to protect themselves on the Internet.

Children using the Internet has become a big concern. Most parents do not realise the dangers involved when their children log onto the Internet. When children are online, they can easily be lured into something dangerous. When children talk to others online, they do not realise they could actually be talking to a harmful person.

In addition, children may also receive pornography online by mistake; therefore, causing concern among parents everywhere. Whether surfing the Web, reading newsgroups, or using e-mail, children can be exposed to extremely inappropriate material. Pornographic sites tend to make sure they are the first sites to be listed in any search area. Some critics say that parents are responsible for their own children on the Internet because there are available services to protect children.

To keep children safe, parents and teachers must be aware of the dangers. They must actively guide and guard their children online.There are a number of tools available today that may help keep the Internet environment safer for children. Musicians are also concerned with disadvantages to the Net such as, accessibility and freedom. They are upset because the Internet provides their music online at no charge to consumers. File-sharing software, such Kazaa, Emule and may others provides copyrighted songs to all Internet users.

The main concern is-the music is free! Musicians feel "they are not getting paid for their work". It is almost impossible to close down all file-sharing services; there are too many of them to count. Another major disadvantage of the Internet is privacy. Electronic messages sent over the Internet can be easily snooped and tracked, revealing who is talking to whom and what they are talking about.

As people surf the Internet, they are constantly giving information to web sites. People should become aware that the collection, selling, or sharing of the information they provide online increases the chances that their information will fall into the wrong hands. When giving personal information on the Internet, people should make sure the Web site is protected with a recognizable security symbol. On the other hand, this does not mean they are fully protected because anyone may obtain a user's information.

Today, not only are humans getting viruses, but computers are also. Computers are mainly getting these viruses from the Internet; yet, viruses may also be transmitted through floppy disks. However, people should mainly be concerned about receiving viruses from the Internet. Some of these dangerous viruses destroy the computer's entire hard drive, meaning that the user can no longer access the computer. Virus protection is highly recommended. In conclusion, today's society is in the middle of a technological boom. People can either choose to take advantage of this era, or simply let it pass them by. The Internet is a very powerful tool. It has many advantages; however, people need to be extremely aware of the disadvantages as well.

EXTRANET

INTRODUCTION

A company LAN, or local area network, can house a private Internet-like environment called an *intranet*. The intranet is basically a set of HTML pages relating to internal company business, for employee's eyes only, and is not available to the Internet. If access to or from the Internet is provided, it will be through a firewall gateway that will require a username and password. In this case the intranet becomes an extranet. In short, an extranet is the extension of an intranet to include public access.

An extranet can allow public access to employees, customers, clients or partners. The extranet uses Internet protocols so users can navigate with a browser, but resides on the company's private server rather than on a public Internet server. Extranet access from the Internet can be controlled through various architectures that are password or username specific. In other words, areas of the extranet will be available according to password credentials. This limits users to extranet pages relevant to the business they might be conducting, while keeping other areas of the extranet private and secure.

One very valuable application for an extranet is customer service. Online patches, upgrades, downloads, knowledge bases, and an interactive *Help Desk* are just a few examples of ways to serve a client base using an extranet. Extranet chat boards where customers help each other with company products can also build customer confidence and brand loyalty, while saving valuable human resources. Chat boards are also a rich source for potential future product and support development.

Another resource an extranet can provide is the ability to create secure areas for interaction between an organization and its partners or resellers. Development, dissemination of marketing information and tools, data sharing, research, sales reports and more are all possible using an extranet environment. An extranet can also connect to other extranets through the common language of Internet protocols. This makes it invaluable to organizations involved in collaborative efforts and opens the door to greater creative opportunities. In the past, geography was a significant hindrance to collaboration, but extranet technology bridges that gap effortlessly and virtually cost-free.

Extranets can revolutionize the way a company does business, improve the bottom line, enrich the customer base, and create opportunities that remain out of reach without an extranet. If interested in finding out more about what an extranet can do for your business, consult an extranet site developer. The Internet popularized instant communications with far-flung computers via the simple click of a mouse.

Anyone with a Web browser can follow links and hop from site to site, gleaning information that companies and people have decided to publish. That same point and click access can be used to speed communication and enhance collaboration between a company and its partners and customers. But what happens when a company needs to share information that is confidential? That's where the "extranet" comes in.

EXPLANATION

An extranet has the appearance and feel of a website, but adds levels of security to prevent unwanted viewers from clicking through to private data. Similar to an intranet—a private Internet for people inside a company—an extranet widens the circle to privileged outsiders.

An extranet can streamline the sharing of information, as well as applications and services. For example, a public relations agency may want to review marketing materials with a client. Rather than e-mail a large file, or fax it, or send it via costly overnight mail, the agency could put the materials on a private website. An extranet. The agency might also want to use this extranet to collaborate with clients, sharing calendars, project management tools, and other applications.

"An extranet allows the organization to have a closer, interactive relationship with its customers, partners, etc., without the need for complete management of the users or their IT environment," says Ray Wagner, research vice president with Gartner Inc., of Stamford, Conn. An extranet is similar to an intranet but it is made accessible to selected external partners such as business partners, suppliers, key customers, etc, for exchanging data and applications and sharing information.

As with an intranet, an extranet can also provide remote access to corporate systems for staff who spend lots of time out of the office, for instance those in sales or customer support, or home workers. Extranet users should be a well-defined group and access must be protected by rigorous identification routines and security features. An Extranet is similar to an Intranet but it is made accessible to selected external partners such as business partners, suppliers, key customers etc, for exchanging data and applications and sharing information. As with an Intranet, an Extranet can also provide remote access to corporate and organisational systems for staff who spend lots of time out of the office, for instance those in sales, customer support, or home workers.

Extranets offer a cost effective and efficient way for businesses to connect with their trading partners. It also means that your business partners and suppliers can access the information they need 24 hours a day. The ability of the extranet to automate the trading tasks between you and your trading partners can lead to enhanced business relationships and help to integrate your business firmly within their supply chain. Within the tourism industry we have delivered customised extranet solutions that are now helping run day-today business processes on a worldwide level.

Businesses of all sizes are under increasing pressure to use online ordering, electronic order tracking and inventory management. At the same time small businesses are keen to meet the demands of larger companies in terms of working flexibly, adopting new technologies and enabling the exchange of business information and transactions. An Extranet can offer a range of benefits to your organisation or business from lowering costs, to producing faster results and improving the quality of service to customers.

ADVANTAGES

- Improved business relationships with key trading partners because of the close collaborative working that extranets support
- Improved customer service by giving customers direct access to information and enabling them to resolve their own queries
- A single user interface between you and your business partners
- Improving the security of communications between you and your business partners, since exchanges can take place under a controlled and secure environment
- Shared news of product development exclusively with partner companies
- Flexible working for your own staff, as an extranet allows remote and mobile staff to access core business information 24 hours a day, irrespective of location
- More integrated supply chains through the use of online ordering, order tracking and inventory management
- Reduced costs by making manuals and technical documentation available online to trading partners and customers
- More effective collaboration between business partners-perhaps members of a project team-by enabling them to work online on common documentation

USING EXTRANET

Businesses of all sizes are under increasing pressure to use online ordering, electronic order tracking and inventory management. At the same time small businesses are keen to meet the demands of larger companies in terms of working flexibly, adopting new technologies and enabling the exchange of business information and transactions.

Extranets offer a cheap and efficient way for businesses to connect with their trading partners. It also means that your business partners and suppliers can access the information they need 24 hours a day. The ability of the extranet to automate the trading tasks between you and your trading partners can lead to enhanced business relationships and help to integrate your business firmly within their supply chain.

WORKING

Extranet functionality comes in different forms. A public website is a simple extranet, Wagner says. "If it has interactivity, it's a little more complex. If it has a limited user base that's controlled by the organization in some way, it's even more complex," Wagner says. "If it has real applications that allow business transactions, collaboration, or sharing of corporate intellectual property to occur, it's very complex and requires significant resource outlay, planning, and security."

Extranets also require measures to ensure privacy and security of information. Some of the security methods that can protect extranets from unauthorized access include the use of virtual private networks (VPNs), firewalls, user authentication and/or encryption.

Extranets for Small Business

One way for a small business to provide an extranet is through hosted applications, like WebEx's Web Office, Trichys' Work Zone, and Microsoft SharePoint Services. In addition, Microsoft plans to release Microsoft Office Live, a hosted version of the Office application suite that allows groups to collaborate.

Sharing information via a hosted workspace is often easier on the bottom line, which is important to the small or fast-growing business, says Karen Leavitt, vice president of WebEx. "It's far more cost effective to put information into a hosted workspace, a shared repository on the Web to exchange information in real time with your clients," Leavitt says. Hosted applications are great for small businesses without an IT department, she says. "There is no setup at all," she says. "Everything is hosted on the Web."

Besides saving a company the cost of running a more expensive server-based application, like Microsoft Exchange, such collaboration services help a company to accelerate revenues. "If a sales guy can literally meet with six different prospects in a day by conducting Web meetings with them, rather than getting on a plane and doing one or two, they have more opportunities to close business for the company," Leavitt says.

USES

Understand what the Internet is and know some of its main uses.

Some of its main uses are to:

- Integrate the operations of multinational corporations.
- Provide access to and share information and databases.
- Transfer and share files between computers.
- Facilitate business transactions.
- Share resources.
- Promote scientific co-operation between research institutions.
- Provide a communications channel for the military.

WORLD WIDE WEB

DEFINITION

The World Wide Web or WWW is a part of the Internet. The WWW consists of all the sites that can be accessed using a web browser such as Mozilla, Netscape, Internet Explorer or Opera. In order for a browser to access a web site, the web site must contain files that have a particular format constructed using HyperText Markup Language or HTML.

These sites are developed using special web development applications. It is possible to create simple web sites using a word processor by saving the document in HTML format. The HTML documents are stored as web pages on special servers known as web servers.

These run special web server software such as Apache Web Server or Internet Information Services. The WWW enables the free flow of information across the world. Developments in technology have made access easier and faster. As a result the WWW also became known as the Information Superhighway. Most of the activities listed under the Internet in the previous section are now actually carried out using the Internet.

In other words, the sites are created in HTML, or a similar format, are installed on web servers and are accessed by web browsers. The World Wide Web is here to stay, but if you have not yet learned how to use it, you may feel a little bit intimidated. Search engines, browsers, article directories, and instant messaging programmes all seem a little confusing at first.

Browser

A browser is simply a programme used to access the Internet. The most popular are Internet Explorer,Firefox, and Opera. Your computer probably already has an Internet browser installed on it. Each browser works a little bit differently, but they all have an address bar where you type the website address you wish to visit. That is the first step in using the Internet.

Search Engine

Most people access the Internet using a search engine. A search engine is a website that contains a programme designed to search the Internet and retrieve pages that match your search criteria. For instance, if you want to look at information about poodles, you would type "poodles" into the search engine box, and the software would search the Internet and pull up relevant websites that relate to poodles. You would choose the sites you wanted to visit based on their short descriptions. Some of the most popular search engines are MSN, Google, Yahoo!, and Ask.com. Using the Internet with a search engine is sometimes called "surfing."

Subject Directories

If you would prefer to visit a site that already has relevant information on your topic categorized for you to see, try a subject directory. These are like giant libraries that you can search by topic. As you navigate the directory, you gradually make your way to the site you want. You would then be provided with a wealth of information on poodles, all categorized by real people, not software. Some popular subject directories include Yahoo!, Internet Public Library, About.com, and the WWW Virtual Library.

E-mail

E-mail refers to electronic mail, and is one of the most basic forms of communication on the Internet and there are many companies who offer e-mail archiving services as well as others which help manage this system. When you send an e-mail, you type up your letter, put your recipient's e-mail address in the address line, hit send, and the letter is instantly sent to the recipient's "inbox," or e-mail programme.

TELEPHONE NETWORK IN COMPUTING

PSTN

The PSTN or Public Switched Telephone Network refers to the originally telephone network. From a communications perspective it was slow and unreliable. Some of the exchanges on a PSTN may still make use of mechanical switches to route telephone calls. These add additional noise to the line. When lines are noisy, signals have to be resent repeatedly between the source and the destination. The PSTN makes use of analogue technology. Analogue technology uses continuously variable signals. An example of an analogue signal is ordinary speech. Newer digital technologies make use of pulses of fixed magnitude and duration.

In order to improve connections, it is possible to have an analogue leased line. This is a dedicated permanent telephone connection between two computers using the PSTN.

In order to connect a computer to a telephone network, you need a modem. This is an abbreviation for modulator-demodulator. The function of the modem is to convert the digital signals from the computer into an analogue form suitable for transmission on the PSTN.

ISDN

ISDN or Integrated Services Digital Network is a technological development that is able to make use of the existing PSTN cabling to transmit digital signals. Technically ISDN is an international standard for the transmission of data, voice and video or normal voice or digital telephone lines. ISDN supports rates of up to 64Kbps. An ISDN connection consists of two lines which can be used independently or together to give a combined rate of 128Kbps. If you wish to connect a computer to an ISDN line you need a special ISDN modem. This is a different type of modem to the one used with an analogue line. Its purpose, however, is the same, to convert the digital signals of the computer into a form suitable for transmission on an ISDN line. It is possible to get a dedicated connection between two computers using ISDN. This is called a diginet connection. The older telephone systems make use of electrical currents transmitted through copper cabling. As electric signals are subject to interference, they are not the ideal method of transmitting data.

ADSL

ADSL or Asymmetric Digital Subscriber Lines allow the transmission of high speed digital data over ordinary telephone lines using a modulation technology called DMT or Discrete MultiTone. Ideally, fibre-optic is the ideal medium for high speed digital transmission. As the installation of fibre-optic is expensive, ADSL provides solution until copper cable is replaced by fibre-optic.

COMMUNICATIONS TERMINOLOGY

Analogue Signals

Analogue signals are used on the PSTN as well as for normal AM and FM radio transmissions. An analogue signal is one which varies continuously as, for example, in ordinary speech.

Digital Signals

Digital signals are used in ISDN and ADSL connections. Newer television and radio transmission techniques are also making using of digital technology. Digital signals are two state signals corresponding to a switch which is on or off. The same two state signal can also represent TRUE and FALSE or 1 and 0. Graphically a digital signal is represented as in the diagram above.

Modems

A modem or modulator-demodulator is a device connected between a computer and a telephone line. Its function is to convert the digital signals of the computer into a form suitable for transmission over a telephone line. It must also do the reverse and convert the telephone line signals into a form suitable for the computer. Note that the modem used to connect to an ISDN line is different to that used to connect to an analogue line.

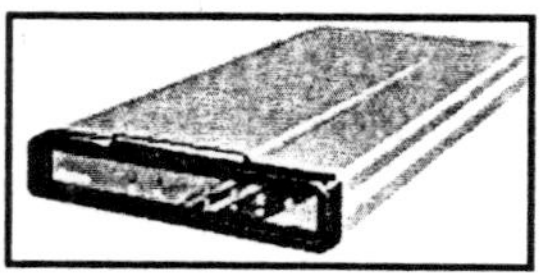

Fig. External Modem

Data Transfer Rates

Each 1 or 0 that is transferred is referred to as a bit. The speed of a data transfer is measured by the number of bits that can be transferred each second or bps (bits per second). This is also sometimes called the baud rate or bandwidth.

High speed lines have their speed measured in kbps or Mbps:

- 1 kbps = 1 024 bps (roughly 1 000 bps)
- 1 Mbps = 1 024 kbps = 1 048 576 bps (roughly 1 000 000 bps)

To put these figures in perspective, the maximum theoretically attainable speed with an analogue line is 56kbps. This figure is very seldom attained and the reality is usually substantially lower. ISDN lines operate at 64 kbps.

4

Central Processing Unit

SIGNED NUMBERS

ADDITION

Adding Unsigned Numbers

Adding unsigned numbers in binary is quite easy. Recall that with 4 bit numbers we can represent numbers from 0 to 15. Addition is done exactly like adding decimal numbers, except that you have only two digits (0 and 1).

The only number facts to remember are that,

0+0 = 0, with no carry,

1+0 = 1, with no carry,

0+1 = 1, with no carry,

1+1 = 0, and you carry a 1.

so to add the numbers 06_{10}=0110_2 and 07_{10}=0111_2 (answer = 13_{10} = 1101_2) we can write out the calculation (the results of any carry is shown along the top row, in italics).

Decimal	Unsigned binary
1 (carry)	110 (carry)
06	0110
+07	+0111
13	1101

The only difficulty adding unsigned numbers occurs when you add numbers that are too large. Consider 13+5.

Decimal	Unsigned binary
0 (carry)	1101 (carry)
13	1101
+05	+0101
18	10010

The result is a 5 bit number. So the carry bit from adding the two most significant bits represents a results that *overflows* (because the sum is too big to be represented with the same number of bits as the two addends).

Adding Signed Numbers

Adding signed numbers is not significantly different from adding unsigned numbers. Recall that signed 4 bit numbers (2's complement) can represent numbers between-8 and 7. To see how this addition works, consider three examples.

Decimal	Signed binary
	1110 (carry)
-2	1110
+3	+0011
1	0001

Decimal	Signed binary
	011 (carry)
-5	1011
+3	+0011
-2	1110

Decimal	Signed binary
	1100 (carry)
-4	1100
-3	+1101
-7	1001

In this case the extra carry from the most significant bit has no meaning. With signed numbers there are two ways to get an overflow--if the result is greater than 7, or less than-8. Let's consider these occurrences now. In this case the extra carry from the most significant bit has no meaning. With signed numbers there are two ways to get an overflow—if the result is greater than 7, or less than-8. Let's consider these occurrences now.

Decimal	Signed binary
	110 (carry)
6	0110
+3	+0011
9	1001

Decimal	Signed binary
	1001 (carry)
-7	1001
-3	+1101
-10	0110

Obviously both of these results are incorrect, but in this case overflow is harder to detect. But you can see that if two numbers with the same sign (either positive or negative) are added and the result has the opposite sign, an overflow has occurred. Typically DSP's, including the 320C5x, can deal somewhat with this problem by using something called saturation arithmetic, in which results that result in overflow are replaced by either the most positive number (in this case 7) if the overflow is in the positive direction, or by the most negative number (-8) for overflows in the negative direction.

Adding Fractions

There is no further difficult in adding two signed fractions, only the interpretation of the results differs. For instance consider addition of two Q3 numbers shown (compare to the example with two 4 bit signed numbers, above).

Decimal	Fractional binary
	1110 (carry)
-0.25	1110
+0.375	+0011
0.125	0001

Decimal	Fractional binary
	011 (carry)
-0.625	1011
+0.375	+0011
-0.25	1110

Decimal	Fractional binary
	1100 (carry)
-0.5	1100
-0.375	+1101
-0.875	1001

If you look carefully at these examples, you'll see that the binary representation and calculations are the same as before, only the decimal representation has changed.

This is very useful because it means we can use the same circuitry for addition, regardless of the interpretation of the results.

Even the generation of overflows resulting in error conditions remains unchanged (again compare with above)

Decimal	Fractional binary
	110 (carry)
0.75	0110
+0.375	+0011
1.125	1001

Decimal	Fractional binary
	1001 (carry)
-0.875	1001
-0.375	+1101
-1.25	0110

2'S COMPLEMENT

We do not just place a 1 in the MSB of a binary number to make it negative. We must take the 2's Complement of the number. Taking the 2's Complement of the number will cause the MSB to become 1.

To obtain the 2's complement of a number is a two step process.

- Take the 1's complement of the number by changing every logic 1 bit in the number to a 0, and change every logic 0 bit to a 1.
- Add 1 to the 1's Complement of the binary number. You now have the 2's Complement of the original number. You will notice that the MSB has become a 1.

The complement of a binary number, also known as the 1's complement, requires us to change every logic 1 bit in a number to a logic 0, and every logic 0 bit to a logic 1. Let's find the 1's complement of 36H or 0011 0110 in binary. In the following table, the 1's Complement is shown in red.

Number format	D7	D6	D5	D4	D3	D2	D1	D0
Unsigned number	0	0	1	1	0	1	1	0
1's Complement	1	1	0	0	1	0	0	1

To obtain the 2's complement of a binary number, we must first obtain the 1's complement of the number and then add 1. In the following table, the 1's complement is RED and the 2's Complement is in BLUE. The 2's complement of 36H or 0011 0110 in binary is:

Number format	D7	D6	D5	D4	D3	D2	D1	D0
Unsigned number	0	0	1	1	0	1	1	0
1's Complement	1	1	0	0	1	0	0	1
2's Complement	1	1	0	0	1	0	1	0

If we are using signed binary numbers and the MSB is already logic 1, it means the value is the 2's complement of the number. The actual numeric value can be determined by taking the 2's complement of the number and keeping track of the minus sign mentally.

Find the decimal value of the signed binary number 0FFH.

Number format	D7	D6	D5	D4	D3	D2	D1	D0
Signed number	1	1	1	1	1	1	1	1
1's Complement	0	0	0	0	0	0	0	0
2's Complement	0	0	0	0	0	0	0	1

Therefore, 0FF is a signed number that has the value in decimal of-1.

USING 2'S COMPLEMENT ADDITION

If we add the 2's Complement of a signed number to another signed number, we are performing the mathematical operation of subtraction. This is, in fact. how many 8-bit microprocessors actually perform subtraction, they perform 2's complement addition.

Let us see if 0FFH is really-1. If we add it to 01H, we expect the result to be 0. One special condition about twos complement addition, overflows (a CARRY OUT which SETS the CARRY FLAG) from the register are ignored. So let's see what happens.

In Decimal	CO	D7	D6	D5	D4	D3	D2	D1	D0
1	X	0	0	0	0	0	0	0	1
–1	X	1	1	1	1	1	1	1	1
0	1	0	0	0	0	0	0	0	0

The last row of the table shows that the result is 0. The 1 in the CO (CARRY OUT) is ignored. If we ignore the CO, the result is 0000 0000. Okay, so it works for a byte. How about a Word? It is the same procedure. Only the MSB is used as the sign bit, so the MSB of the low order byte is a weighted position bit.

For 16-bit numbers:

- 8000H is negative because the high order bit is one.
- 0100H is positive because the high order bit is zero.
- 7FFFH is positive.
- 0FFFFH is negative.
- 0FFFH is positive.

LOOK AHEAD CARRY ADDERS

PURPOSE

- To Understand delays in digital circuits
- To Learn to use the Timing Simulator
- To Design a 16-bit carry-look ahead adder and measure its delay.

BACKGROUND: CIRCUIT DELAYS

Up to now we have been interested in the functional operation of logic circuits. In the previous labs you used the logic simulator to verify that the circuits function properly. However, there is one other important aspect to circuit design: the speed at which it operates. The speed of a digital circuit is very important, as it will determine the maximum frequency at which it can work. Let us consider a PC that has a clock frequency of 800 MHz. That means that each 1.25 ns (*i.e.* period T=1/frequency) the PC will perform a computation! As we will see, this will require clever circuit design.

There are several factors that contribute to the delay. One is the propagation delay due to the internal structure of the gates, another factor is the loading of the output buffers (due to fan out and net delays), and a third factor is the logic circuit itself.

Propagation Delay

When the input signal of a gate changes, the output signal will not change instantaneously as is shown in Figure below.

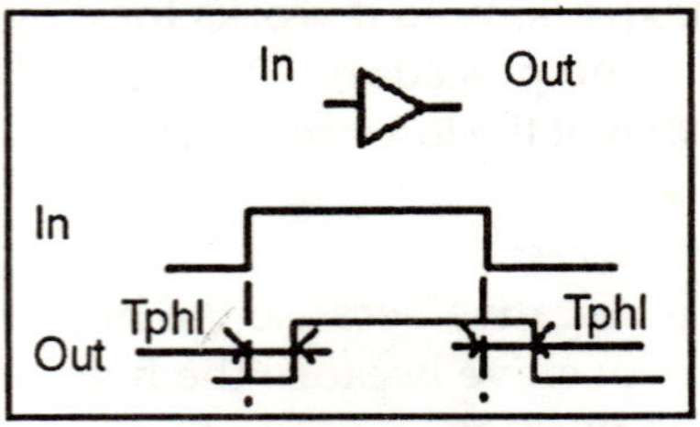

Fig. Propagation Delay of Gates.

The propagation delay (or gate delay) of a gate is the time difference between the change of the input and output signals. There are two types of gate delays, T_{PHL} and T_{PLH}, as indicated in Figure. The value of the propagation delay varies from gate to gate and from logic family to family. In general the more you are willing to pay for a device (or chip), the faster it will be. The FPGAs we are using in the lab have gate delays which vary between 1.5 and 4.5ns. The actual delay depends on the way the logic gates have been mapped into the LUTs (Look up table) of a CLB (Configurable Logic Block). The I/O buffers have delays in the range of 2-4ns.

Fanout and Net Delays

The propagation delay described above is caused by parasitic capacitors inside the gates and the physical limitations of the devices used to build these gates. Another cause of delay is the capacitor associated with the loads seen by a gate. The more capacitors that need to be charged or discharged the longer it will take for the output to change. Also, the longer the interconnection, the more resistance the nets will have. The easiest way to visualize this is to use a hydraulic equivalent of a capacitor and a resistor: a bucket filled with water and a narrow pipe, respectively, as shown in

Figure. The more buckets connected to the drain (*i.e.* the input inverter), the longer it will take to empty them. This delay is the result of the fan out of the inverter.

Delay as a Result of Circuit Topography

Circuits that perform the same function can vary significantly in their speeds. A good example is an adder circuit. The one you designed in the previous lab is called a *ripple-adder* and is considerably slower that a *carry-look-ahead adder* or *CLA [1,3,4]*.

MEASURING CIRCUIT DELAYS

The overall speed of a digital system can be measured on an oscilloscope by comparing the input to the output signals. However, during the design phase, the circuit has not yet been fabricated and therefore, cannot be measured. In that case it is possible to determine the delay of circuits by doing a *Timing Simulation*. The advantage of a simulation is that one can also determine the delay of internal nodes of a circuit. This can be very helpful to understand which nodes or paths are the slowest and thus limit the overall speed of the circuits. These paths are called "Critical path". It is important to understand which paths are critical in a circuit so that one can reduce their delay.

RIPPLE-CARRY VS. CARRY-LOOK-AHEAD ADDERS

One type of circuit where the effect of gate delays is particularly clear, is an ADDER. In this lab you will be measuring the delay of different types of adder circuits. The 4-bit adder you designed and implemented in the previous lab is called a ripple-carry adder because the result of an addition of two bits depends on the carry generated by the addition of the previous two bits. Thus, the Sum of the most significant bit is only available after the carry signal has rippled through the adder from the least significant stage to the most significant stage. This can be easily understood if one considers the addition of the two 4-bit words: $1\,1\,1\,1_2 + 0\,0\,0\,1_2$, as shown in Figure.

$$
\begin{array}{l}
1\ \ 1\ \ 1\ \ 1 \longrightarrow \text{Carry bits} \\
\quad\ 1\ \ 1\ \ 1\ \ 1 \\
+\ \ 0\ \ 0\ \ 0\ \ 1 \\
\hline
1\ \ 0\ \ 0\ \ 0\ \ 0 \\
C_0\, S_3\, S_2\, S_1\, S_0 \rightarrow \text{Sum bits} \\
/ \\
\text{Carry.out}
\end{array}
$$

Fig. Addition of two 4-bit Numbers Illustrating the Generation of the Carry-out Bit.

In this case, the addition of ($1+1 = 10_2$) in the least significant stage causes a carry bit to be generated. This carry bit will consequently generate another carry bit in the next stage, and so on, until the final carry-out bit appears at the output. As a result, the final Sum and Carry bits will be valid after a considerable delay. The carry-out bit of the first stage will be valid after 4 gate delays (2 associated with the XOR gate and 1 each associated with the AND and OR gates).

From the schematic of Figure, one finds that the next carry-out (C2) will be valid after an additional 2 gate delays (associated with the AND and OR gates) for a total of 6 gate delays. In general the carry-out of a N-bit adder will be valid after 2N+2 gate delays. The Sum bit will be valid an additional 2 gate delays after the carry-in signal. Thus the sum of the most significant bit S_{N-1} will be valid after $2(N-1) + 2 + 2 = 2N + 2$ gate delays.

This delay may be in addition to any delays associated with interconnections. It should be mentioned that in case one implements the circuit in a FPGA, the delays may be different from the above expression depending on how the logic has been placed in the look up tables and how it has been divided among different CLBs.

The disadvantage of the ripple-carry adder is that it can get very slow when one needs to add many bits. For instance, for a 32-bit adder, the delay would be about 66 ns if one assumes a gate delay of 1 ns. That would imply that the maximum frequency one can operate this adder would be only 15 MHz! For fast applications, a better design is required.

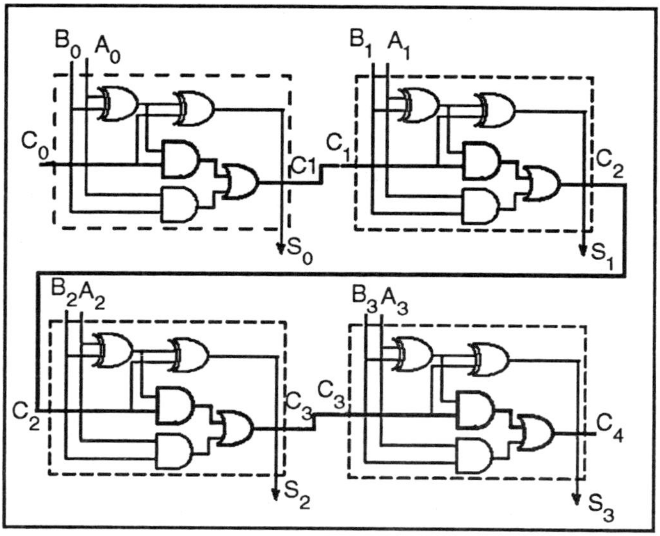

Fig. Ripple-carry Adder, Illustrating the Delay of the Carry Bit.

The carry-look-ahead adder solves this problem by calculating the carry signals in advance, based on the input signals. It is based on the fact that a carry signal will be generated in two cases: (1) when both bits A_i and B_i are 1, or (2) when one of the two bits is 1 and the carry-in (carry of the previous stage) is 1.

Thus, one can write,

- $C_{OUT} = C_{i+1} = A_i.B_i + (A_i$ Å $B_i).C_{i.}$ The "⊕" stands for exclusive OR or XOR. One can write this expression also, as
- $C_{i+1} = G_i + P_i.C_i$ *in which*:
- $G_i = A_i.B_j$
- Pi = (A_i Å B_i)

  are called the Generate and Propagate term, respectively. Lets assume that the delay through an AND gate is one gate delay and through an XOR gate is two gate delays. Notice that the Propagate and Generate terms only depend on the input bits and thus will be valid after two and one gate delay, respectively. If one uses the above expression to calculate the carry signals, one does not need to wait for the carry to ripple through all the previous stages to find its proper value. Let's apply this to a 4-bit adder to make it clear.

- $C_1 = G_0 + P_0.C_0$
- $C_2 = G_1 + P_1.C_1 = G_1 + P1.G_0 + P_1.P_0.C_0$
- $C_3 = G_2 + P_2.G_1 + P_2.P_1.G_0 + P_2.P_1.P_0.C_0$
- $C_4 = G_3 + P_3.G_2 + P_3.P_2.G_1 + P_3P_2.P_1.G_0 + P_3P_2.P_1.P_0.C_0$

Notice that the carry-out bit, C_{i+1}, of the last stage will be available after four delays (two gate delays to calculate the Propagate signal and two delays as a result of the AND and OR gate). The Sum signal can be calculated as follows,

- $S_i = A_i \oplus B_i \oplus C_i = P_i \oplus C_i$. The Sum bit will thus be available after two additional gate delays (due to the XOR gate) or a total of six gate delays after the input signals A_i and B_i have been applied. The advantage is that these delays will be the same independent of the number of bits one needs to add, in contrast to the ripple counter.

The carry-look ahead adder can be broken up in two modules:

– The Partial Full Adder, PFA, which generates Si, Pi and Gi as defined by equations 3, 4 and 9 above; and

– The Carry Look-ahead Logic, which generates the carry-out bits according to equations 5 to 8.

The 4-bit adder can then be built by using 4 PFAs and the Carry Look-ahead logic block as shown in Figure below. The disadvantage of the carry-lookahead adder is that the carry logic is getting quite complicated for more than 4 bits. For that reason, carry-look-ahead adders are usually implemented as 4-bit modules and are used in a hierarchical structure to realise adders that have multiples of 4 bits. Figure below shows the block diagram for a 16-bit CLA adder. The circuit makes use of the same CLA Logic block as the one used in the 4-bit adder.

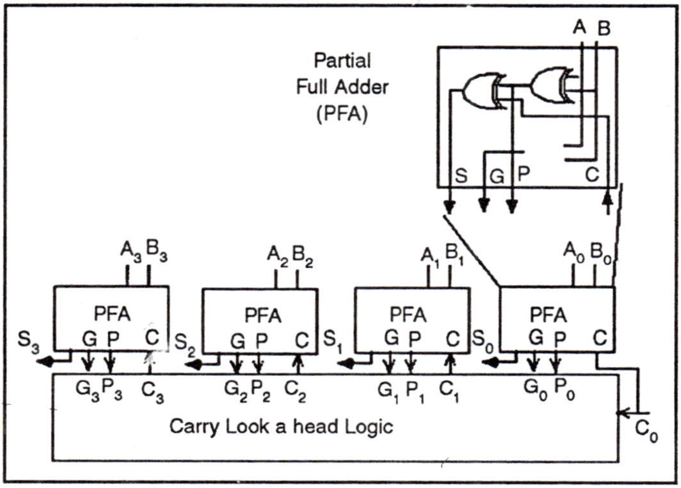

Fig. Block Diagram of a 4-bit CLA.

Notice that each 4-bit adder provides a group Propagate and Generate Signal, which is used by the CLA Logic block. The group Propagate P_G of a 4-bit adder will have the following expressions,

- $P_G = P_3.P_2.P_1.P_0$;
- $G_G = G_3 + P_3G_2 + P_3.P_2.G_1. + P_3.P_2.P_1.G_0$

The group Propagate P_G and Generate G_G will be available after 3 and 4 gate delays, respectively (one or two additional delays than the P_i and G_i signals, respectively).

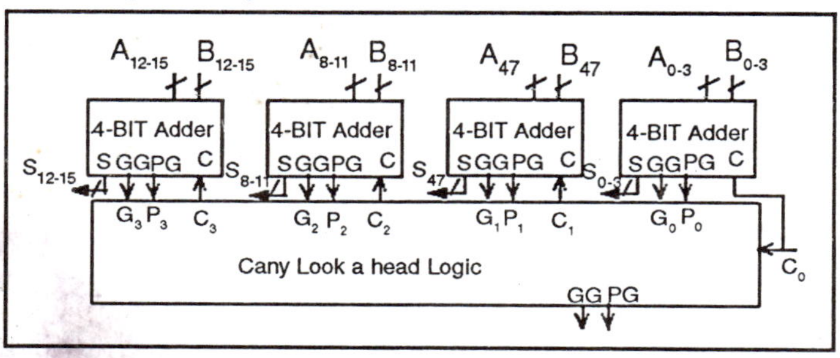

Fig. Block Diagram of a 16-bit CLA Adder.

GENERATE AND PROPAGATE

Why generate and propagate. If you look at the Boolean expressions for p_i and g_i, you will see that they both use only x_i and y_i. Neither depend on the carry. Sincex_i and y_i are available immediately, this gives us hope that we can avoid waiting for carries.

This is how we do it. First, let's write the c_1 which is the carry out for the adding bit 0 of x and y.

$$c_1 = g_0 + p_0c_0$$

Now, we write it for c_2.

$$c_2 = g_1 + p_1c_1$$

At this point, we've used c_1, which we'd rather avoid, because it means waiting for that carry to be computed. However, we *just* defined c_1 as $g_0 + c_0p_0$.

Let's plug that in:

$$\begin{aligned} c_2 &= g_1 + p_1(g_0 + p_0c_0) \\ &= g_1 + p_1g_0 + p_1p_0c_0 \end{aligned}$$

Notice that we no longer have c_1. That means we no longer have to wait for the carry!

Let's go one more step further:

$$c_3 = g_2 + p_2c_2$$

Again, we would prefer to avoid using c_2 since this requires us to wait for the result to propagate across two adders. However, we *already* have a Boolean expression for c_2 (we just computed it a moment ago) that doesn't use any carries except c_0 which we have right away.

$$\begin{aligned} c_3 &= g_2 + p_2c_2 \\ &= g_2 + p_2(g_1 + p_1g_0 + p_1p_0c_0) \\ &= g_2 + p_2g_1 + p_2p_1g_0 + p_2p_1p_0c_0 \end{aligned}$$

Already, you should be able to detect a pattern. By following the same pattern, you'd expect:

$$c_4 = g_3 + p_3g_2 + p_3p_2g_1 + p_3p_2p_1g_0 + p_3p_2p_1p_0c_0$$

MULTIPLICATION

MULTIPLYING UNSIGNED NUMBERS

Multiplying unsigned numbers in binary is quite easy. Recall that with 4 bit numbers we can represent numbers from

0 to 15. Multiplication can be performed done exactly as with decimal numbers, except that you have only two digits (0 and 1). The only number facts to remember are that 0*1=0, and 1*1=1 (this is the same as a logical "and").

Multiplication is different than addition in that multiplication of an n bit number by an m bit number results in an n+m bit number. Let's take a look at an example where n=m=4 and the result is 8 bits

Decimal	Binary
10	1010
×6	×0110
60	0000
	1010
	1010
	+0000
	0111100

In this case the result was 7 bit, which can be extended to 8 bits by adding a 0 at the left. When multiplying larger numbers, the result will be 8 bits, with the leftmost set to 1, as shown.

Decimal	Binary
13	1101
×14	×1110
182	0000
	1101
	1101
	+1101
	10110110

As long as there are n+m bits for the result, there is no chance of overflow. For 2 four bit multiplicands, the largest possible product is 15*15=225, which can be represented in 8 bits.

MULTIPLYING SIGNED NUMBERS

There are many methods to multiply 2's complement numbers. The easiest is to simply find the magnitude of the two multiplicands, multiply these together, and then use the original sign bits to determine the sign of the result. If the multiplicands had the same sign, the result must be positive, if the they had different signs, the result is negative. Multiplication by zero is a special case (the result is always zero, with no sign bit).

MULTIPLYING FRACTIONS

As you might expect, the multiplication of fractions can be done in the same way as the multiplication of signed numbers. The magnitudes of the two multiplicands are multiplied, and the sign of the result is determined by the signs of the two multiplicands.

There are a couple of complications involved in using fractions. Although it is almost impossible to get an overflow (since the multiplicands and results usually have magnitude less than one), it is possible to get an overflow by multiplying-1x-1 since the result of this is +1, which cannot be represented by fixed point numbers.

The other difficulty is that multiplying two Q3 numbers, obviously results in a Q6 number, but we have 8 bits in our result (since we are multiplying two 4 bit numbers). This means that we end up with two bits to the left of the decimal point. These are sign extended, so that for positive numbers they are both zero, and for negative numbers they are both one. Consider the case of multiplying-1/2 by-1/2:

Decimal	Fractional binary
–0.5	1100
×0.5	×0100
–0.25	0000
	0000
	+111100
	11110000

This obviously presents a difficulty if we wanted to store the number in a Q3 result, because if we took just the 4 leftmost bits, we would end up with two sign bits. So what we'd like to do is shift the number to the left by one and then take the 4 leftmost bit. This leaves us with 1110 which is equal to-1/4, as expected.

On a 16 bit DSP two Q15 numbers are multiplied to get a Q30 number with two sign bits. On the 320C50 there are two ways to accomplish this. The first is to use the p-scaler immediately after the multiplier, or the postscaler after the accumulator. to shift the result to the left by one

Example for Multiplication

$$13 \times 11 = 143$$

The paper-and-pencel method:

$$
\begin{array}{cccccccc}
 & & & & 1 & 1 & 0 & 1 \\
 & & & \times & 1 & 0 & 1 & 1 \\
\hline
 & & & & 1 & 1 & 0 & 1 \\
 & & & 1 & 1 & 0 & 1 & \\
 & & 0 & 0 & 0 & 0 & & \\
+ & 1 & 1 & 0 & 1 & & & \\
\hline
1 & 0 & 0 & 0 & 1 & 1 & 1 & 1
\end{array}
$$

Improve the method so that only 2 numbers are added each time:

$$
\begin{array}{cccccccc}
 & & & & 1 & 1 & 0 & 1 \\
 & & & \times & 1 & 0 & 1 & 1 \\
\hline
 & & & & 1 & 1 & 0 & 1 \\
 & & + & 1 & 1 & 0 & 1 & \\
\hline
 & & 1 & 0 & 0 & 1 & 1 & 1 \\
 & & 0 & 0 & 0 & 0 & & \\
\hline
 & & 1 & 0 & 0 & 1 & 1 & 1 \\
+ & 1 & 1 & 0 & 1 & & & \\
\hline
1 & 0 & 0 & 0 & 1 & 1 & 1 & 1
\end{array}
$$

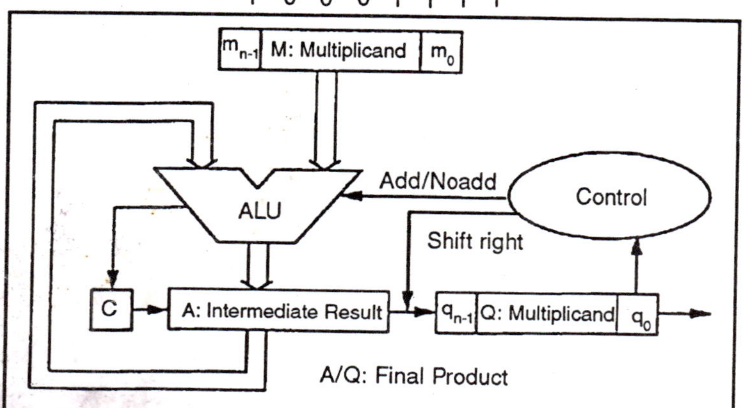

Hardware for Multiplication

Algorithm for Hardware Multiplication

```
Do n times:
{
      if (q0 = 1) then A ← A + M;
      right shift A and Q by 1 bit
}
```

Note: When A and Q are right shifted, the MSB of A is filled with 0 and the LSB of A becomes the MSB of Q, and the LSB of Q is lost.

Example

$$13 \times 11 = 143$$

Always use three registers M, A, and Q. Initially, the multiplicand 13 =$(1101)_2$ is in M, the multiplier 11 = $(10111)_2$ is in Q, and A is zero.

	[M]	1101		
	[A]	0000	[Q]	1011
q0 = 1, add A = [A] + [M]	+	1101		
	0	1101		1011
right shift A/Q	0	0110		1101
q0 = 1, add A = [A] + [M]	+	1101		
	1	0011		1101
right shift A/Q	0	1001		1110
q0 = 0,right shift, A/Q	0	0100		
q0 = 1, add A = [A] + [M]	+	1101		
	1	0001		1111
right shift A/Q	0	1000		1111

The upper half of the product $(1010001111)_2$ = 143 is in register A, while the lower half is in register Q.

Example for Division

$$274 \div 13 = 21\frac{1}{13}$$

```
                 000010101          Quotient
Divisor   1101 ) 100010010          Dividend
                 -1101
                 -----
                   10000
                   -1101
                   -----
                     1110
                    -1101
                    -----
                        1         Remainder
```

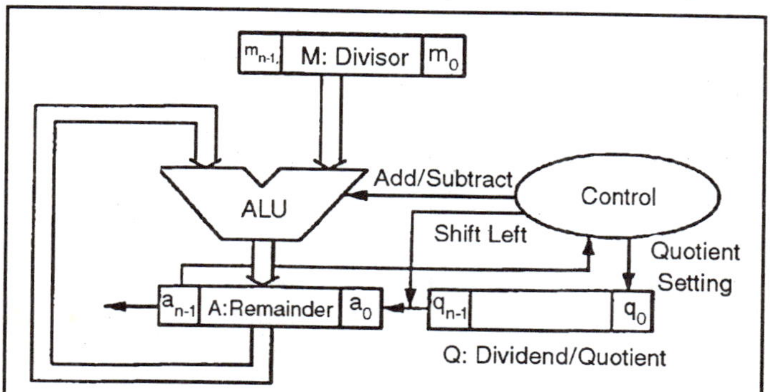

Hardware for Division

Algorithm for Hardware Division (Restoring)

Do n times:

```
{
    left shift A and Q by 1 bit
    A ← A-M;
    if A < 0 (a_{n-1} = 1), then q0 ← 0,A ← A +
    M  (restore)
    else q0 ← 1
}
```

Note: When A and Q are left shifted, the MSB of Q becomes the LSB of A, and the MSB of A is lost. The LSB of Q is made available for the next quotient bit.

Example

$$8 \div 3 = 2\frac{2}{3}$$

Initially, the divisor $3 = (0011)_2$ is in register M, the

dividend 8 = $(1000)_2$ is in register Q, and register A is zero. Note that subtraction by 3 = $(0011)_2$ is implemented by adding its 2's complement 1101.

	[M]	**1101**		
	[A]	**0000**	**[Q]**	**1011**
left shift A/Q		0001		000.
A = [A]–[M]	+	1101		
A < 0		1101		0000
A = [A] + [M]	+	0011		
		0001		0000
left shift A/Q		0010		000.
A = [A]–[M]	+	1101		
A < 0		0011		0000
A = [A] + [M]	+	0011		
		0010		0000
left shift A/Q		1100		000.
A = [A]–[M]	+	1101		
A > 0		0001		0001
left shift A/Q		0010		001.
A = [A]–[M]	+	1101		
A < 0		1111		0010
A = [A] + [M]	+	0011		
		0010		1111

The quotient $(0010)_2 = 2$ is in register Q, and the reminder $(0010)_2 = 2$ is in register A.

Algorithm for Hardware Division (Non-restoring)

In the algorithm above, if the subtraction produces a non-positive result (A > 0), registers A and Q are left shifted and the next subtraction is carried out. But if the subtraction produces a negative result (A < 0), the dividend need be first restored by adding the divisor back before left shift A and Q and the next subtraction:

- If A ≤ 0, then 2A–M (left shift and subtract);
- If A ≥ 0, then 2(A + M)–M = 2A + M (restore, left shift and subtract).

Note that when A < 0, the restoration is avoided by combining the two steps. This leads to a faster non-restoring division algorithm:

Algorithm for Hardware Division (Non-restoring)

Do n times:

```
{    left shift A and Q by 1 bit
     if (previous A ≥ 0) then A → A-M
     else A → A + M;
     if (current A ≥ 0) then q0 → 1
     else q0 → 1
}
     if (A < 0) then  (remainder must be
        positive)
```

	[M]	0011		
	[A]	0000	[Q]	1000
left shift A/Q		0001		000.
A = [A]–[M]	+	1101		
A < 0		1110		0000
left shift A/Q		1100		000.
A = [A] + [M]	+	0011		
A < 0		1111		0000
left shift A/Q		1110		000.
A = [A] + [M]	+	0011		
A > 0		0001		0001
left shift A/Q		0010		001.
A = [A]–[M]	+	1101		
A < 0		1111		0010
A = [A] + [M]	+	0011		
		0010		1111

The quotient $(0010)_2$ = 2 is in register Q, and the reminder $(0010)_2$ = 2 is in register A. The restoring division requires two operations (subtraction followed by an addition to restore) for each zero in the quotient. But non-restoring division only requires one operation (either addition or subtraction) for each bit in quotient.

BOOTHS ALGORITHM AND ARRAY MULTIPLIER

DEFINITION OF AN ALGORITHM

In the introduction, we gave an informal definition of an algorithm as "a set of instructions for solving a problem" and we illustrated this definition with a recipe, directions to a friend's house, and instructions for changing the oil in a car engine. You also created your own algorithm for putting letters and numbers in order. While these simple algorithms are fine for us, they are much too ambiguous for a computer. In order for an algorithm to be applicable to a computer, it must have certain characteristics. We will specify these characteristics in our formal definition of an algorithm.

An algorithm is a well-ordered collection of unambiguous and effectively computable operations that when executed produces a result and halts in a finite amount of time. With this definition, we can identify five important characteristics of algorithms.

- Algorithms are well-ordered.
- Algorithms have unambiguous operations.
- Algorithms have effectively computable operations.
- Algorithms produce a result.
- Algorithms halt in a finite amount of time.

These characteristics need a little more explanation, so we will look at each one in detail.

Algorithms are Well-ordered

Since an algorithm is a collection of operations or instructions, we must know the correct order in which to execute the instructions. If the order is unclear, we may perform the wrong instruction or we may be uncertain which instruction should be performed next. This characteristic is especially important for computers. A computer can only execute an algorithm if it knows the exact order of steps to perform.

Algorithms have Unambiguous Operations

Each operation in an algorithm must be sufficiently clear

so that it does not need to be simplified. Given a list of numbers, you can easily order them from largest to smallest with the simple instruction "Sort these numbers." A computer, however, needs more detail to sort numbers. It must be told to search for the smallest number, how to find the smallest number, how to compare numbers together, etc.

The operation "Sort these numbers" is ambiguous to a computer because the computer has no basic operations for sorting. Basic operations used for writing algorithms are known as primitive operations or primitives. When an algorithm is written in computer primitives, then the algorithm is unambiguous and the computer can execute it.

Algorithms Produce a Result

In our simple definition of an algorithm, we stated that an algorithm is a set of instructions for solving a problem. Unless an algorithm produces some result, we can never be certain whether our solution is correct. Have you ever given a command to a computer and discovered that nothing changed? What was your response? You probably thought that the computer was malfunctioning because your command did not produce any type of result.

Without some visible change, you have no way of determining the effect of your command. The same is true with algorithms. Only algorithms which produce results can be verified as either right or wrong.

Algorithms Halt in a Finite Amount of Time

Algorithms should be composed of a finite number of operations and they should complete their execution in a finite amount of time. Suppose we wanted to write an algorithm to print all the integers greater than 1. Our steps might look something like this:

DIVISION AND LOGIC OPERATIONS

LOGICAL OPERATIONS

In the "truth tables" below, the input bits are in bold, and the results are plain.

And

The logical AND operation compares 2 bits and if they are both "1", then the result is "1", otherwise, the result is "0".

	0	1
0	0	0
1	0	1

Or

The logical OR operation compares 2 bits and if either or both bits are "1", then the result is "1", otherwise, the result is "0".

	0	1
0	0	1
1	1	1

XOR

The logical XOR (Exclusive OR) operation compares 2 bits and if exactly one of them is "1" (*i.e.,* if they are different values), then the result is "1"; otherwise (if the bits are the same), the result is "0".

	0	1
0	0	1
1	1	0

Not

The logical NOT operation simply changes the value of a single bit. If it is a "1", the result is "0"; if it is a "0", the result is "1". Note that this operation is different in that instead of comparing two bits, it is acting on a single bit.

0	1
1	0

FLOATING POINT ARITHMETIC OPERATION

FLOATING POINT ARITHMETIC

Arithmetic operations on floating point numbers consist

of addition, subtraction, multiplication and division the operations are done with algorithms similar to those used on sign magnitude integers (because of the similarity of representation)—example, only add numbers of the same sign. If the numbers are of opposite sign, must do subtraction.

ADDITION

Example on decimal value given in scientific notation:

$$\begin{array}{r} 3.25 \times 10 ** 3 \\ +\ 2.63 \times 10 ** -1 \\ \hline \end{array}$$

first step: align decimal points second step: add:

$$\begin{array}{r} 3.25 \quad \times 10 ** 3 \\ +\ 0.000263 \times 10 ** 3 \\ \hline 3.250263 \times 10 ** 3 \end{array}$$

(presumes use of infinite precision, without regard for accuracy)third step: normalize the result (already normalized!) example on fl pt. value given in binary:

.25 = 0 01111101 00000000000000000000000
100 = 0 10000101 10010000000000000000000

to add these fl. pt. representations, step 1: align radix points shifting the mantissa LEFT by 1 bit DECREASES THE EXPONENT by 1 and shifting the mantissa RIGHT by 1 bit INCREASES THE EXPONENT by 1 we want to shift the mantissa right, because the bits that fall off the end should come from the least significant end of the mantissa,

-> choose to shift the.25, since we want to increase it's exponent.
-> shift by

$$\begin{array}{r} 10000101 \\ -01111101 \\ \hline 00001000 \end{array}$$ (8) places.

0 01111101 00000000000000000000000 (original value)
0 01111110 10000000000000000000000 (shifted 1 place)
(note that hidden bit is shifted into msb of mantissa),
0 01111111 01000000000000000000000 (shifted 2 places)

0 10000000 00100000000000000000000 (shifted 3 places)
0 10000001 00010000000000000000000 (shifted 4 places)
0 10000010 00001000000000000000000 (shifted 5 places)
0 10000011 00000100000000000000000 (shifted 6 places)
0 10000100 00000010000000000000000 (shifted 7 places)
0 10000101 00000001000000000000000 (shifted 8 places)

Step: Add (don't forget the hidden bit for the 100)

    0 10000101 1.10010000000000000000000 (100)
    +0 10000101 0.00000001000000000000000 (.25)
    ----
    0 10000101 1.10010001000000000000000

Step: normalize the result (get the "hidden bit" to be a 1) it already is for this example.result is

0 10000101 10010001000000000000000

Subtraction

like addition as far as alignment of radix points then the algorithm for subtraction of sign mag. numbers takes over before subtracting, compare magnitudes (don't forget the hidden bit!) change sign bit if order of operands is changed.don't forget to normalize number afterward.

Multiplication

Example on decimal values given in scientific notation:

    3.0 × 10 ** 1
    +0.5 × 10 ** 2

algorithm: multiply mantissas add exponents

    3.0 ×10 ** 1
    + 0.5 ×10 ** 2

    1.50× 10 ** 3

example in binary: use a mantissa that is only 4 bits so that I don't spend all day just doing the multiplication part.

    0 10000100 0100
    × 1 00111100 1100

mantissa multiplication: 1.0100

(don't forget hidden bit) × 1.1100

```
       --------
      00000
     00000
    10100
   10100
  10100
 -------
1000110000
```

becomes 10.00110000

Add exponents: always add true exponents (otherwise the bias gets added in twice)biased:

```
 10000100
+00111100
```

```
 10000100 01111111 (switch the order of the subtraction,
-01111111 - 00111100 so that we can get a negative value)
 00000101 01000011
```

true exp true exp is 5. is–67
add true exponents 5 + (–67) is–62.

Re-bias exponent:–62 + 127 is 65. unsigned representation for 65 is 01000001. put the result back together (and add sign bit). 1 01000001 10.00110000 normalize the result: (moving the radix point one place to the left increases the exponent by 1.) 1 01000001 10.00110000 becomes 01000010 1.000110000 this is the value stored (not the hidden bit!): 1 01000010 000110000

Division

Similar to multiplication.

True division: Do unsigned division on the mantissas (don't forget the hidden bit) subtract TRUE exponents. The IEEE standard is very specific about how all this is done. Unfortunately, the hardware to do all this is pretty slow.

Some comparisons of approximate times:

2's complement integer add	1 time unit
fl. pt add	4 time units
fl. pt multiply	6 time units
fl. pt. divide	13time units

There is a faster way to do division. Its called division by reciprocal approximation. It takes about the same time as a fl. pt. multiply. Unfortunately, the results are not always the same as with true division.

Division by reciprocal approximation: instead of doing a/b they do a × 1/b. figure out a reciprocal for b, and then use the fl. pt. multiplication hardware. example of a result that isn't the same as with true division.

True division:	3/3	= 1 (exactly)
Reciprocal approx:	1/3	=.33333333
	3 ×.33333333	=.99999999, not 1

It is not always possible to get a perfectly accurate reciprocal.

ISSUES IN FLOATING POINT

Note: this discussion only touches the surface of some issues that people deal with. Entire courses could probably be taught on each of the issues.

Rounding

Arithmetic operations on fl. pt. values compute results that cannot be represented in the given amount of precision. So, we must round results. There are MANY ways of rounding. They each have "correct" uses, and exist for different reasons. The goal in a computation is to have the computer round such that the end result is as "correct" as possible. There are even arguments as to what is really correct.

Methods of Rounding

Round towards 0: Also called truncation. Figure out how many bits (digits) are available. Take that many bits (digits) for the result and throw away the rest. This has the effect of making the value represented closer to 0.

Example:

.7783 if 3 decimal places available.778

if 2 decimal places available.77

round towards + infinity—regardless of the value, round towards +infinity.

Example:

1.23 if 2 decimal places, 1.3

– 2.86 if 2 decimal places,-2.8

round towards-infinity—regardless of the value, round towards-infinity.

Example:

1.23 if 2 decimal places, 1.2

– 2.86 if 2 decimal places,-2.9

in binary—rounding to 2 digits after radix point round towards + infinity—

1.1101

|

1.11 | 10.00

— — —

1.001

|

1.00 | 1.01

— —

round towards-infinity—

1.1101

|

1.11 | 10.00

— — —

1.001

|

1.00 | 1.01

— —

round towards zero (TRUNCATE)—

1.1101

|

1.11 | 10.00

— — —

1.001

|

1.00 | 1.01

— —

–1.1101

|

–10.00 I -1.11

— — —

–1.001

I

–1.01 I -1.00

— —

Round towards Nearest

Odd case: If there is anything other than 1000... to the right of the number of digits to be kept, then rounded in IEEE standard such that the least significant bit (to be kept) is a zero.

1.1111

I

1.11 I 10.00

— — —

1.1101

I

1.11 I 10.00

— — —

1.001 (ODD CASE)

I

1.00 I 1.01

— —

–1.1101 (1/4 of the way between)

I

–10.00 I -1.11

— — —

–1.001 (ODD CASE)

I

–1.01 I -1.00

— —

Note: this is a bit different than the "round to nearest" algorithm for the "tie" case.5 learned in elementary school for decimal numbers.

Use of Standards

—> allows all machines following the standard to exchange data and to calculate the exact same results.

—> IEEE fl. pt. standard sets parameters of data representation (# bits for mantissa vs. exponent)

—> Pentium architecture follows the standard

Overflow and Underflow

Just as with integer arithmetic, floating point arithmetic operations can cause overflow. Detection of overflow in fl. pt. comes by checking exponents before/during normalization. Once overflow has occurred, an infinity value can be represented and propagated through a calculation. Underflow occurs in fl. pt. representations when a number is to small (close to 0) to be represented. (show number line!) if a fl. pt. value cannot be normalized (getting a 1 just to the left of the radix point would cause the exponent field to be all 0's) then underflow occurs.

HW VS. SW COMPUTING

Floating point operations can be done by hardware (circuitry) or by software (programme code).

-> a programmer won't know which is occurring, without prior knowledge of the HW.

-> SW is much slower than HW. by approx. 1000 times.

A difficult (but good) exercise for students would be to design a SW algorithm for doing fl. pt. addition using only integer Operations. SW to do fl. pt. operations is tedious. It takes lots of shifting and masking to get the data in the right form to use integer arithmetic operations to get a result—and then more shifting and masking to put the number back into fl. pt. format. A common thing that manufacturers used to do is to offer 2 versions of the same architecture, one with HW, and the other with SW fl. pt. ops.

PROCESSOR ORGANIZATION

DEFINITION

Heretofore it has been known that the apparatus of a digital computer might be arranged in a manner such as to allow accessing to the data storage bits of the computer memory in either of two distinct modes. That is, it has been taught that a system might be developed whereby data can be written into the memory in a word-oriented mode and read from the memory in a bit-oriented mode or vice-versa. That is, data might be written into the memory such that all bits of one word are written simultaneously and one bit of all words are read simultaneously or conversely, one bit of all words are written simultaneously and all bits of one word are read simultaneously.

However, "corner-turning" problems have been inherent in prior techniques. These "corner-turning" problems are well understood by those skilled in the art. An oft-used example of such problems is the acquisition, storage, and accessing of radar data. It can be readily understood that if a radar system acquires a plurality of data at various ranges on one azimuth and stores that data in an azimuth-oriented manner and does this for several azimuths it must then devise a unique method to access this stored data if it later desires to access all data at the same range but different azimuths.

In other words, if data is acquired and stored in an azimuth-oriented mode and is later to be accessed in a range-oriented mode then unique apparatus or methods must be utilized to make such accessing. In the past, systems have required either complex logic circuitry, redundancy of circuitry or an increased number of memory access lines so as to be above to "turn the corner" from a bit-oriented access to a word-oriented access or vice-versa. Particular approaches towards circumventing the "corner-turning" problem have been numerous. A typical approach to the solution has been shown in U.S. Letter Pat. 3,277,449 for the Orthogonal Computer designed by William Shooman. Certain articles by Mr. Showman further define andenhance the teachings of this patent.

Particularly, chapter 15, entitled "Orthogonal Processing" of the book Parallel Processor Systems, Technologies and Applications edited by L. C. Hobbs and published by Spartan Books in 1970 basically outlines the teachings of the patent. It is readily observable from an understanding of the Shooman Patent that the invention described therein requires both vertical and horizontal accessing means, and vertical and horizontal arithmetical means. In other words, the Shooman invention, and others which have sought to circumvent the "corner-turning" problem, fundamentally teach two separate computers operating upon the same memory. Such systems are extremely expensive due to the requirements of the duplication ofaccess circuitry and arithmetic units.

Further, it has been known that computer systems known as associative processors might be designed whereby arithmetic, search, or other logical operations might be performed upon a plurality of data simultaneously. Such systems have proven themselves to be quite effective in the rapid processing of data. However, heretofore such systems have generally been quite inflexible as to mode of operation; that is, such systems have been capable of simultaneously processing all bits of one word, or one bit of all words, but no given system has been capable of performing simultaneous operations in both modes without the duplication of much of its circuitry such as to use different logic and arithmetic circuitry for each of the two modes.

Therefore, it is the general object of the instant invention to present a novel solid state associative processor organization wherein a unique solid state memory array is coupled with the key apparatus of an associative processor to form an associative array wherein associative or parallel operations may be performed upon data in either a word-oriented or a bit-oriented mode and wherein each mode utilizes the same read-write lines and arithmetic unit.

A further object of the invention is to provide a solid state associative processor organization wherein a plurality of the aforementioned associative arrays may be operated upon in parallel so as to be capable of simultaneously receiving and processing data from a large number of sources.

A further object of the invention is to provide a control system whereby the control programmes necessary for the parallel operation of a plurality of associative arrays may themselves be processed with a speed conducive to that of the associative arrays. Still a further object of the invention is to provide a unique computer organization which is not only capable of the parallel processing of a large volume of data from various sources and capable of processing the control programme with a speed conducive to the data processing speed of the system, but to do so in a manner which is accurate in operation, highly flexible, adaptable to various uses, and quite economical.

The aforesaid objects of the invention and other objects which will become apparent as the description proceeds are achieved by a digital computer wherein operations may be simultaneously performed on a plurality of data in both a bit-oriented mode and a word-oriented mode comprising a plurality of solid state memory arrays, the data storage arrangements of which are such that access may be made to the data storage bits thereof in either a bit-oriented mode or a word-oriented mode, and of suchcharacter that a single set of data input/output lines is required for writing data into the arrays or reading data from the arrays in both modes and a plurality of arithmetic units, one associated with each solid state memory array, providing the means for performing, in both word-oriented and bit-oriented modes, parallel logical and arithmetic operations on the data associated with the solid state memory arrays.

GENERAL REGISTER ORGANIZATION

When a large number of registers are included in the CPU, it is most efficient to connect them through a common bus system. The registers communicate with each other not only for direct data transfers, but also while performing various micro-operations. Hence it is necessary to provide a common unit that can perform all the arithmetic, logic and shift micro-operation in the processor.

BUS ORGANIZATION FOR SEVEN CPU REGISTERS

The output of each register is connected to true multiplexer (mux) to form the two buses A & B. The selection lines in each multiplexer select one register or the input data for the particular bus. The A and B buses forms the input to a common ALU. The operation selected in the ALU determines the arithmetic or logic micro-operation that is to be performed. The result of the micro-operation is available for output and also goes into the inputs of the registers.

The register that receives the information from the output bus is selected by a decoder. The decoder activates one of the register load inputs, thus providing a transfer both between the data in the output bus and the inputs of the selected destination register. The control unit that operates the CPU bus system directs the information flow through the registers and ALU by selecting the various components in the systems.

$$R_1 \rightarrow R_2 + R_3$$

- *MUX A selection (SEC A)*: To place the content of R2 into bus A
- *MUX B selection (sec B)*: To place the content of R3 into bus B
- *ALU operation selection (OPR)*: To provide the arithmetic addition (A + B)
- *Decoder destination selection (SEC D)*: To transfer the content of the output bus into R_1

These form the control selection variables are generated in the control unit and must be available at the beginning of a clock cycle. The data from the two source registers propagate through the gates in the multiplexer and the ALU, to the output bus, and into the into of the destination registers, all during the clock cycle intervals.

CONTROL WORD

There are 14 binary selection inputs in the units, and their combined value specified a control word. It consists of four fields three fields contain three bits each, and one field has five bits. The three bits of SEL A select a source register for the A input of the ALU. The three bits of SEL B select a source register for the B input of the ALU. The three bit of SEC D select a destination register using the decoder and its seven load outputs. The five bits of OPR select one of the operations in the ALU. The 14-bit control word when applied to the selection inputs specify a particular micro-operation.

Table. Encoding of Register Selection Fields

Binary code	SEL A	SEL B	SEL D
000	Input	Input	None
001	R_1		
010	R_2		
011	R_3	S	S
100	R_4	A	A
101	R_5	M	M
110	R_6	E	E
111	R_7		

Table. Encoding of ALU Operation.

OPR & elect	Operation	Symbol
00000	Transfer A	TSFA
00001	Increment A	INCA
00010	Add A + B	ADD
00101	Subtract A-B	SUB
00110	Decrement A	DEC A
01000	AND A and B	AND
01010	OR A and B	OR
01100	XOR A and B	XOR
01110	Complement A	COMA
10000	Shift right A	SHRA
11000	Shift left A	SHLA

Examples of Micro-operation for the CPU

Symbolic Designation

Micro operation	SECA	SEC B	SEL D	OPR	Control word			
$R_1 \rightarrow R_2 - R_3$	R_2	R_3	R_1	SUB	010	011	001	00101
$R_4 \rightarrow R_5 \text{ V } R_5$	R_4	R	R_4	OR	100	101	100	0101
$R_6 \rightarrow R_6 + 1$	R_6	–	R_6	MCA	110	000	110	00001
$R_7 \rightarrow R_1$	R_1	–	R_7	TSFA	001	000	111	00000
Output $\rightarrow R_2$	R_2	–	None	TSFA	010	000	000	00000
Output $\rightarrow$ Input	Input	–	None	TSFA	000	000	000	00000
$R_4 \rightarrow$ SHL R4	R_4	–	R_4	SHLA	100	000	100	11000
$R_5 \rightarrow 0$	R_5	R_5	R_5	XOR	101	101	101	01100

STOCK ORGANIZATION

A useful feature that is included in the CPU of most computers is a stack or last-in first out (LIFO) list. A stack is a storage device that stores information in such a manner that the item stored last is the first item retrieved.

The operation a stack can be companied to a stack of trays. The stack in Digital Computer is essentially a memory unit with an address register that can count only (after an initial value is loaded into it.)

The register that holds the address for the stack is called a Stack Pointer (SP) because its values always points at the top item in the stack.

The two operations:

- Push (insert)
- Pop (delete)

REGISTER STACK

A stack can be placed in a portion of a large memory as it can be organized as a collection of a finite number of memory words as register. In a 64-word stack, the stack pointer contains 6 bits because $2^6 = 64$.

The one bit register FULL is set to 1 when the stack is full, and the one-bit register EMTY is set to 1 when the stack is empty.

DR is the data register that holes the binary data to be written into on read out of the stack. Initially, SP is decide to O, EMTY is set to 1, FULL = 0, so that SP points to the word at address O and the stack is masked empty and not full.

Push	SP → SP + 1	Increment stack pointer
	M [SP] → DR	Unit item on top of the Stack
	It (SP = 0) then	(FULL → 1) check it stack is full
	EMTY → 0	Mask the stack not empty.
Pop	DR → [SP]	Read item trans the top of stack
	SP → SP –1	Decrement SP
	It (SP = 0)	Then (EMTY → 1) check it stack is empty
	FULL → 0	Mark the stack not full.

INSTRUCTION FORMATS

The most common fields found in instruction format are:

- An operation code field that specified the operation to be performed
- An address field that designates a memory address or a processor registers.
- A mode field that specifies the way the operand or the effective address is determined.

Computers may have instructions of several different lengths containing varying number of addresses. The number of address field in the instruction format of a computer depends on the internal organization of its registers. Most computers fall into one of three types of CPU organization.

Single accumulator organization	Add × AC → AC + M [×]
General register organization	Add R1, R2, R3 R → R2 + R3
Stack organization	Push ×

Three Address Instruction

Computer with three addresses instruction format can use each address field to specify either processor register are memory operand.

ADD	R_1, A, B	$A_1 \rightarrow M [A] + M [B]$	
ADD	R_2, C, D	$R_2 \rightarrow M [C] + M [B]$	X = (A + B) * (C + A)
MUL X, R_1, R_2	M [X] R_1 * R_2		

The advantage of the three address formats is that it results in short programme when evaluating arithmetic expression. The disadvantage is that the binary-coded instructions require too many bits to specify three addresses.

Two Address Instruction

Most common in commercial computers. Each address field can specify either a processes register on a memory word.

MOV	R_1, A	$R_1 \rightarrow M [A]$	
ADD	R_1, B	$R_1 \rightarrow R_1 + M [B]$	
MOV	R_2, C	$R_2 \rightarrow M [C]$	X = (A + B) * (C + D)
ADD	R_2, D	$R_2 \rightarrow R_2 + M [D]$	

MUL	R_1, R_2	$R_1 \rightarrow R_1 * R_2$
MOV	X_1 R_1	M [X] $\rightarrow R_1$

One Address Instruction

It used an implied accumulator (AC) register for all data manipulation. For multiplication/division, there is a need for a second register.

Load	A	AC → M [A]	
Add	B	AC → AC + M [B]	
Store	T	M [T] → AC	X = (A +B) × (C + A)
Load	C	AC → M (C)	All operations are done
Add	D	AC → AC + M (D)	between the AC register
Ml	T	AC → AC + M (T)	and a memory operand.
Store	X	M [×]→ AC	It's the address of a temporary memory location required for storing the intermediate result.

Zero – Address Instruction

A stack organized computer does not use an address field for the instruction ADD and MUL. The PUSH and POP instruction, however, need an address field to specify the operand that communicates with the stack (TOS → top of the stack).

Push	A	Tos → A
Push	B	Tos → B
Add		Tos → (A + B)
Push	C	Tos → C
Push	D	Tos → D
Add		Tos → (C + D)
Mul		Tos → (C + D) * (A + B)
Pop	X	M [X] Tos

ADDRESSING MODES

The operation field of an instruction specifies the operation to be performed. This operation must be executed on some data stored in computer register as memory words.

The way the operands are chosen during programme execution is dependent on the addressing mode of the instruction.

The addressing mode specifies a rule for interpreting or modifying the address field of the instruction between the operand is activity referenced. Computer use addressing mode technique for the purpose of accommodating one or both of the following provisions.

- To give programming versatility to the uses by providing such facilities as pointer to memory, counters for top control, indexing of data, and programme relocation.
- To reduce the number of bits in the addressing fields of the instruction.

OPERATION CYCLE OF THE COMPUTER

- Fetch the instruction from memory
- Decode the instruction
- Execute the instruction

Programme Counter (PC) keeps track of the instruction in the programme stored in memory.

PC holds the address of the instruction to be executed next and in incremented each time an instruction is fetched from memory.

- Implied mode
- Immediate mode
- Register mode
- Register mode
- *Register*: Indirect mode
- Auto increment/Auto decrement mode
- Direct address mode
- Indirect address mode
- Relative address mode
- Indexed addressing mode
- Base register addressing mode

Opcode	Mode	Address

INSTRUCTION FORMAT WITH MODE FIELD

Relative Address

The content of PC is added to the address part of the instruction in order to obtain the effective address,

Ex: PC = 825 + 1 + 24

Indexed Addressing Mode

The content of index register is added to the address part of the instruction in order to obtain the effective address.

Base Register Addressing Mode

The content of a base register is added to the address bank of the instruction to obtain the effective address.

Indirect Address

Effective Address = Address part of instruction + content of CPU register.

DATA TRANSFER AND MANIPULATION

Computer provides an extensive set of instructions to give the user the flexibility to carryout various computational task. Most computer instruction can be classified into three categories.

- Data transfer instruction
- Data manipulation instruction
- Programme control instruction

Data transfer instruction cause transferred data from one location to another without changing the binary instruction content. Data manipulation instructions are those that perform arithmetic logic, and shift operations. Programme control instructions provide decision-making capabilities and change the path taken by the programme when executed in the computer.

Data Transfer Instruction

Data transfer instruction move data from one place in the computer to another without changing the data content. The most common transfers are between memory and processes registers, between processes register and input or output, and between processes register themselves.

Table. Typical Data Transfer Instruction

Name	Mnemonic
Load	LD
Store	ST
Move	MOV
Exchange	XCH
Input	In
Output	Out
Push	Push
Pop	Pop

Data Manipulation Instruction

It performs operations on data and provides the computational capabilities for the computer. The data manipulation instructions in a typical computer are usually divided into three basic types.

- Arithmetic Instruction
- Logical bit manipulation Instruction
- Shift Instruction.

Arithmetic Instruction

Name	Mnemonic
Increment	INC
Decrement	DEC
Add	Add
Subtract	Sub
Multiply	MUL
Divide	DIV
Add with carry	ADDC
Subtract with basses	SUBB
Negate (2's complement)	NEG

Logical and Bit Manipulation Instruction

Name	Mnemonic
Clear	CLR

Complement	COM
And	AND
Or	OR
Exclusive-Or	XOR
Clear carry	CLRC
Set carry	SETC
Complement carry	COMC
Enable interrupt	ET
Disable interrupt	OI

Shift Instruction

Instructions to shift the content of an operand are quite useful and one often provided in several variations. Shifts are operation in which the bits of a word are moved to the left or right. The bit-shifted in at the and of the word determines the type of shift used. Shift instruction may specify either logical shift, arithmetic shifts, or rotate type shifts.

Name	Mnemonic
Logical shift right	SHR
Logical shift left	SHL
Arithmetic shift right	SHRA
Arithmetic shift left	SHLA
Rotate right	ROR
Rotate left	ROL
Rotate mgmt through carry	RORC
Rotate left through carry	ROLC

RISC and CISC ARCHITECTURE

Characteristics of CISC architecture are:

- A large no. of instruction-typically from 100 to 250 instruction.
- Some instruction that perform specialized tasks and one used infrequently.
- A large variety of addressing modes – typically from 5 to 20 different modes.
- Variable length instruction format
- Instruction that manipulate operates in memory.

RISC CHARACTERSTICS

The concept of RISC arithmetic involves an attempt to reduce execution time by simplifying the instruction set of the computer.

The major characteristics of a RISC processes are:

- Relatively few instructions
- Relatively few addressing modes
- Memory access limited to load and store instruction
- All operations done within the registers of the CPU.
- Fixed-length, easily decoded instruction format
- Single-cycle instruction execution
- Handmaiden rather than micro programmed control.

PARALLEL PROCESSING

Parallel processing is a term used to denote a large class of techniques that are used to provide simultaneously data-processing tasks for the purpose of increasing the computational speed of the computer.

Instead of processing each instruction sequentially as in a conventional computer, a parallel processing system is able to perform concurrent data processing to achieve faster execution time.

The system may have two or more processor operating concurrently. The purpose of parallel processing is to speed up the computer processing capability and increase its throughput. The amount of hardware increases with parallel processing, hence the cost increases.

PIPELINING

Pipelining is a technique of decomposing a sequential process into sub-operation with each sub-process being executed in a special dedicated segment that operator concurrently with all other segment.

A pipeline can be visualized as a collection of processing segments through which binary information flows. Each segment performs partial processing dictated by the way the task is portioned.

The result obtained from the computation in each segment

is transferred to next segment in the pipeline. The final result is obtained after the data have passed through all segments.

Example: Ai * Bi + Ci for all I = 1,2,3, ...7

Each sub operation is to be implemented in a segment within a pipeline.

Each segment has one or two registers and a combinational circuit. R_1 through R5 are registers that receive new data with every clock pulse. The multiplier and adder combinational circuits.

The sub-operations performed in each segment of the pipeline are:

$R_1 \rightarrow Ai, R_2 \rightarrow Bi$	Input Ai and Bi
$R_3 \rightarrow R_1 * R_2\ R_4 \rightarrow Ci$	Multiply and Input ci
$R_1 \rightarrow R_3 + R_4$	Add Ci to product

Table. Content of Registers in Pipeline Example.

Clock pulse number	Segment 1 R_1	R_2	Segment 2 R_3	R_4	Segment 5 R_5
1.	A_1	B_1	-	-	-
2.	A_2	B_2	$A_1 * B_1$	C_1	-
3.	A_3	B_3	$A_2 * B_2$	C_2	$A_1 * B_1 + C_1$
4.	A_4	B_4	$A_3 * B_3$	C_3	$A_2 * B_2 + C_2$
5.	A_5	B_5	$A_4 * B_4$	C_4	$A_3 * B_3 + C_3$
6.	A_6	B_6	$A_5 * B_5$	C_5	$A_4 * B_4 + C_4$
7.	A_7	B_7	$A_6 * B_6$	C_6	$A_5 * B_5 + C_5$
8.	-	-	$A_7 * B_7$	C_7	$A_6 * B_6 + C_6$
9.	-	-	-	-	$A_7 * B_7 + C_7$

GENERAL CONSIDERATION

Task as the total operation performed going through all the segments in the pipeline

Space-time Diagrams

The behaviour of a pipeline can be illustrated with a space-time diagram. The horizontal axis displays the time in clock cycles and the vertical axis give the segment no.

Example	Task – 6, Segment – 4							
1	2	3	4	5	6	7	8	9
T_1	T_2	T_3	T_4	T_5	T_6			
	T_1	T_2	T_3	T_4	T_5	T_6		
		T_1	T_2	T_3	T_4	T_5	T_6	
			T_1	T_2	T_3	T_4	T_5	T_6

Formula: K + (n – 1) (time taken)

K = segment no.

N = tasks.

Speed-up = $nt_n/(K+n-1)\ t_p = t_n/t_p$ (if $t_n = k\ t_p$)

ARITHMETIC PIPELINE

Usually found in very high speed computers; They are used to implement floating-point operation, multiplication of fixed-point numbers, and similar computation encountered in scientific problems. A pipeline multiplier is essentially an array multiplier with special adders designed to minimize the carry propagation time through the partial products floating-point operation are easily decomposed into sub operations.

$X = A * 2^a$

$X = B * 2^b$

Sub operations that are performed in from segments are:

- Compare the exponents
- Align the mantissas
- Add/subtract the mantissas
- Normalize the result

Instruction Pipeline

Pipeline processing can occurs not only in the data stream, but in the instruction stream as well. An Instruction pipeline reads consecutive instruction from memory while previous instruction one being executed in other segments. This causes the instruction fetch and execute phase to overlap and perform simultaneous operations.

Most of the cases, the computer needs to process each instruction (with the following segments of steps:

- Fetch the instruction from memory
- Decode the instruction

- Calculate the effective address
- Fetch the operands from memory
- Execute the instruction
- Store the result in the proper place.

The design of an instruction pipeline will be most efficient it the instruction cycle is divided into segments of cycle duration. The time that-each step takes to fulfill its function depends on the instruction and the way it is executed.

In general there are three major difficulties that cause the instruction pipeline to deviate from its normal operation.

- Resource conflicts
- Data dependency
- Branch difficulties

Solution of Data Dependency (Techniques)

- Hardware interlocks
- Operand forwarding
- Delayed load

Handling Branch Instruction

- Pre-fetch target instruction
- Branch target butter (BTB)
- Loop buffer
- Branch predictions
- Delayed branch

RISC Pipeline

RISC has the ability to use an efficient instruction pipeline. The simplicity of the instruction set can be utilized to implement on instruction pipeline using a small number of sub-operations, with each being executed in one clock cycle. The data transfer in RISC are limited to load and store instruction.

They usually need three/four stage of pipelining. One of the major advantage of RISC over CISC is to execute instruction at the rate of one/clock cycle. The advantage of RISC over CISC is that RISC can achieve pipeline segments, requiring just one clock cycle. While CISC user many segments in its pipeline, with the longest segment requiring or more clock cycle.

Example: Three segment Instruction Pipeline

I	Instruction fetch
A	ALU operation
E	Execute Instruction

VECTOR PROCESSING

Some problems are characterized by the fact that they require a vast number of computations that will take a conventional computer days or aware weeks to complete. Computer with vector processing capabilities are in demand in specialized application. The following are representative application areas where vector processing is to the utmost importance.

- Long-range weather forecasting
- Petroleum explorations
- Seismic data analysis
- Aerodynamics and space flight simulations.
- Artificial intelligence and export system.
- Mapping the human genuine.
- Image processing.

An Instruction format for an instruction format includes five fields: Operation Code/Base address Source/base address source 2/base address destination/vector length. This is essentially a three address instruction with three fields specifying the base address of the operand and an additional field that given the length of the data items in the vector. This assumes that a vector operand resides in memory.

Example Matrix Multiplication

The matrix multiplication is one of the most computational intensive operation performed in computers with vector processes. The multiplication of two matrices (n × n) consist of n^2 inner product or n^3 multiply-add operation.

a_{11}	a_{12}	a_{13}	b_{11}	b_{12}	b_{13}	c_{11}	c_{12}	c_{13}
a_{12}	a_{22}	a_{23}	b_{12}	b_{22}	b_{23}	c_{12}	c_{22}	c_{23}
a_{31}	a_{32}	a_{33}	b_{31}	b_{32}	b_{33}	c_{31}	c_{32}	c_{33}

The product matrix C is a 3 × 3 matrix where element are related to the elements of A & B by the inner product: In general, the inner product consists of the scan of k product term of the term.

$C = A_1 B_1 + A_2 B_2 + A_3 A_3 + \text{-----} + A_k B_k$

We can break down the summation into from section:

C = A1 B1 + A5 A5 + Aa Ba + AB BB +————
+ A2 B2 + A6 B6 + A10 B10 + A14 B14 +————
+ A 3 B3 + A7 B7 + A11 B11 + A15 B15 +————
+ A4 B4 + A8 B8 + A12 B12 + A16 B16 +-————

Assume that the Floating Point multiplier pipeline and Floating Point Adder pipeline have four segments each. All segment register in the multiplier and adder are initialized to 0. Therefore, the output of the adder is 0 for the first eight cycles until both pipes are full. At the beginning of the 9th cycle, the output of the adder is A_1B_1 and the output of the multiplier in A_5B_5. Thus the ninth cycle starts the addition $A_1B_1 + A_5B_5$ in the adder pipeline and so on.

Array Processors

An array processor is a processor that performs computations on large arrays of data. The term is used to refer two different types of processors. An attached array processor is an auxiliary processor attached to a general-purpose computer. It is intended to improve the performance of the host computer in specific numerical computation tasks.

An SIMD array processor is a processor that has a single instruction on multiple data organization. It manipulates vector instruction by means of multiple functional units responding to a common instruction.

Attached Array Processor

Its purpose is to enhance the performance of the computer by providing vector processing for complex scientific application. It achieves high performance by means of parallel processing with multiple functional units. It includes the arithmetic unit containing one or more pipelined Floating Point Adder and Multipliers. The array processors can be programmed by the user to accommodate a variety of complex arithmetic problem.

SIMD Array Procerssor

An SIMD Array Processor is a computer with multiple processing units operating in parallel. The processing units are synchronized to perform the same operation under the common control units, thus providing a SIMD organization.

It contains a set of processing elements (PEs), each having a local memory M. Each processor element includes an ALU, a floating-print Arithmetic Unit, and working registers. The master control unit controls the operations in the PE. The main memory is used for storage of the programme.

The function of the Master control Unit is to decode the instruction and determine how the instruction is to be executed. Scalar and programme control instructions are directly executed with in the Master Control Unit. Vector instructions are broadcast to all PE simultaneously. Each PE uses operand stored in its local memory. Vector operands are distributed to the local memories prior to the parallel execution of the instructions.

5

Control Unit

INSTRUCTIONS

EXECUTION PORTS

Executing one OP after another would obviously not make any use of parallel execution units. To make sure that the out-of-order execution is actually working, Intel is using the 'Renamer and Allocator' as well as the 'Reorder-Unit'. The 'Integer/FP Renamer/Allocator' is found before the Reservation Station, and as the name already says it, this unit is responsible for integer as well as FP and multimedia OPs. Athlon does this work a bit more sophisticated. The units that take care of the out-of-order execution are the Integer Scheduler and the FP Scheduler, both able to hold a quite impressive number of OPs (18/36).

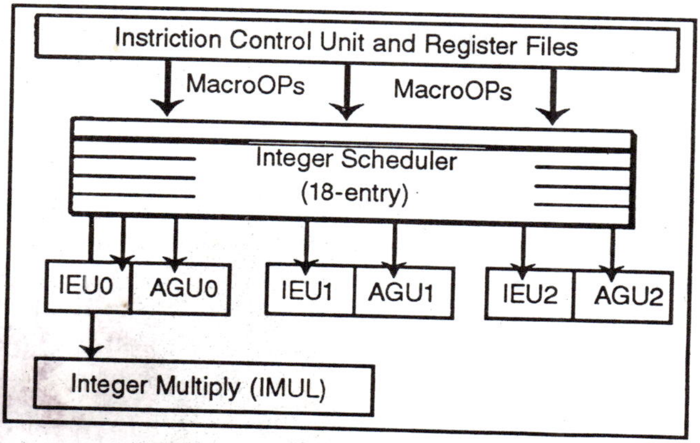

Fig. Athlon's Integer Execution Path.

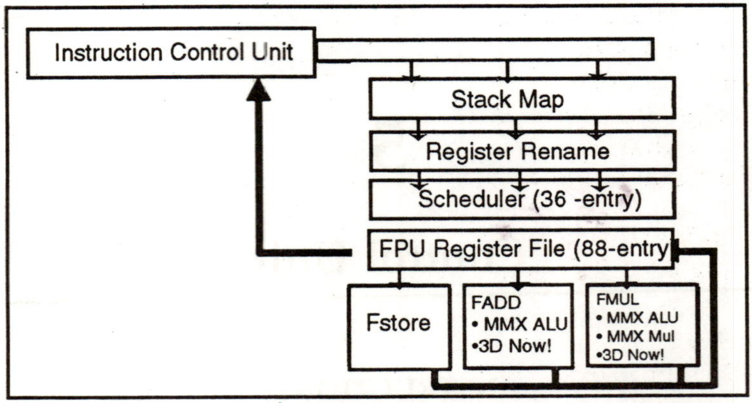

Fig. Athlon's Floating Point and Multimedia Execution Path.

The control unit is the part of a computer that controls the computer's operation. Basically, each part of the computer requires control signals to arrive at particular times for each instruction of the computer's software. The control unit provides those control signals.

The control unit is the part of a computer that controls the computer's operation. Basically, each part of the computer requires control signals to arrive at particular times for each instruction of the computer's software. The control unit provides those control signals. At one time control units were ad-hoc logic, and they were difficult to design. Now they are designed as a microprogram that is stored in a control store. Words of the microprogram are selected by a sequencer and the bits from those words directly control the different parts of the computer, including the registers, arithmetic and logic unit, instruction register, bus, input/output and computer storage.

In modern computers, each of these subsystems may have its own subsidiary controller, but the control unit is the top dog that controls the computer overall.

A control unit for a CISC ISA can... have to deal with instructions that involve tens and even hundreds of minor states. There would thus be thousands of logic expressions to generate the control signals. CAD tools can simplify and minimize these and even lay them out on the silicon automatically, but it is still a large block of irregular logic on the chip. The control unit is a finite state machine that takes as its inputs the IR, the status register (which is partly filled by the status output from the ALU), and the current major state of the cycle. Its rules are encoded either in random logic, a Programmable Logic Array (PLA), or Read-Only Memory (ROM), and its outputs are sent across the processor to each point requiring coordination or direction for the control unit.

For example the outputs needed for the portion of the instruction/data path shown in Discussion 13 are Jump/Branch/ NextPC, IR Latch, Read Control, Load Control, ALU Function Select, Load/Reg-Reg, Reg R/W.

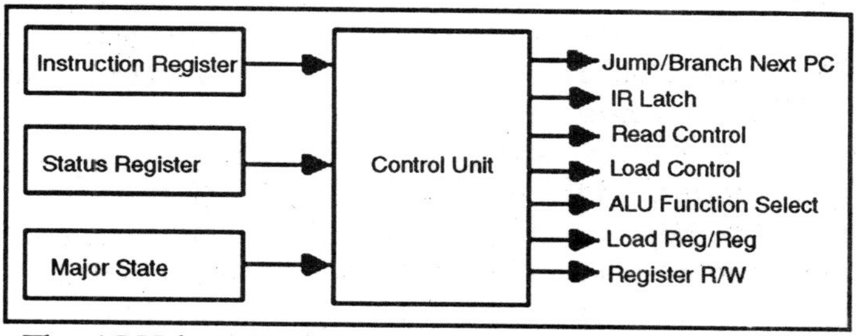

The ALU function select takes the instruction op code and translates it into a given function of the ALU (either one line per ALU function or a compact binary code for the function). The Jump/Branch/PC depends on the instruction type and in a RISC architecture these may be directly coded in the op code. Read control occurs at the start of an instruction cycle. IR latch and occurs at the end of the fetch state. Load control happens at the end of the data fetch state of a load instruction. Load Reg/Reg again depends on the op-code. Register R/W is in the start of the data fetch stage and at the write back stage of an operation. It thus depends on the major state and the instruction.

A CISC architecture typically uses a more complex control unit. As we've noted before, the IR is often multiple words, and the control unit has to look at different parts of the IR at different stages of execution. In fact, the entire IR may not be available at once, requiring interlocks with fetch logic to ensure the contents of the IR are valid.

There are many more control signals coming out of a CISC control unit, partly to control the more complex addressing logic, but also to directly connect to the many special purpose registers. In a RISC architecture, the registers are accessed uniformly in a block so a simple decoder in the register file can select the particular register. In a CISC architecture, there are restrictions on the particular registers that can be used by a given instruction and these are enforced by the control unit.

To begin the design of a control unit, we start by listing every control signal in the instruction/data path of the processor. This becomes a list of the control unit's outputs. As input, it has the instruction register, any status information (such as branch flags, interrupts, etc.) from the processor, and a "major state" which simply keeps track of where we are in the execution of an instruction. We always begin an instruction with state 0, which corresponds to Fetch. During that state, the control unit outputs the necessary signals to route the contents of the PC to the memory address port, to select and clock the memory until it responds with data from that location, and then cause this data to be latched into the IR.

In a CISC architecture, the Fetch may only retrieve the first part of an instruction, and (depending on bits in the IR that are then decoded by the control unit) more words may need to be fetched. In a RISC architecture, a single Fetch retrieves a complete instruction, so we may proceed to the next major state, which is usually to begin fetching data from the registers, while we decode the instruction.

In a RISC architecture, "decoding an instruction" mainly means that the instruction type field determines what the control unit will do for the remainder of the instructions. If you think of the CU as a finite state machine, the bits in the type field select the next state following the decode.

In terms of a program's logic, this is like selecting a branch in a Switch statement – each branch of the Switch contains the series of steps to be performed for one type of instruction. For example, after decoding a Jump instruction, the control unit outputs the signals required to combine the address portion of the instruction with the upper bits of the PC and load the result back into the PC. The CU then returns to the Fetch step. Thus, a Jump has three major states (Fetch, Decode, Complete). For a memory Load instruction, the CU first sends one of the selected register values (the address) to the address port of the memory (via a multiplexer) and signals the memory to fetch this location. When the memory returns the value, then the CU sends signals to the necessary multiplexer(s) and the register file so that the memory data goes over the Dest bus and is stored in the designated register. Thus, a Load has four major states.

So, for each type of instruction, and for each major state in each type of instruction, we look at the list of control signals and decide what value each signal must have. In some cases, the value doesn't matter (*e.g.*, if memory isn't selected, it doesn't matter whether it is set to read or write, because it simply won't do anything in either case). You can think of this as a large 2-dimensional table indexed by instruction type and major state. Within each cell of the table is a list of the control signal and their values.

One last bit of control output that we've neglected is the control of the major state itself. This is usually a register, as shown above, that is input to the CU. But it also receives its next value on each clock from the CU. In the above example, the Jump proceeds from State 0 (Fetch) to State 1 (Decode) to State 3 (Complete) and then goes back to State 0. While a Load adds a State 4. In some designs, the state register also encodes the instruction type. Thus, it is really referring to the different states of the finite state machine (FSM) rather than the major steps of the instructions. So, for example, the FSM states for a Load might be the sequence 0, 1, 12, 13. The latter two distinguish Memory and Write Back from the Complete stage of the Jump. In other designs, we might see Jump going through states 0, 1, 2, and Load going through 0, 1, 2, 3, with the type field used to distinguish the different behaviour of the latter states. This is all just a matter of using somewhat different ways of naming the same things. The important point is just that the CU has the inputs it needs to know what it is supposed to be doing on the present clock and what it will do next. In the CU design process, this translate to ensuring that one of the control signals on the list is the "next state" signal, and that we always specify this in every cell of our table.

Multi Cycle Data Path

Unlike the way this is drawn in the text, it is quite obvious here that each level of the controller's finite state machine corresponds to a clock cycle (or major state). This view clearly shows the commonality of the first two major states, prior to the decoding of the instruction. The third stage is a typical fanning out of the finite state machine to deal with the different cases of the instruction types. Thus, we can see that the machine is arranged in a table where the rows are major states, and the columns are major instruction types. Because the new PC values have been computed, the Jump and Branch types can be finished early. The memory read takes the longest (5 major states). Each of these states produces a set of control signals that cause the multiplexers to select the appropriate inputs, and the various registers to latch at the proper time. This is determined by looking at each device requiring control and determining for each state whether it is necessary to issue a signal on that particular control line.

Note that in the text, the circuitry controlled by the status from the ALU is shown external to the control for simplicity. But in a more general controller that must handle multiple conditions, this logic would not be separated. Because there are ten distinct states, and the book chooses to encode the instruction type in the major state (really the FSM state number) the state register for this machine must have four bits.

One common approach to implementing a controller is to have the major state be implemented by a counter register and within each of these states the different columns are represented by the state register (which in a RISC architecture could just be the instruction type code). The major state counter simply increments on each clock cycle, and when a column of states finishes early, its last state generates a reset signal to the major state counter. Another issue that is not addressed here is what happens when there is a memory delay. We are still assuming that memory returns in a single cycle. The simplest case is to stall the finite state machine until the fetch is complete. This is done by having a memory wait signal that is input to the finite state machine. Each memory fetch state has a next state arc that loops back to itself whenever memory wait is asserted.

Simple Data Path Example: PDP-8

The DEC PDP-8 is a frequently cited example of an almost trivial datapath. We'll quickly take a look at it and note some differences in the implementation approach. The PDP-8 is a 12-bit word machine with a single register (called the Accumulator). It thus falls into the class of single address computers. The majority of the instructions are specified by the upper 3 bits of a 12-bit word. In the DEC scheme, the high order bit is number 0 and the low order bit is 11. Operations 0 through 5 use an addressing scheme in which bit 3 determines whether the address is direct or indirect, and bit 4 determines whether it refers to an address in the current 128-word "page" or the page that starts at address 0. The processor organization is as follows, note that for the sake of further simplification, the Current Page mode logic has been omitted:

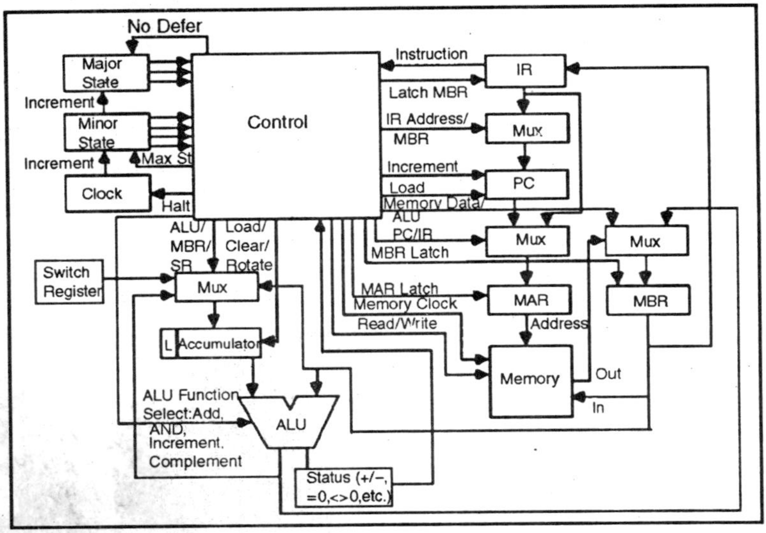

The processor has three major states: Fetch, Defer (Indirect address fetch), and Execute.

Here is an example of an instruction execution:

- 1077—add location 77 directly to the accumulator
- Major State 1 (Fetch)
- Minor State 1 MAR <-PC
- Minor State 2 MBR <-Mem(MAR), PC <-PC + 1
- Minor State 3 Latch MBR into IR
- Minor State 4 Decode Instruction = Add, Mode = Direct (no defer), Page = 0, Max St, No defer
- Major State 2 (Execute)
- Minor State 1 MAR <-00000 + IR6..IR11
- Minor State 2 MBR <-Mem(MAR), ALU Function = Add
- Minor State 3 Acc <-ALU result, Max St
- Now let's look at some of these control lines to see what logic expressions drive them:
- No defer = (Major State = 1) AND (IR5 = 0)
- Latch MBR = (Major State = 1) AND (Minor State = 3)
- Increment PC = (Major State = 1) AND (Minor State = 2)
- IR address/MBR = (IR0..IR2 = 4 or 5) AND (IR3 = 1)
- Load PC = (Major State = 3) AND (Minor State = 3) AND (IR0..IR2 = 4 or 5)
- Memory Data/ALU = (Major State = 3) AND (IR0..IR2 = 3)
- MBR Latch = ((Major State = 1) AND (Minor State = 2)(OR)(Major State = 2) AND (Minor State = 2)(OR ((Major State = 3) AND (Minor State = 2) AND (IR0..IR2 < 4))

And so on. Essentially for each of the control signals we identify all of the conditions that could cause it to be asserted and add them to the expression for the given signal.

Microcode

In many CISC architectures the control unit can feed back to the major (and minor) states and has internal registers and a ROM. It can thus cause portions of an instruction to be extended or repeated as necessary. The minor states, registers. additional control logic, and ROM form a finite state machine called a microcode engine. In the microcode engine, the opcode from the IR becomes a jump address into the ROM. A micro-PC can be used to step through a series of fetches from the ROM starting at that point, with each fetch resulting in control signals being sent out and providing feedback to the major and minor state values.

An alternative to using a micro-PC is to have each instruction explicitly specify the address of its successor. Thus, one of the fields in the micro-op may be the address of the next instruction. This allows jumps to be used anywhere in the microcode with no time penalty—consider that if a separate instruction had to be employed for a jump, it would add a cycle to the execution of the ISA instruction.

The microcode instruction set can contain a subroutine jump so that common sequences of control outputs can be reused. This is typically present in systems that employ a microPC rather than a next instruction field. There is typically just one subroutine return register, so nesting of subroutines is not allowed. Thus, the subroutine jump may be implemented as a normal jump with a signal issued that stores the current micro-PC value into the return register. And the subroutine ends with a Return operation rather than a jump to another location. The Return operation issues a signal that loads the return register back into the micro-PC. In a system with an explicit next instruction field, the current address plus one is stored into the return register and it is implicit that the next location holds the next instruction following the subroutine call. (An alternative is to have both a subroutine jump address and a next instruction address, and simply return to the same instruction, but this requires the instruction format to be larger than necessary for most operations.

Microinstruction Format Design

From the preceding discussion of how sequential execution, jumps, and calls are executed we can gather that the microinstruction needs to include control information for the microengine itself. In the simplest microinstruction formats, each bit represents a control signal that is sent out to the datapath. Thus, when a microinstruction is fetched, the bits in the instruction are connected to control wires and cause actions to occur in the datapath.

For example, in our PDP-8 example, there are 14 control signals that are driven by a single bit, and three others that each require multiple bits, for a total of 23 bits. Each of the first 20 bits of this microinstruction corresponds to a control signal in the PDP-8. For example, bit 0 might be the Halt, bit 1 the No defer, bit 2 the Max St., bit 3 Acc.

Load, bit 4 Acc. clear, etc. This simple representation is effective but inefficient. For example, it uses 4 bits to select the ALU function but only one of those bits should be asserted at any time. Thus, we can save some memory by storing the number of the active bit and using an external "decoder" circuit to translate the two bits into the four lines that control the ALU. In a simple design such as the PDP-8, it may seem that this (two bit) savings is trivial, but in a CISC ISA, the number of control signals can be quite large and it is important to minimize the number of bits in the microinstruction format. Every location in the microcode memory has to store the same set of bits, so any waste of bits is multiplied by the number of words.

Microinstruction format designs are often classified by the width of the word employed. One approach is to have a very wide word that contains all of the control signals necessary to drive the system. Such a design is referred to as a "horizontal" microinstruction format. Another approach is to use a narrower word, with a sequence of microinstructions being required to drive all of the control signals. This is called a "vertical" microinstruction format.

At first glance, it appears that a vertical microinstruction is inherently slower—it takes a sequence of operations to accomplish what the horizontal microinstruction can do in a single cycle. But consider that in many cases, individual control lines are asserted only in certain minor states. If all of these are grouped together by minor state, then they can reuse some of the bits of the microword by having their outputs first fed to a "demultiplexer" that steers them to the proper signal lines according to the current minor state.

Horizontal microcode has been employed in massively parallel array processors where every processor in the system shares a single controller. Often the controller is itself a full-fledged computer, and so the microinstruction both contains traditional machine code for the controller itself as well as the control signals that are distributed to the processors that make up the array. A typical horizontal microinstruction for this type of machine is 128 bits wide (16 bytes). Thus, every effort is made to reduce the number of words required. It is important to note, however, that this is an unusual application of microcode.

One other problem with horizontal microcode is that it is difficult to drive such a large number of signals simultaneously. The switching of so many drivers at once can cause the power supply voltage to sag momentarily (the same as when your lights dim as you turn on a big appliance). This in turn causes noise to appear on signal lines that can cause erroneous behaviour in other parts of the computer. Avoiding this requires careful circuit design and sometimes clever tricks, such as ensuring that the signals are asserted in a series of slightly offset time steps.

Microcode

Of course, the whole reason for using microcode is to manage the complexity of a CISC ISA's control unit. Most RISC designs, even those that have fairly complex implementations, are still sufficiently regular that their control units can be directly constructed from a FSM built with combinational logic. (The advantage of using combinational logic is that it is easier to build a fast decoder with it than with a microcode ROM.)

However, for a CISC ISA, the speed decrease resulting from the use of microcode is often outweighted by the need to manage the complexity of controlling the architecture (a slow processor is, after all, more useful than a faster one that doesn't work). In a CISC architecture there may be a large number of instruction types, each with different fields referring to a wide range of registers that have asymmetrical functions, or referring to one or more memory operands with as many as 20 different addressing modes. (The DEC VAX, Intel 80X86/ Pentium, and Intel iAPX 432 are prime examples).

A control unit for a CISC ISA can thus have to deal with instructions that involve tens and even hundreds of minor states. There would thus be thousands of logic expressions to generate the control signals. CAD tools can simplify and minimize these and even lay them out on the silicon automatically, but it is still a large block of irregular logic on the chip.

More importantly, if a mistake is discovered later (*i.e.*, one of the logic expressions is wrong), then it may be necessary to resimplify the entire design and lay it out again, which could mean a redesign of the rest of the chip to accommodate a change in the size of the control unit. This is obviously a very costly error. Unfortunately, it is also common. Even with the best design and simulation tools, several commercial chips have gone into production with errors that were discovered later. An early 68000 design had a bug that would cause the processor to hang in certain cases, Intel shipped half a million Pentium processors with an error in the floating-point division instruction before it was caught, and has had bugs in earlier processors.

Since errors do occur, manufacturers of CISC processors use microcode to reduce the cost of correcting the errors (and to help simplify the initial design, which in itself helps to reduce errors). A bug-fix in a microcoded controller is just a matter of changing the ROM, which does not affect the size of the controller at all. It is a very low-cost correction. In addition, a microcoded design is easier to enhance because unused op-codes can be turned into new machine instructions by simply extending the microcode. This simplicity of extension may be another factor that has lead to the increasingly complex ISAs produced by CISC manufacturers.

At one point, it was even thought that allowing the user to add to the microcode was a good idea. If a user has a particular operation that they want to accelerate, they can code it up as a new instruction in the microcode. Such machines were said to have "writeable control stores." The VAX 11/780, the first model in the VAX line, was one of the most widely sold of these machines. However, the feature was rarely used for two reasons: first, the compilers could not take advantage of the custom instructions so the user had to programme in assembly language; second, the microcode is tied to the machine implementation (it refers to the particular control signals in the design) so it is not even portable to another model of the same architecture.

Nanocode

In some cases, such as the Motorola 68000, there is also a nanocode engine. The 68000 uses 544 17-bit words in its microengine and 336 68-bit words in its nanocode engine. It thus has 32,096 bits of ROM. If everything had been done with 68-bit words, it would have required 36,992 bits.

The M68000 microcode is very unusual in that the microcode implicitly calls the nanocode. Each microcode instruction causes a corresponding nanocode engine instruction to be fetched automatically. The nanocode bits are actually the control signals that get distributed across the machine. The microcode instructions thus have only to determine what the next instruction will be. They have two formats, one for an unconditional jump (perhaps just to the next location) or a conditional jump (two bits of the jump address are reserved for the result of the conditional test). This would seem to imply that there are as many nanocode instructions as microcode instructions. Yet we can see that there are 208 fewer. This is accomplished by carefully assigning the addresses so that common nanocode operations can have multiple microcode locations corresponding to them. The address space allows for 1024 instructions, and they are arranged so that if a bit (or several) is ignored, the same nanocode address is produced.

Comparison of Some Microcode Engines

- *Motorola* 68000: 544 17-bit microwords, plus 336 68-bit nanowords

- *DEC LSI*-11: 2048 22-bit microwords
- *IBM* 3033 *mainframe*: 2048 108-bit microwords plus 2048 126-bit microwords
- *Texas instruments* 8800: 32K 128-bit microwords in user-programmable RAM

UMass/Hughes IUA-2: 64K 128-bit microwords in RAM

The STARTECH SD6 tuning kit consists of a computer-controlled auxiliary control unit. Thanks to an included model-specific wire harness and detailed installation instructions the plug-and-play module can be installed in less than 30 minutes by any authorized Chrysler/Jeep dealer.

At one time control units were ad-hoc logic, and they were difficult to design. Now they are designed as a microprogram that is stored in a control store. Words of the microprogram are selected by a sequencer and the bits from those words directly control the different parts of the computer, including the registers, arithmetic and logic unit, instruction register, bus, input/output and computer storage.

DISK CONTROLLER INCLUDING FORMAT

The present invention relates to a disk controller and, more particularly, to an optical disk controller for an optical disk having a spirally formed track. An optical disk is employed as one of the data storage units in an information processing system. An optical disk controller performs a data transfer operation between the disk and a host processor.

The optical disk controller includes in general a buffer memory for temporarily storing write data from the host processor and read data from the disk, a format control unit for converting the write data from the buffer memory into data to be recorded on the disk and the data reproduced from the disk into the read data, and a system controller for responding to commands from the host processor to control the data transfer flow. Further included in the disk controller are a servo controller for controlling the focus and tracking of an optical beam on the disk and a drive controller for ordering, under the control of the system controller, the servo controller to perform a seek operation in which the optical beam moves to a target track and a jump operation in which the optical beam jumps to the adjacent track.

When the system controller receives a data transfer command from the host processor, it requests the seek operation of the drive controller, so that the optical beam moves rapidly to the target track. At a time when a target sector on that track is searched, the format controller starts to operate in a data write mode to record the write data from the buffer memory on the disk and in a data read mode to supply the buffer memory with the read data responsive to the data recorded on the disk. In the data write mode, the write data is transferred from the host processor to the buffer memory, and in the data read mode, the read data is transferred from the buffer memory to the host processor. Thus, the data transfer is executed between the disk and the host processor.

However, sometimes in the data write mode no write data has been transferred to the buffer memory at a time the target sector is searched and that the write data transfer to the buffer memory is suspended. Also in the data read mode, the buffer memory is often filled with the read data which are not transferred to the host processor yet.

In such cases, the data read/write operation is of course suspended until the write data arrives in the buffer memory or until the buffer memory has a vacancy for accepting the read data.

On the other hand, the disk continues to rotate. Since the track on the disk is formed spirally, therefore, the accessible sector advances in sequence, so that the target sector is not searched again even when the write data is transferred to the buffer memory or the vacancy for the read data is formed in the buffer memory.

Therefore, the format controller informs the system controller of a fact that the data read/write operation is suspended due to the above reason. In response thereto, the system controller requests the jump operation of the drive controller to back the optical beam up by one track. To back the optical beam up is called hereinafter "jump back".

DESCRIPTION OF THE DRAWINGS

The above and other objects, advantages and features of the present invention will be more apparent from the following description taken in conjunction with the accompanying drawings, in which:

Referring now to Figure, an optical disk controller according to an embodiment of the present invention includes an interface circuit 8 which receives and supplies commands and data from and to a host processor 14 via a system bus 15. The commands such as a data write command and a data read command from the host processor 14 are supplied to a system controller 11 via a controller bus 13.

The system controller 11 responds to the commands thus supplied and calculates ID (Identification) information indicative of a physical address of a sector from which a data read/write operation starts and the number of sectors to be subjected to the data read/write and further generates seek information for moving rapidly an optical beam 31 to a target track on an optical disk 1.

The seek information is supplied via a bus 110 to a drive controller 6, whereas read/write command information is supplied via a bus 13 to a format control unit 7 and a memory control unit 10. The data to be written into the disk 1, *i.e.* write data from the host processor 14, are temporarily stored into a buffer memory 9 through the interface circuit 8 and an internal bus 12. The buffer memory 9 is of a FIFO (first-in first-out) type.

The data to be transferred to the host processor 14, *i.e.* read data derived from the disk 1, are also temporarily stored into the buffer memory 9 and then transferred to the host processor 14 through the interface circuit 8 and the system bus 15. The memory control unit 10 manages the buffer memory 9 through a control line 10 and thus detects the presence/absence of the write data into the memory 9 and the presence/absence of a vacancy for the read data in the memory 9. The detection output is outputted as ready information 102.

On the other hand, the disk 1 is rotated by a spindle motor 2 and the data read/write is carried out by an optical beam 31 from an optical head circuit 3. This circuit 3 produces focus and tracking information 32 for the beam 31, which information is in turn supplied to a servo controller 5. In response thereto, the controller 5 performs the rotation speed control of the motor 2 and the focus and tracking control of the beam 31 through control data 51 and 52. The servo controller 5 is further supplied with a seek control information and track jump information 61 from a drive controller 6. In response thereto, the servo controller 5 opens the servo control loop to move the beam 31 as the seek operation and the track jump operation.

The optical head circuit 3 communicates via a data line 71 with a format control unit 71 with respect to data to be recorded on the disk 1 and data reproduced from the disk 1. The format control unit 7 receives the write data from the buffer memory 9 in the data write mode and then supplies them to the head circuit 3 as data to be recorded. In the data read mode, on the other hand, it receives the data from the head circuit 3 and then supplies them to the buffer memory 9 as the read data. In accordance with the present invention, the format control unit 7 generates a jump back signal 72 by itself, and the jump back signal 72 is in turn supplied directly to the servo controller 5 without intervention of the system controller 11 and the drive controller 6.

Turning to Figure, the format control unit 7 includes a decoder 702 decoding or demodulating serial data 7021 which are supplied from the head circuit 3 as data recorded on the disk 1. The data derived from the decoder 702 is converted into parallel data by a serial-parallel/parallel-serial conversion circuit 703. The serial data are further supplied to a synchronizing pattern detector 704. This detector 704 detects predetermined patterns such as a sector mark indicative of the beginning of a sector, an address mark indicative of the beginning of ID information and a data mark indicative of the beginning of data and supplies this detection information to a sequence controller 710 via a bus 7041 to synchronize the controller 710. When ID information indicative of a current sector is obtained in the conversion circuit 702, it is transferred to a current ID register 705. The read-out data obtained in the circuit 703 in the data read mode is transferred to the buffer memory 9 via the bus 12. In the data write mode, on the other hand, the write data from the buffer memory 9 is transferred to the conversion circuit 703 and then converted into serial data which are in turn encoded or modulated by an encoder 701. Serial data 7011 to be recorded on the disk 1 are thus obtained and supplied to the head circuit 3.

ID information stored in the current ID register 703 is changed each time an accessible sector is changed. The ID information is compared by a comparator 706 with an output of a selector 707. This selector 707 selects and outputs the content of a target ID register 708 when a selection signal 7071 is at the low level. On the other hand, the high level of the signal 7071 causes the selector 707 to select and output the content of a suspended ID register 709. The target ID register 708 is loaded by the system controller 11 with ID information indicative of a sector from which data read/write operation starts. The suspended ID register 709 captures the content of the current ID register 705 in response to an ID fetch signal 7091.

The output 7061 of the comparator 706 is supplied to the sequence controller 710 which also receives a read ready signal 1021 and a write ready signal 1022 as data ready information 102 from the memory control unit 10. The sequence controller 710 responds to the synchronizing information 7041, the comparison output signal 7061, data ready information 102 and command information from the controller 11 and generates a set of sequence control signals 7101 for performing a sequence of operations. The sequence control signals 7101 contain the selection signal 7071 and ID fetch signal 7091. The controller 710 further generates the jump back signal 72 which is in turn supplied directly to the servo controller 5.

Referring to Figure, there is shown a tracking servo loop circuit and a jump back control circuit in the servo controller 5 and a part of the optical head circuit 3. A laser beam 31 from a laser diode 305 as an optical source is applied to the disk 1, through a beam splitter 303 and a lens 301. The laser beam reflected from the disk 1 is supplied to a read-out control circuit 304 by the beam spritter 303. The circuit 304 produces the serial data 7021 to be supplied to the format control unit 7. The circuit 304 further produces tracking information of the beam 31 and supplies it to a tracking error producing circuit 305 in which tracking error information is produced and then supplied through a phase compensation circuit 306, a selector 307 and a driver 308 to a tracking actuator 302 to carry out a tracking control. The circuit 306 compensates the phase delay of the actuator 302. The serial data 7011 to be recorded is supplied to a recording control circuit 316 to drive the laser diode 305.

The selector 307 receives the tracking error compensation signal from the circuit 306, a jump back drive signal 721 from a jump back circuit 720 and a seek drive signal 611 from the drive controller 6 and selects and outputs one of them in response to the levels of a jump back instruction signal 722 and a seek instruction signal 612. Specifically, when only the signal 722 takes the active level, the jump back drive signal 721 is selected and outputted. The seek drive signal 611 is selected when the signal 612 is at the active level. When both the signals 612 and 722 are at the inactive level, the tracking error compensation signal is selected.

The jump back circuit 720 includes two S-R type flip-flops 310 and 311, a NAND gate 312, an AND gate 313, a P-channel transistor 314, an N-channel transistor 315, a delay circuit 309 and a tracking cross detector 318 which are connected as shown. Accordingly, the jump back signal 72 from the sequence controller 710 of the format control unit 7 sets both flip-flops 310 and 311 to change the signal 722 to the active level and turn the transistor 314 ON. The tracking servo loop is thereby made open. The actuator 302 is driven by the V_{DD} level, so that the laser beam 31 starts to move back to a track that is just before the current track. When the laser beam 31 crosses an intermediate point between two tracks, the detector 318 produces the detection output to reset the flip-flop 311. The transistor 314 is thereby turned OFF, whereas the transistor 315 is turned ON to stop the lens 301. The output of the detector 318 is delayed by a predetermined time by the delay circuit 309, and the delayed output resets the flip-flop 310. As a result, the tracking servo loop is formed again. The one-track jump back operation is thus completed.

An operation will be described below with reference to FIGS. 1 to 3 and further to Figure illustrating the track configuration on the disk 1. When the host processor 14 issues data read/write command, the system controller 11 responds to command and produces and stores into the target ID register 708 ID information indicative of the physical address of a sector from which the data read/write operation starts, denoted by a read/write commencement sector 101 in Figure. The system controller 11 further requests the sequence controller 710 to initiate a sequence flow for data read or write and supplies the drive controller 6 with seek information for moving the laser beam 31 to the neighbourhood of the read/write commencement sector 101 by the seek operation.

In response thereto, the drive controller 6 produces the seek drive signal 611 with making the signal 612 active, so that the laser beam 31 moves to the neighbourhood of the sector 101. The signal 612 is thereafter changed to the inactive level to activate the tracking servo loop. The serial data 7021 from the read-out control circuit 304 are thereby supplied to the decoder 702 and the synchronizing pattern detector 704. As described above, ID information to be stored in the current ID register 705 is changed each time the accessible sector varies. Since the selection signal 7071 is at the low level in an initial state, the content of the target ID register 708, *i.e.* the ID information of the data read/write commencement sector 101, is compared by the comparator 706 with the content of the current ID register 705.

When the comparator 706 produces the active level signal 7061 to inform that the read/write commencement sector 101 is accessible, the sequence controller 710 checks the level of data ready information 1021 before requesting the memory control unit 10 to transfer data between the buffer memory 9 and the conversion circuit 703. The write ready signal 1022 of the data ready information 102 is in the active level when write data is stored in the buffer memory 9 in the data write mode, and the read ready signal 1021 thereof is in the active level when the buffer memory 9 has a vacancy for accepting the read-out data in the data read mode. The sequence controller 710 monitors the ready signal 1021 or 1022 in accordance with the operation mode to be executed. When the monitored ready signal 1021 or 1022 is in the inactive level at a time the comparison output signal 7061 becomes active, the data read/write cannot be performed. Therefore, the sequence controller 710 generates the jump back signal 72. Consequently, as already described with reference to Figure, the laser beam 31 jumps back to a track 105 that is just before a track 104 on which the read/write commencement sector 101 exists.

The sequence controller 710 further generates the ID fetch signal 7091, so that ID information of the read/write commencement sector 101 is stored in the suspended ID register 709 as a read/write-suspended sector information. The selection signal 7071 is thereafter changed to the high level to cause the selector 707 to select the register 709.

When the laser beam 31 shifts from the track 105 to the track 104 by the rotation of the disk 1 and the ID information of the sector 101 is then stored in the current ID register 705, the comparator 706 generates again the active level output signal 7061. Assuming that the write data is stored in the buffer memory 9 from the host processor 14 or the buffer memory 9 has a vacancy for accepting the read data before the active level signal 7061 is generated again, the monitored ready signal 1021 or 1022 is at the active level at a time the signal 7061 becomes active.

Accordingly, the sequence controller 710 requests the data transfer of the memory control unit 10. In the data write mode, the write data is thereby transferred from the buffer memory 9 to the conversion circuit 703. In the data read mode, on the other hand, the read data is transferred from the conversion circuit 703 to the buffer memory 9.

If the monitored ready signal 1021 or 1022 is still at the inactive level when the signal 7061 comes active again, the jump back operation is repeated.

After the data read/write operation starts from the sector 101, the sequence controller 710 checks the monitored ready signal 1021 or 1022 irrespective of the level of the comparison signal 7061 each time the content of the current ID register 705 changes.

As denoted by a suspended sector 102 in Figure, assume that the mentioned ready signal 1021 or 1022 is at the inactive level when the ID information indicative of the sector 102 is stored in the current ID register 705. The sequence controller 710 therefore generates the jump back signal 72 to back the track to be accessed by one. The ID information of the sector 102 is stored into the suspended ID register 709. After the jump back operation is completed, the content of the current ID register 705 changes in sequence. When the current ID register 705 stores the ID information indicative of the suspended sector 102, the comparison output signal 7061 becomes active. In response thereto, the sequence controller 710 requests again the jump back operation or requests the data transfer for the sector 102 in accordance with the monitored ready signal 1021 or 1022.

After the data read/write operation for the sector 102 is completed, the sequence controller 710 checks the ready signal 1021 or 1022 irrespective of the comparison output signal 7061 each time the content of the current ID register changes, as described hereinbefore.

Thus, the format control unit 7 detects whether or not the data read/write for the currently accessible sector is performed and then generates by itself, the jump back signal 72 when the data read/write is disabled. The jump back signal 72 controls directly the jump back circuit 720 to perform one-track jump back operation. Therefore, the access time is free from delay due to the response time of the system controller 11 and the drive controller 6. Moreover, the processing load of the system controller 6 is reduced.

The disk controller is required to execute a write-verify operation in which data from the host processor are recorded on the disk and thereafter the recorded data is read out and checked for errors. This operation is executed in general as follows. That is, the format control unit informs the system controller of the completion of data recording. In response thereto, the system controller requests the seek operation of the drive controller to back the optical beam by a predetermined number of tracks. Thereafter, the format control unit receives a verifying command from the system control.

In such an operation, as shown in Figure, if the data write commencement sector 101 is close to a data write end sector 103, while it is sufficient to back the beam 31 by two tracks, due to the delay of response time of the controllers 11 and 6, the beam 31 has already passed the write commencement sector 101 at the time the beam 31 is backed by two tracks. For this reason, the beam 31 requires to be backed by three tracks, resulting in that the initiation of the verifying operation is delayed.

A circuit construction for solving the above problem is shown in FIGS. 5 and 6 as another embodiment of the present invention, in which the same components as those shown in FIGS. 2 and 3 are denoted by the same reference numerals to omit further description thereof.

The format control unit according to the present embodiment further includes an S-R type flip-flop 750, an AND gate 751, a down counter 752 and a sector register 753, and a track register 754 is provided in the sequence controller 710. The sector register 753 is loaded with the number of sectors to be subjected to data recording from the system controller 11. The track register 754 is loaded with the number of tracks to be backed up from the system controller 11.

The jump back operation which may be performed in the data write mode responsive to the write-verify operation is omitted because it is the same as the former embodiment.

By the generation of the comparison output signal 7061 due to the write commencement sector 101 becoming accessible, the flip-flop 750 is set to open the AND gate 751 and the content of the sector register 753 is loaded to the down counter 752. The sequence controller generates a count signal 7511 every time the write data is recorded on the sector, so that the content of the down counter 752 is decremented one by one. When the count value reaches zero, *i.e.* when the data write operation to the write end sector 103 is completed, the sequence controller 710 outputs the content, of the track register 754 onto the data line 7541 and thereafter generates the jump back signal 72.

Turning to Figure, the jump back circuit 720 according to the present embodiment further includes a down counter 760, a zero detector 761, an AND gate 762 and an OR gate 763. The data on the line 7541 is loaded to the down counter 760. By the jump back signal 72 being thereafter generated, one-track jump back operation is executed and the content of the down counter 760 is decremented by one. The signal from the delay circuit 309 representative of the completion of one-track jump back operation passes through the AND gate 762 and then sets the flip-flops 310 and 311 as the jump back signal. The one-track jump back operation is thereby performed again. Since the content of the down counter 760 reaches zero, the detector 761 closes the AND gate 762. The output from the delay circuit 309 is thereby masked. Thus, the jump back operation for backing the beam 31 by two tracks is performed immediately. The comparator 706 thereafter generates the active level output signal 7061 for initiating the verifying operation.

It is apparent that the present invention is not limited to the above embodiments but may be modified and changed without departing from the scope and spirit of the invention. For example, in place of the selector 707, two comparators can be provided, one of which compares the current ID register with the target ID register and the other of which compares the current ID register with the suspended ID register, one of outputs of these comparator being selected. Moreover, a part of the buffer memory can be provided in the format control unit.

INSTRUCTION CYCLES

INTRODUCTION

In order to programme at an elementary level, it is not necessary to understand in detail the internal structure of the processor that one is using. However, in order to do efficient programming, such an understanding is required. The purpose of this chapter is to present the basic hardware concepts necessary for understanding the operation of the Z80 system. The complete microcomputer system includes not only the microprocessor unit (here the Z80), but also other components. This chapter presents the Z80 proper, while the other devices (mainly input/output) will be present in a separate chapter.

We will review here the basic architecture of the microcomputer system, then study more closely the internal organization of the Z80. We will examine, in particular, the various registers. We will then study the programme execution and sequencing mechanism. From a hardware standpoint, this chapter is only a simplified presentation. The reader interested in gaining detailed understanding is referred to our book ref. C201 ("Microprocessors," by the same author).

The Z80 was designed as a replacement for the Intel 8080, and to offer additional capabilities. A number of references will be made in this chapter to the 8080 design.

SYSTEM ARCHITECTURE

The architecture of the microcomputer system appears in Figure. The microprocessor unit (MPU), which will be a Z80 here, appears on the left of the illustration. It implements the functions of a *central-processing unit* (CPU) within one chip: it includes an *arithmetic-logical unit* (ALU), plus its internal registers, and a*control unit* (CU), in charge of sequencing the system.

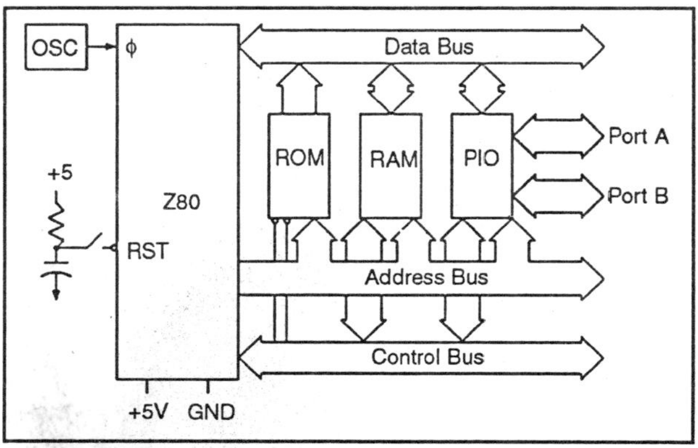

Fig. Standard Z80 System.

The MPU creates three *buses*: an 8-bit bidirectional *data bus*, which appears at the top of the illustration, a 16-bit unidirectional *address bus*, and a *control bus*, which appears at the bottom of the illustration. Let us describe the function of each of the buses.

The *data bus* carries the data being exchanged by the various elements of the system. Typically, it will carry data from the memory to the MPU or from the MPU to the memory or from the MPU to an input/output chip. (An input/output chip is a component in charge of communicating with an external device.) The *address bus* carries an address generated by the MPU, which will select one internal register within one of the chips attached to the system. This address specifies the source, or the destination, of the data which will transit along the data bus.

The *control bus* carries the various synchronization signals required by the system. Having described the purpose of the buses, let us now connect the additional components required for a complete system. Every MPU requires a precise timing reference, whichis supplied by a *clock* and a *crystal*. In most "older" microprocessors, the clock-oscilator is external to the MPU and requires an extra chip. In most recent microprocessors, the clock-oscilator is usually incorporated within the MPU. The quartz crystal, however, because of its bulk, is always external to the system. The crystal and the clock appear on the left of the MPU box in Figure.

Let us now turn our attention to the other elements of the system. Going from the left to right on the illustration, we distinguish: The ROM is the *read-only memory* and contains the *programme* for the system. The advantage of the ROM memory is that its contents are permanent and do not disappear whenever the system is turned off. The ROM, therefore, always contains a *bootstrap* or a *monitor* programme (their function will be explained later) to permit initial system operation. In a process-control environment, nearly all the programmes will reside in ROM, as they will probably never be changed. In such a case, the industrial user has to protect the system against power failure; programmes must not be volatile. They must be in ROM. However, in a hobbyist environment, or in a programme-development environment (when the programmer tests his programme), most of the programmes will reside in RAM, so that they can be easily changed. Later, they may remain in RAM, or be transferred into ROM, if desired. RAM, however, is volatile. Its contents are lost when power is turned off.

The RAM (*random-access memory*) is the read/write memory for the system. In the case of a control system, the amount of RAM will typically be small (for data only). On the other hand, in a programme development environment, the amount of RAM will be large, as if will contain programmes plus development software. All RAM contents must be loaded prior to use from an external device.

Finally the system will contain one or more interface chips so that it may communicate with the external world. The most frequently used interface chip is the PIO or*parallel input/output* chip. It is the one shown on the illustration. This PIO, like all other chips in the system, connects to all three buses and provides at least two 8-bit ports for communication with the outside world. For more details on how and acutal PIO works, refer to book C201 or, for specifics of the Z80 system.

All the chips are connected to all three buses, including the control bus. The functional modules which have been described need not necessarily reside on a single LSI chip. In fact, we could use *combination chips,* which may include both PIO and a limited amount of ROM or RAM. Still more components will be required to build a real system. In particular, the buses need to be *buffered*. Also *decoding logic* may be used for the memory RAM chips, and, finally, some signals may need to be amplified by *drivers*. These auxiliary circuits will not be described here as they are not relevant to programming. The reader interested in specific assembly and interfacing techniques is referred to book C207 "Microprocessor Interfacing Techniques."

INSIDE A MICROPROCESSOR

The large majority of all microprocessor chips on the

market today implement the same architecture. This "standard" architecture will be described here. It is shown in Figure below. The modules of this standard microprocessor will now be detailed, from right to left.

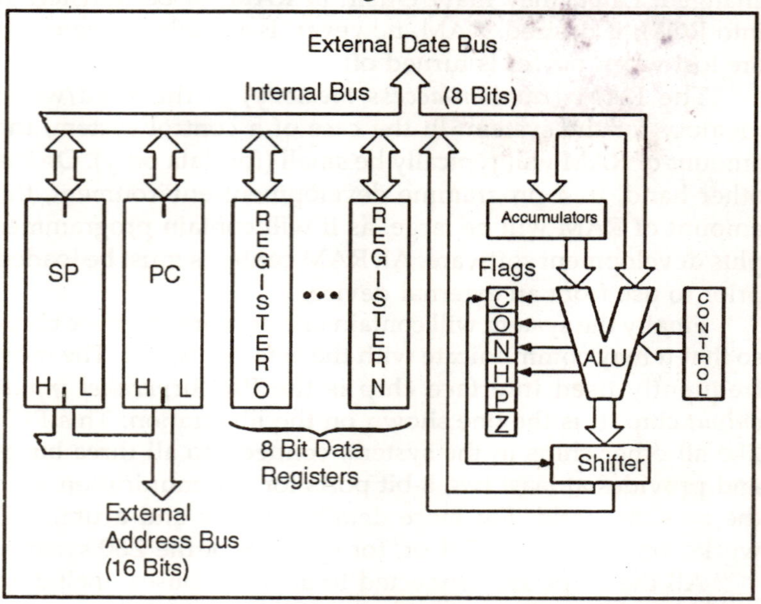

Fig. "Standard" Microprocessor Architecture.

The *control box* on the right represents the control unit which synchronizes the entire system. Its role will be clarified within the remainder of this chapter. The *ALU* performs arithmetic and logic operations. A special register equips one of the inputs of the ALU, the left input here. It is called the accumulator. (Several accumulators may be provided.) The accumulator may be referenced as input and output (source and destination) within the same instruction.

The ALU must also provide *shift* and *rotate* facilities. A shift operation consists of moving the contents of a byte by one or more positions to the left or to the right. This is illustrated in Figure. Each bit has been moved to the left by one position. The details of shifts and rotations will be presented in the next chapter.

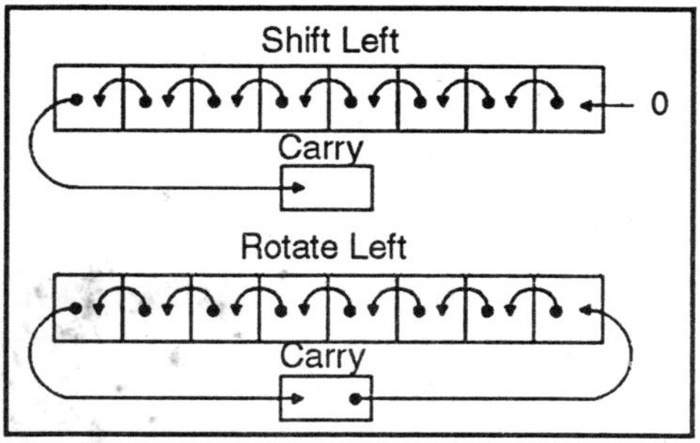

Fig. Shift and Rotate.

The shifter may be on the ALU output, as illustrated in Figure or may be on the accumulator input. To the left of the ALU, the *flags* or *status register* appear. Their role is to store exceptional conditions within the microprocessor. The contents of the flags registers may be tested by specialized instructions, or may be read on the internal data bus. A *conditional* instruction will cause the execution of a new programme, depending on the value of one of these bits. The role of the status bits in the Z80 will be examined later in this chapter.

Setting Flags

Most of the instructions executed by the processor will modify some or all of the flags. It is important to always refer to the chart provided by the manufacturer listing which bits will be modified by the instructions. This is essential in understanding the way a programme is being executed. Such a chart for the Z80 is shown in Figure.

The Registers

Let us look now at above Figure. On the left of the illustration, the registers of the microprocessor appear. Conceptually, one can distinguish the *general-purpose registers* and the *address registers.*

The General-Purpose Registers

General-purpose registers must be provided in order for the ALU to manipulate data at high speed. Because of restrictions on the number of bits which is reasonable to provide within an instruction, the number of (directly addressable) registers is usually limited to fewer than eight. Each of these registers is a set of eight flip-flops, connected to the bidirectional internal data bus. These eight bits can be transferred simultaneously to or from the data bus. The implementation of these registers in MOS flip-flops provide the fastest level of memory available, and their contents can be accessed within tens of nanoseconds.

Internal registers are usually labeled from 0 to n. The role of these registers is not defined in advance: they are said to be "general-purpose." They may contain any data used by the programme. These general-purpose registers will normally be used to store eight-bit data. On some microprocessors, facilities exist to manipulate two of these registers at a time. They are then called "register pairs." This arrangement facilitates the storage of 16-bit quantities, whether data or addresses.

The Address Registers

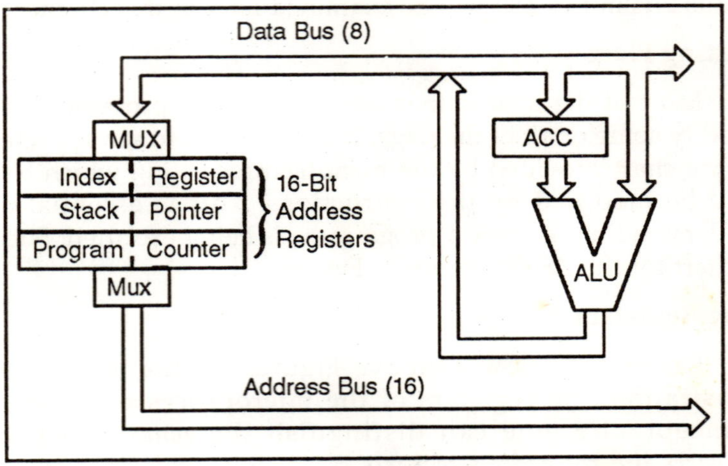

Fig. The 16-bit Address Registers Create the Address Bus.

Address registers are 16-bit registers intended for the storage of addresses. They are also often called *data counters* or *pointers*. They are double registers, *i.e.*, two eight-bit registers. Their essential characteristic is to be connected to the address bus. The address registers create the address bus. The address bus appears on the left and the bottom part of the illustration in Figure below. The only way to load the contents of these 16-bit registers is via the data bus. Two transfers will be necessary along the data bus in order to transfer 16 bits. In order to differentiate between the lower half and the higher half of each register, they are usually labelled as L (low) or H (high), denoting bits 0 through 7, and 8 through 15, respectively. This label is used whenever it is necessary to differentiate the halves of these registers. At least two address registers are present within most microprocessors. "MUX" in Figure stands for multiplexer.

PROGRAMME COUNTER (PC)

The *programme counter* must be present in any processor. It contains the address of the next instruction to be executed. The presence of the programme counter is indispensable and fundamental to programme execution. The mechanism of programme execution and the automatic sequencing implemented with the programme counter will be described in the next section. Briefly, execution of a programme is normally sequential. In order to access the next instruction, it is necessary to bring it from the memory into the microprocessor. The contents of the PC will be deposited on the address bus, and transmitted towards the memory.

In a few exceptional microprocessors, such as the two-chip F8, there is no PC on the microprocessor. This does not mean that the system does not have a programme counter. The PC happens to be implemented directly on the memory chip, for reasons of efficiency.

Stack Pointer (SP)

The *stack* has not been introduced yet and will be described in the next section. In most powerful, general-purpose microprocessors, the stack is implemented in "software", *i.e.,* within the memory. In order to keep track of the top of this stack within the memory, a 16-bit register is dedicated to the *stack pointer* or *SP*. The SP contains the address of the top of the stack within the memory. It will be shown that the stack is indispensable for interrupts and for subroutines.

Index Register

Indexing is a memory-addressing facility which is not always provided in microprocessors. The various memory-addressing techniques will be described in Chapter 5. Indexing is a facility for accessing blocks of data in the memory with a single instruction. An *index register* will typically contain a displacement which will be automatically added to a base (or it might contain a base which would be added to a displacement).

The Stack

A *stack* is formally called an LIFO structure (last-in, first-out). A stack is a set of registers, or memory locations, allocated to this data structure. This first element introduced into the stack is always at the bottom of the stack. The element most recently deposited in the stack is on top of the stack. The analogy can be drawn with a stack of plates on a restaurant counter. There is a hole in the counter with a spring in the bottom. Plates are piled up in the hole. With this organization, it is guaranteed that the plate which has been put first in the stack (the oldest) is always at the bottom. The one that has been placed most recently on the stack is the one which is on top of it. This example also illustrates another characteristic of the stack. In normal use, a stack is only accessible via two instructions: "push" and "pop" (or "pull"). The *push* operation results in depositing one element on top of the stack (two in case of the Z80). The *pull* operation consists of removing one element from the stack. In the case of a microprocessor, it is the *accumulator* that will be deposited on top of the stack.

The availability of a stack is required to implement three programming facilities within the computer system: subroutines, interrupts, and temporary data storage. The role of the stack during interrupts will be explained in Chapter 6 (Input/Output Techniques). Finally, the role of the stack in saving data at high speed will be explained during specific application programmes.

A stack may be implemented in two ways:

- A fixed number of registers may be provided within the microprocessor itself. This is a "hardware stack." It has the advantage of high speed. However, it has the disadvantage of a limited number of registers.
- Most general-purpose microprocessors choose another approach, the software stack, in order not to restrict the stack to a very small number of registers. This is the approach chosen in the Z80. In the software approach, a dedicated register within the microprocessor, here register SP, stores the stack pointer, *i.e.*, the address of the top element of the stack (or, sometimes, the address of the top element of the stack plus one).

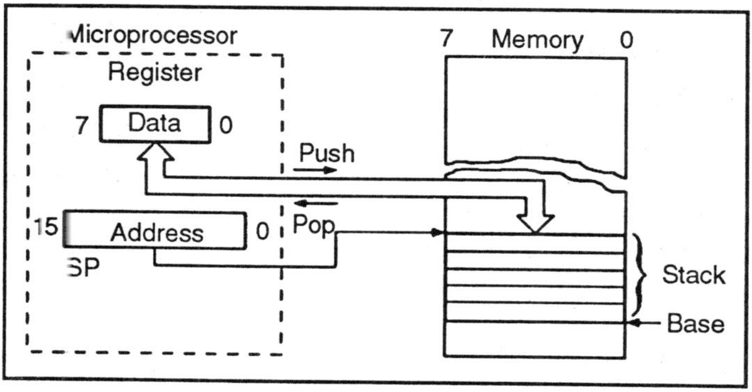

Fig. The Two Stack-Manipulation Instructions.

INSTRUCTION EXECUTION CYCLE

Let us now refer to Figure below: The microprocessor unit appears on the left, and the memory appears on the right. The memory chip may be a ROM or a RAM, or any other chip which happens to contain memory. The memory is used to store instructions and data. Here, we will fetch one instruction from the memory to illustrate the role of the programme counter. We assume that the programme counter has valid contents. It now holds a 16-bit address which is the address of the next instruction to fetch in the memory. Every processor proceeds in three cycles:

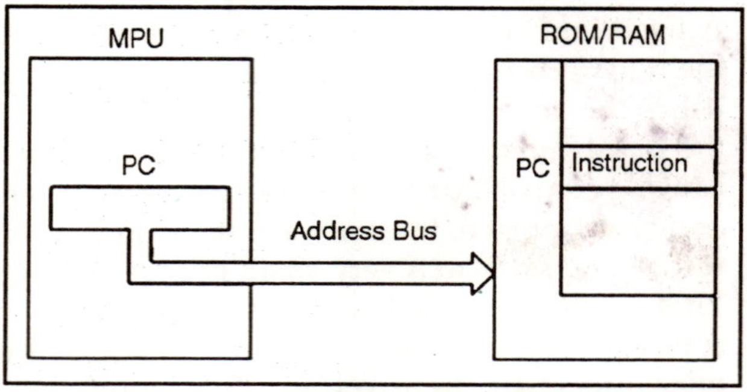

Fig. Fetching an Instruction from the Memory.

Fetch

Let us now follow the sequence. In the first cycle, the contents of the programme counter are deposited on the address bus and gated to the memory (on the address bus). Simultaneously, a read signal may be issued on the control bus of the system, if required. The memory will receive the address. This address is used to specify one location within the memory. Upon receiving the read signal, the memory will decode the address it has received, through internal decoders, and will select the location specified by the address. Let us briefly summarize the sequencing: the contents of the programme counter are output on the address bus. A read signal is generated. *The memory cycles,* and perhaps 300 nanoseconds later, the instruction at the specified address is deposited on the data bus (assuming a single byte instruction). The microprocessor then reads the data bus and deposits its contents into a specialized internal register, the IR register. The IR is the *instruction register*: it is eight-bits wide and is used to contain the instruction just fetched from the memory. The fetch cycle is now completed. The 8 bits of the instruction are now physically in the special internal register of the MPU, the IR register. The IR appears on the left of Figure below. It is not accessible to the programmer.

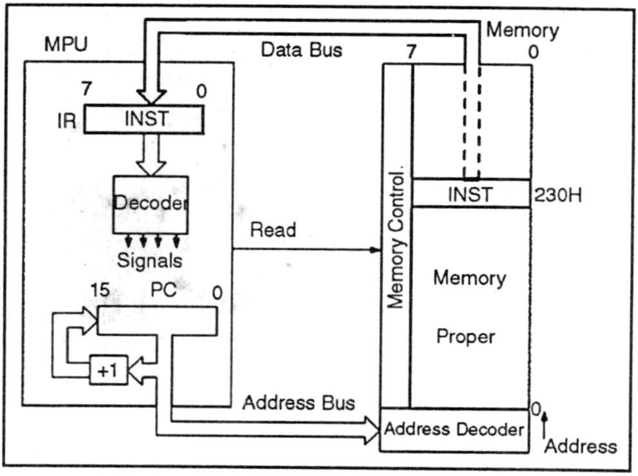

Fig. Automatic Sequencing.

DECODING AND EXECUTION

Once the instruction is contained in IR, the control unit of the microprocessor will decode the contents and will be able to generate the correct sequence of internal and external signals for the execution of the specified instruction. There is, therefore, a short decoding delay followed by an execution phase, the length of which depends on the nature of the instruction specified. Some instructions will execute entirely within the MPU. Other instructions will fetch or deposit data from or into the memory. This is why the various instructions of the MPU require various length of time to execute. This duration is expressed as a number of (clock) cycles.

FETCHING NEXT INSTRUCTION

An automatic mechanism must therefore be provided by a simple incrementer attached to the programme counter. This is illustrated inFigure. Every time that the contents of the programme counter (at the bottom of the illustration) are placed on the address bus, its contents will be incremented and written back into the programme counter. As an example, if the programme counter contained the value "0", the value

"0" would be output on the address bus. Then the contents of the programme counter would be incremented and the value "1" would be written back into the programme counter. In this way, the next time that the programme counter is used, it is the instruction at address 1 that will be fetched.

It must be stressed that the above descriptions are simplified. In reality, some instructions may be two-or even three-bytes long, so that successive bytes will be fetched in this manner from memory. However, the mechanism is identical. The programme counter is used to fetch successive bytes of an instruction as well as to fetch successive instructions themselves. The programme counter, together with its incrementer, provides an automatic mechanism for pointing to successive memory locations.

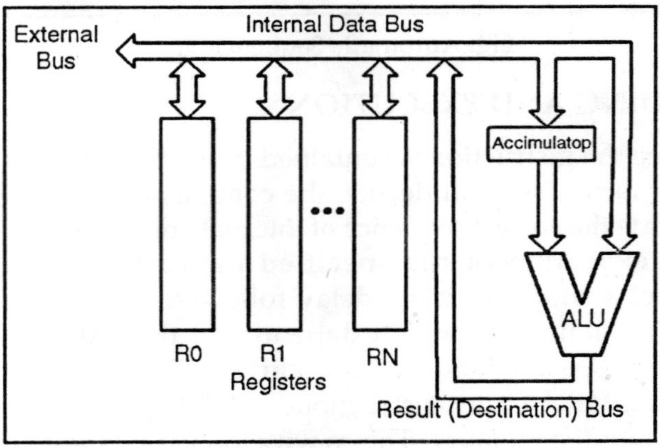

Fig. Single-Bus Architecture.

We will now execute an instruction within the MPU. A typical instruction will be, for example: R0 = R0 + R1. This means: "ADD the contents of R0 and R1, and store the results in R0." To perform this operation, the contents of R0 will be read from register R0, carried via the single bus to the left input of the ALU, and stored in the buffer register there. R1 then will be selected and its contents will be read onto the bus, then transferred to the right input of the ALU. This sequence is illustrated in Figures. At this point, the right input of the ALU is conditioned by R1, and the left input of the ALU is conditioned by the buffer register, containing the previous value of R0. The operation can be performed. The addition is performed by the ALU, and the result appears on the ALU output, in the lower right-hand corner of Figure. The result will be deposited on the single bus, and will be propagated back to R0. This means, in practice, that the input latch of R0 will be enabled, so that data can be written into it. Execution of the instruction is now complete. The results of the addition are in R0. It should be noted that the contents of R1 have not been modified by this operation.

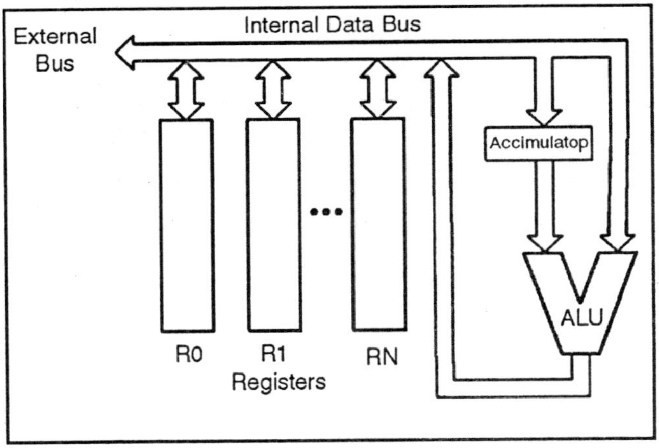

Fig. Execution of an Addition-R0 into ACC

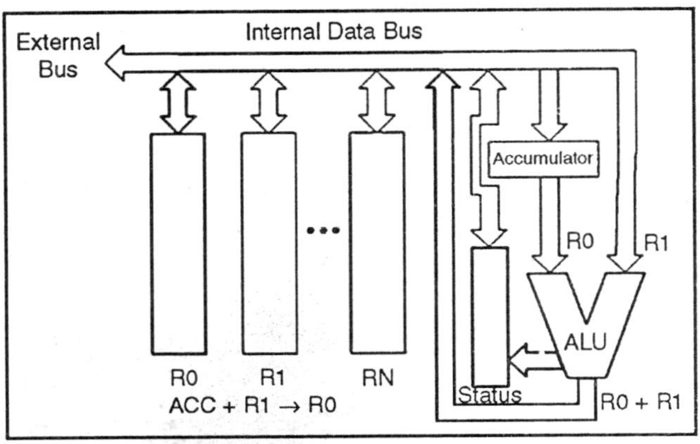

Fig. Result is Generated and Goes into R0

The buffer register on the left input of the ALU was necessary in order to *memorize* the contents of R0, so that the single bus could be used again for another transfer. However, a problem remains.

INTERNAL ORGANIZATION OF Z80

The terms necessary in order to understand the internal elements of the microprocessor have been defined. We will now examine in more detail the Z80 itself, and describe its capabilities. The internal organization of the Z80 is shown in figure below. This diagram presents a logical description of the device. Additional interconnections may exist but are not shown. Let us examine the diagram from right to left.

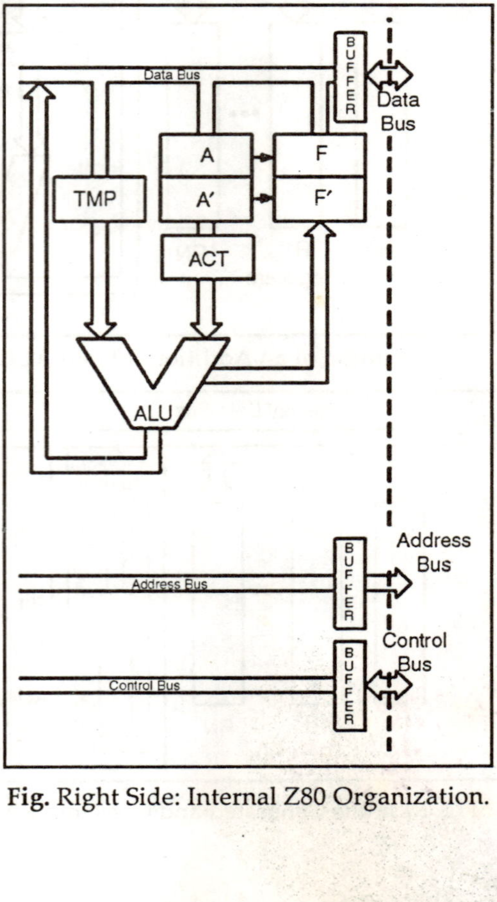

Fig. Right Side: Internal Z80 Organization.

The accumulator register, which has been described in the previous section, is identified as A on the right input path of the ALU. This is the register labeled ACT (temporary accumulator). Here, the left input of the ALU is also equipped with a *temporary register*, called TMP. The *flags register* is called "F" in the Z80, and is shown on the right of the accumulator register. The contents of the flags register are essentially conditioned by the ALU, but it will be shown that some of its bits may also be conditioned by other modules or events.

The accumulator and the flags registers are shown as double registers labeled respectively A, A′ and F, F′. This is because the Z80 is equipped internally with two sets of registers A + F, and A′ + F′. However, only *one* set of these registers may be used at any one time. A special instruction is provided to exchange the contents of A and F with A′ and F′. In order to simplify the explanations, only A and F will be shown on most of the diagrams which follow. The reader should remember that he has the option of switching to the alternate register set A′ and F′ if desired.

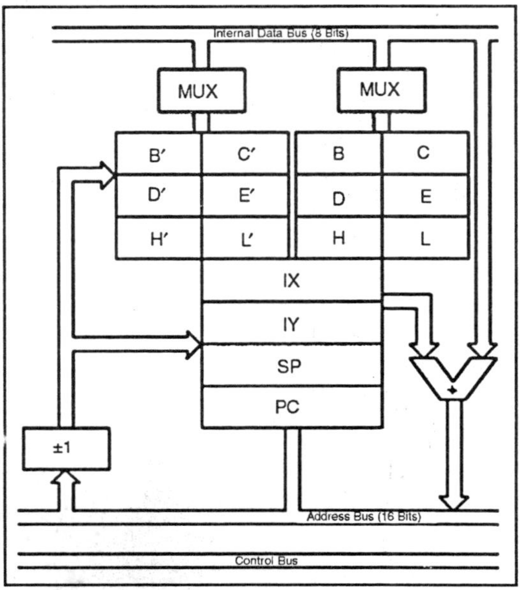

Fig. Centre: Internal Z80 Organization (Register Block)

A large block of registers is shown at the centre of the illustration. On top of the block of registers, two identical groups can be recognized. Each one includes six registers labeled B, C, D, E, H, L. These are the *general-purpose eight-bit registers* of the Z80. There are two peculiarities of the Z80 with respect to standard microprocessors which has been described.

First, the Z80 is equipped with *two* banks of register, *i.e.*, two identical groups of 6 registers. Only six may be used at any one time.

However, special instructions are provided to switch between the two banks of registers. One bank, therefore, behaves as an internal memory, while the other one behaves as a working set of internal registers. The possible uses of the special facility will be described in the next chapter.

Conceptually, it will be assumed, for the time being, that there are only six working registers, B, C, D, E, H, and L, and the second register bank will temporarily be ignored, in order to avoid confusion.

The MUX symbol which appears above the memory bank is an abbreviation for *multiplexer*. The data coming from the internal data bus will be gated through the multiplexer to the selected register. However, only one of these registers can be connected to the internal data bus at any one time.

A second characteristic of these six registers, in addition to being general-purpose eight-bit registers, is that they are equipped with a connection to the *address bus*. This is why they have been grouped in *pairs*. For example, the contents of B and C can be gated simultaneously onto the 16-bits address bus which appears at the bottom of the illustration. As a result, this group of 6 registers may be used to store either eight-bit data or else 16-bit *pointers* for memory addressing.

The third group of registers, which appears below the two previous ones in the middle of figure above, contains four "pure" address registers. As in any microprocessor, we find the programme counter (PC) and the stack pointer (SP). Recall that the programme counter contains the address of the next instruction to be executed. The stack pointer points to the top of the stack in the memory. In the case of the Z80, the stack pointer points to the *last actual entry* in the stack. (In other microprocessors, the stack pointer points just above the last entry.) Also, the stack grows *"downwards" i.e.* towards the lower addresses.

This means that the stack pointer must be *decremented* any time a new word is *pushed* on the stack. Conversely, whenever a word is *removed* (popped) from the stack, the stack pointer must be *incremented* by one. In the case of the Z80, the "push" and "pop" always involve two words at the same time, so that the contents of the stack pointer will be decremented or incremented by two.

Looking at the remaining two registers of this group of four registers, we find a new type of register which has not been described yet: two *index registers,* labeled IX (Index Register X) and IY (Index Register Y). These two registers are equipped with a special adder shown as a miniature V-shaped ALU on the right of these registers in Figure. A byte brought along the internal data bus may be added to the contents of IX or IY.

This byte is called the *displacement,* when using an indexed instruction. Special instructions are provided which will automatically add this displacement to the contents of IX or IY and generate an address. This is called *indexing.* It allows convenient access to any sequential block of data. This important facility will be described in Chapter 5 on addressing techniques. Finally, a special box labeled "+/-1" appears below and to the left of the block of registers. This is an increment/ decrement.

The contents of any of the register pairs SP, PC, BC, DE, HL (the "pure address" registers) may be automatically incremented or decremented every time they deposit an address on the internal address bus. This is an essential facility for implementing automated *programme loops* which will be described in the next section. Using this feature it will be possible to access successive memory locations conveniently.

Let us move to the left side of the illustration. One register pair is shown, isolated on the left: I and R. The I register is called the *interrupt page address register*. Its rol will be described in the section on interrupts of Chapter 6 (Input/Output Techniques). It is used only in a special mode where an indirect call to a memory location is generated in response to an interrupt. The I register is used to store the high-order part of the indirect address. The lower part of the address is supplied by the device which generated the interrupt.

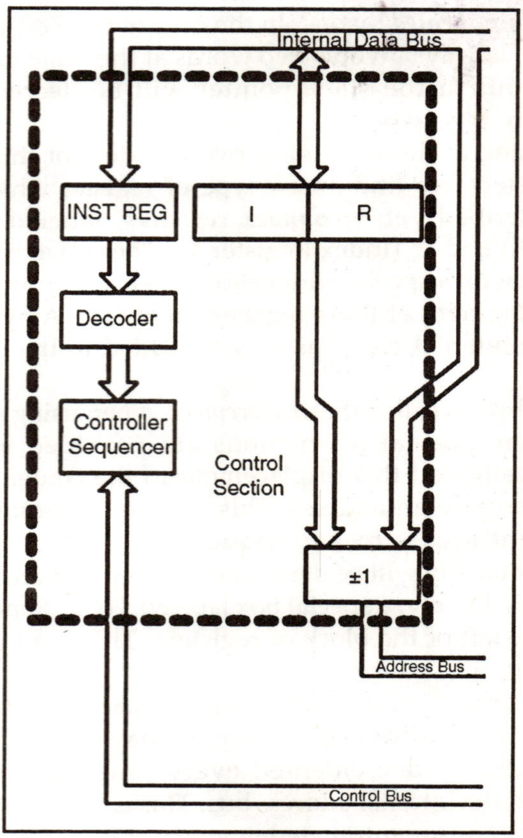

Fig. Left Side: Internal Z80 Organization (Control Section)

The R register is the *memory-refresh register*. It is provided to refresh dynamic memories automatically. Such a register has traditionally been located outside the microprocessor, since it is associated with the dynamic memory. It is a convenient feature which minimizes the amount of external hardware for some types of dynamic memories. It will not be used here for programming purposes, as it is essentially a hardware feature . However, it is possible to use it as a software clock, for example.

Let us move now to the far left of the illustration. There the control section of the microprocessor is located. From top to bottom, we find first the *instruction register* IR, which will contain the instruction to be executed. The IR register is totally distinct from the "I, R" register pair described above. The instruction is received from the memory via the data bus, is transmitted along the internal data bus and is finally deposited into the instruction register. Below the instruction register appears the *decoder* which will send signals to the controller-sequencer and cause the execution of the instruction within the microprocessor and outside it.

All the logical elements in the Z80 have now been described. It is not essential to understand the detailed operation of the Z80 in order to start writing programmes. However, for the programmer who wishes to write efficient codes, the speed of a programme and its size will depend upon the correct choice of registers as well as the correct choice of techniques. To make a correct choice, it is necessary to understand how instructions are executed within the microprocessor. We will therefore examine here the execution of typical instructions inside the Z80 to demonstrate the role and use of the internal registers and buses.

INSTRUCTION FORMATS

The Z80 instructions are listed in Chapter 4. Z80 instructions may be formated in one, two, three or four bytes. An instruction specifies the operation to be performed by the microprocessor. From a simplified standpoint, every instruction may be represented as an opcode followed by an optional literal or address field, comprising one or two words. The opcode field specifies the operation to be carried out. In strict computer terminology, the opcode represents only those bits which specify the operation to be performed, exclusive of the register pointers which it might incorporate. In the microprocessor world, it is convenient to call opcode the operation code itself, as well as any register pointers which it might incorporate. This "generalized opcode" must reside in an eight-bit word for efficiency (this is the limiting factor on the number of instructions available in a microprocessor).

The 8080 uses instructions which may be one, two, or three bytes long. However, the Z80 is equipped with additional indexed instructions, which require one more byte.

In the case of the Z80, opcodes are, in general, one byte long, except for special instructions which require a two-byte opcode.

Some instructions require that one byte of data follow the opcode. In such a case, the instruction will be a two-byte instruction, the second byte of which is data (except for indexing, which adds an extra byte).

In other cases, the instruction might require the specification of an address. An address requires 16 bits and, therefore, two bytes. In that case, the instruction will be a three-byte or a four-byte instruction. For each byte of the instruction, the control unit will have to perform a memory fetch, which will require four clock cycles. The shorter the instruction, the faster the execution.

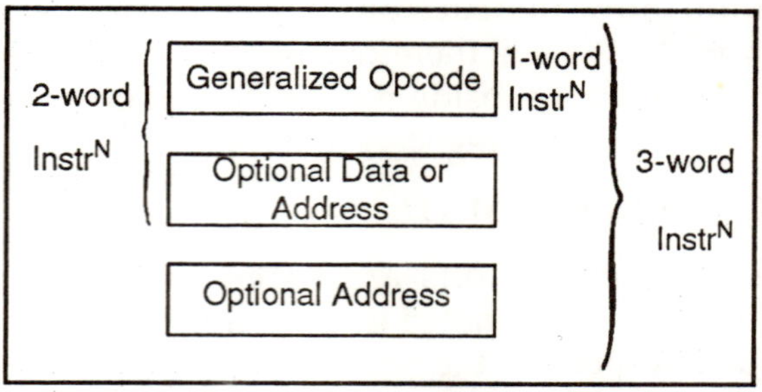

Fig. Typical Instruction Formats.

One-Word Instruction

One-word instructions are, in principle, fastest and are favoured by the programmer. A typical such instruction for the Z80 is: LD r,r′

- *This instruction means*: "Transfer the contents of register r′ into r." This is a typical "register-to-register" operation. Every microprocessor must be equipped with such instructions, which allow the programmer to transfer information from any of the machine's registers intc another one. Instructions referencing special registers of the machine, such as the accumulator or other special-purpose registers, may have a special opcode.

After execution of the above instruction, the contents of r will be equal to the contents of r′. The contents of r′ will *not* have been modified by the read operation.

Every instruction must be represented internally in a binary format. The above representation "LD r,r′ " is symbolic or *mnemonic*. It is called the *assembly-language*representation of an instruction. It is simply meant as a convenient symbolic representation of the actual binary encoding for that instruction. The binary code which will represent this instruction inside the memory is: 0 1 D D D S S S (bits 0 to 7).

This representation is still partially symbolic. Each of the letters S and D stands for a binary bit. The three D's, "D D D", represent the three bits pointing to the*destination* register. Three bits allow selection of one out of eight possible registers. The codes for these registers appear in Figure. For example, the code for register B is "0 0 0", the code for register C is "0 0 1", and so on. Similarly, "S S S" represents the three bits pointing to the *source* register. The convention here is that register r′ is the source, and that register r is the destination. The placement of bits in the binary representation of an instruction is not meant for the convenience of the programmer, but for the convenience of the control section of the microprocessor, which must decode and execute the instruction. The *assembly-language* representation, however, is meant for the convenience of the programmer. It could be argued that LD r,r′ should really mean: "Transfer contents of r into r′." However, the convention has been chosen in order to maintain compatibility with the binary representation in this case. It is naturally arbitrary.

Two-Word Instruction

ADD A, n

This simple two-word instruction will add the contents of the second byte of the instruction to the accumulator. The contents of the second word of the instruction are said to be a "literal." They are data and are treated as eight bits without any particular significance. They could happen to be a character or numerical data. This is irrelevant to the operation.

The code for this instruction is:

1 1 0 0 0 1 1 0 followed by the 8-bit byte "n"

This is an *immediate* operation. "Immediate," in most programming languages, means that the next word, or words, within the instruction contains a piece of data which should not be *interpreted* (the way an opcode is). It means that the next one or two words are to be treated as a *literal*. The control unit is programmed to "know" how many words each instruction has. It will, therefore, always fetch and execute the right number of words for each instruction. However, the longer the possible number of words for the instruction, the more complex it is for the control unit to decode.

Three-Word Instruction

LD A, (nn)

The instruction requires three words. It means: "Load the accumulator from the memory address specified in the next two bytes of the instruction." Since addresses are 16-bits long, they require two words.

In binary, this instruction is represented by:

0 0 1 1 1 0 1 0:	8 bits for the opcode
Low address:	8 bits for the lower part of the address
High address:	8 bits for the upper part of the address

EXECUTION OF INSTRUCTIONS IN Z80

We have seen that all instructions are executed in three phases: fetch, decode, execute. We now need to introduce some definitions. Each of these phases will require several clock cycles.

The Z80 executes each phase in one or more logical cycles, called a "machine cycle." The shortest machine cycle lasts three clock cycles.

Accessing the memory requires three cycles for any operands, four clock cycles for the initial fetch. Since each instruction must be fetched first from memory, the fastest instruction will require four clock cycles. Each machine cycle is labeled M1, M2, etc., and will require three or more clock cycles, or "states," labeled T1, T2, etc.

FETCH Phase

The FETCH phase of an instruction is implemented during the first three states of machine cycle M1; they are called T1, T2, and T3. These three states are common to all instructions of the microprocessor, as all instructions must be fetched prior to execution.

The FETCH mechanism is the following:

T1: PC OUT

The first step is to present the address of the next instruction to the memory. This address is contained in the programme counter (PC). As the first step of any instruction fetch, the contents of PC are placed on the address bus. At this point, an address is presented to the memory, and the memory address decoders will decode this address in order to select the appropriate location within the memory.

Several hundred ns (a nanosecond is 10^{-9} second) will elapse before the contents of the selected memory location become available on the output pins of the memory, which are connected to the data bus.

It is standard computer design to use the memory read time to perform an operation within the microprocessor.

The operation is the incrementation of the programme counter:

T2: PC = PC + 1

While the memory is reading, the contents of the PC are incremented by 1. At the end of state T2, the contents of the memory are available and can be transferred within the microprocessor:

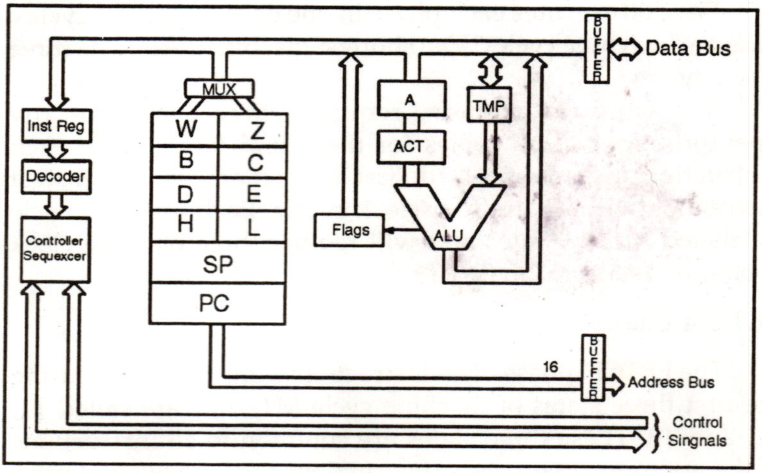

Fig. Instruction Fetch-(PC) Is Sent to the Memory.

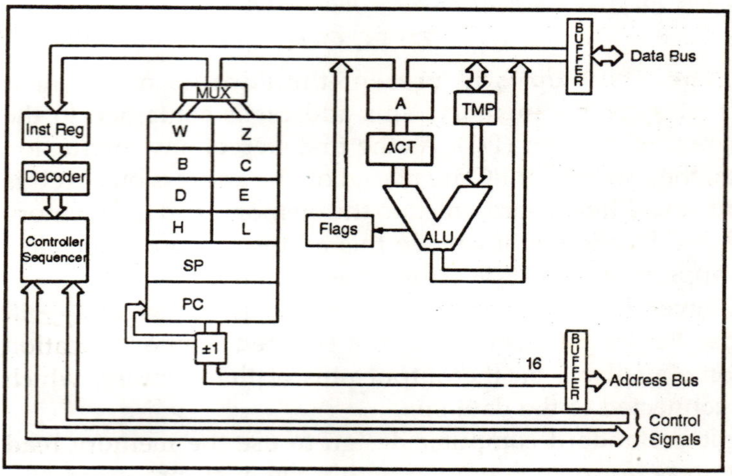

Fig. PC Is Incremented.

DECODE and EXECUTE Phases

During state T3, the instruction which has been read out of the memory is deposited on the data bus and transferred into the instruction register of the Z80, from which point it is decoded.

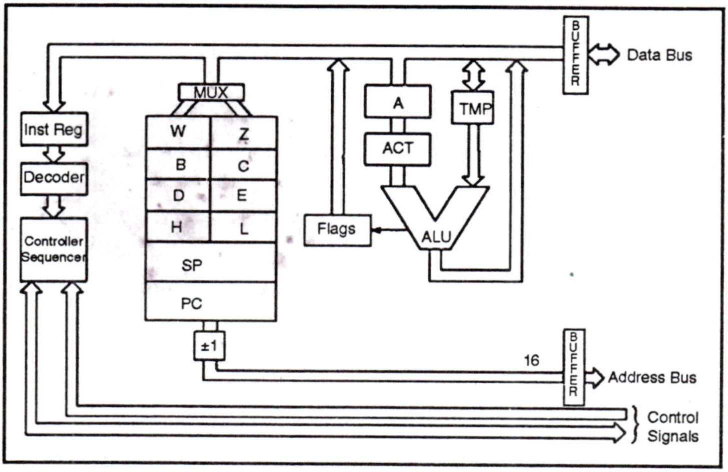

Fig. The Instruction Arrives from the Memory into IR.

It should be noted that states T4 of M1 will always be required. Once the instruction has been deposited into IR during T3, it is necessary to *decode* and *execute* it.

This will require at least one machine state, T4. A few instructions require an extra state of M1 (state T5). It will be skipped by the processor for most instructions. Whenever the execution of an instruction requires more than M1, *i.e.*, M1, M2 or more cycles, the transition will be directly from state T4 of M1 into T1 of M2.

Let us examine an example. The detailed internal sequencing for each example is shown in the tables of Figure. As these tables have not been released for the Z80, the 8080 tables are used instead. They provide an indepth understanding of the instruction execution.

LD D, C

This corresponds to MOV r1,r2 for the 8080. Refer to item 1 of Figure. By coincidence, the destination register in this example happens to be named "D". The transfer is illustrated in Figure below.

This instruction has been described in the previous section. It transfers the contents of register C, denoted by "C", into register D.

		01	
Mnemonic:		MOV r1,r2	
Op code:		$D_7D_6D_5D_4$	$D_3D_2D_1D_0$
		0 1 D D	D S S S
M1 [1]	T1	PC OUT STATUS	
	T2 [2]	PC = PC + 1	
	T3	INST → TMP/IR	
	T4	(SSS) → TMP	
	T5	TMP → (DDD)	

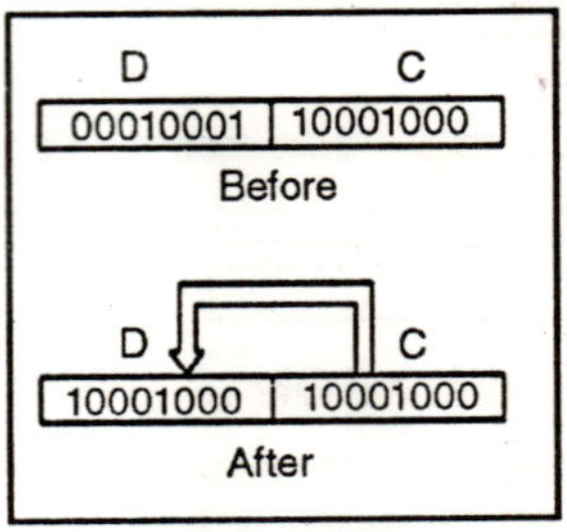

Fig. Transferring C into D

The first three states of cycle M1 are used to fetch the instruction from the memory. At the end of T3, the instruction is in IR, the Instruction Register, from which point it can be decoded.

During T4: (S S S) → TMP

The contents of C are deposited into TMP.

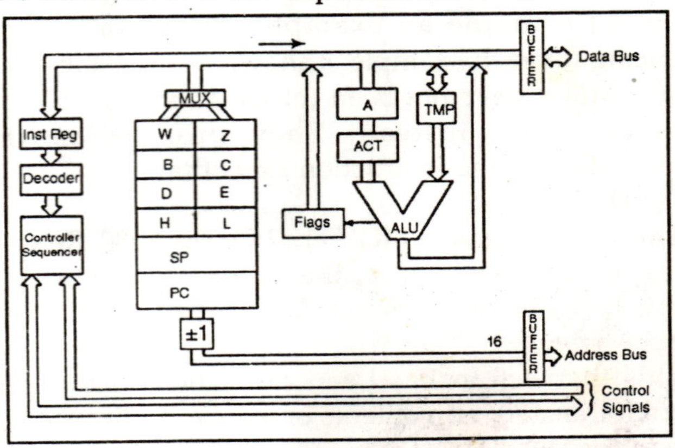

Fig. The Contents of C Are Deposited into TMP

During T5: (TMP) → DDD

The contents of TMP are deposited into D. This is shown in Figure below.

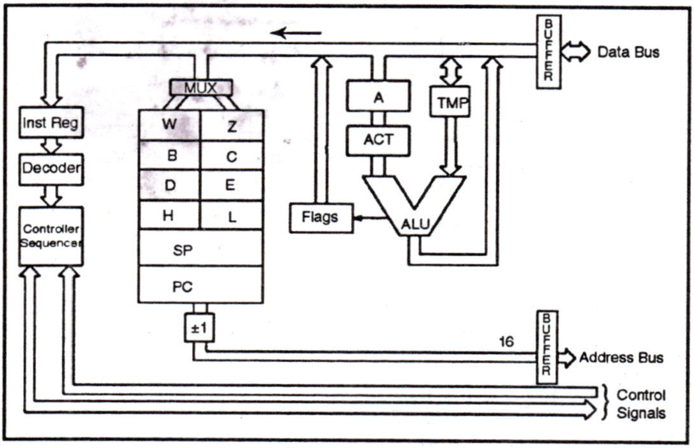

Fig. The Contents of TMP Are Deposited into D.

Execution of the instruction is now complete. The contents of register C have been transferred into the specified destination register D. This terminates execution of the instruction. The other machine cycles M2, M3, M4, and M5 will not be necessary and execution stops with M1.

It is possible to compute the duration of this instruction easily. The duration of every state for standard Z80 is the duration of the clock: 500 ns. The duration of this instruction is the duration of five states, or 5 × 500 = 2500 ns = 2.5 us. With a 400 ns clock, 5 × 400 = 2000 ns = 2.0 us.

The Z80 Chip

For completeness, the signals of the Z80 microprocessor chip will be examined here. It is not indispensable to understand the functions of the Z80 in order to be able to programme it. The reader who is not interested in the details of the hardware may therefore skip this section.

The pinout of the Z80 appears on Figure above. On the right side of the illustration, the address bus and the data bus perform their usual role, as described in the beginning of this chapter. We will describe here the function of the signals on the control bus. They are shown on the left of Figure below.

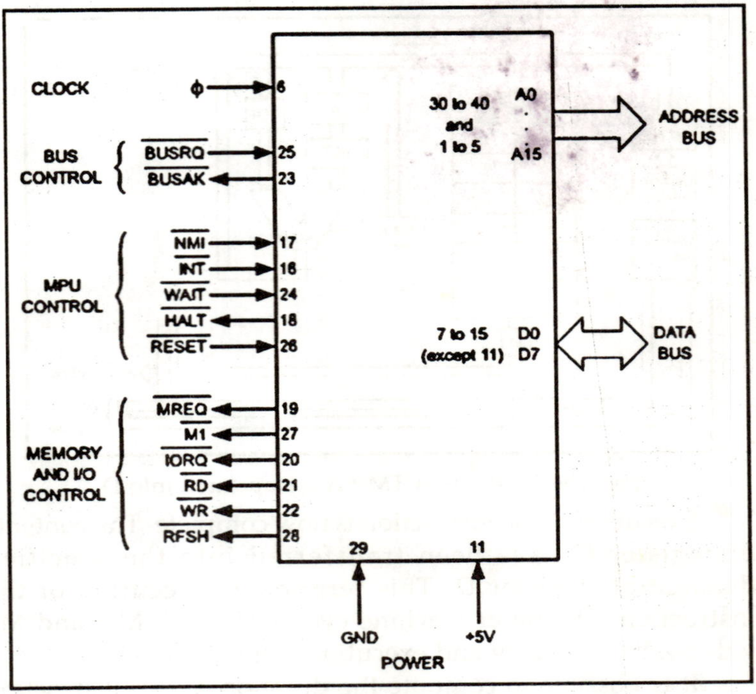

Fig. Z80 MPU Pinout.

The control signals have been partitioned in four groups. They will be described, going from the top of Figure above towards the bottom. The clock input is PHI. The Z80 requires an external 330-ohm pull-up resistor. It is connected to the PHI input and to 5 volts. However, at 4 Mhz, and external clock driver is required.

The two bus-control signals, BUSRQ and BUSAK, are used to disconnect the Z80 from its buses. They are mainly used by the DMA, but could also be used by another processor in the system.

BUSRQ is the bus-request signal. It is issued to the Z80. In response, the Z80 will place its address bus, data bus and tristate output control signals in the high-impendance state, at the end of the current machine cycle. BUSAK is the acknowledge signal issued by the Z80 once the buses have been placed in the high-impendance state.

INTERNAL STATUS AND SEQUENCING

Six Z80 control signals are related to its internal status or to its sequencing:

- INT and NMI are the two interrupt signals. INT is the usual interrupt request. Interrupts will be described in Chapter. A number of input/output devices may be connected to the INT interrupt line. Whenever an interrupt request is present on this line, and when the internal interrupt enable flip-flop (IFF) is enabled, the Z80 will accept the interrupt (provided the BUSRQ is not active). It will then generate an acknowledge signal: IORQ (issued during the M1 state).
- NMI is the non-maskable interrupt. It is always accepted by the Z80 and it forces the Z80 to jump to location 0066 hexadecimal.
- WAIT is a signal used to synchronize the Z80 with slow memory or input/output devices. When active, this signal indicates that the memory or the device is not yet ready for the data transfer. The Z80 CPU will then enter a special wait state until the WAIT signal becomes inactive. It will then resume normal sequencing.
- HALT is the acknowledge signal supplied by the Z80 after it has executed the HALT instruction. In this state, the Z80 waits for an external interrupt and keeps executing NOPs to continually refresh memory.
- RESET is the signal which usually initializes the MPU. It sets the programme counter, register I and R to "0". It disables the interrupt enable flip-flop and sets the interrupt mode to "0". It is normally used after power is applied to the board.

Memory and I/O Control

Six memory and I/O signals are generated by the Z80.

They are:

- *MREQ is the memory request signal*: It indicates that the address present on the address bus is valid. A read or write operation can then be performed on the memory.
- *M1 is machine cycle 1*: This cycle corresponds to the fetch cycle of an instruction.
- *IORQ is the input/output request*: It indicates that the I/O address present on bits 0-7 of the address bus is valid. An I/O read or write operation can then be carried out. IORQ is also generated together with M1 when the Z80 acknowledges an interrupt. This information may be used by external chips to place the interrupt response vector on the data bus. (Normal I/O operations never occur during the M1 state. The combination IORQ plus M1 indicates an interrupt acknowledge situation.)
- *RD is read signal*: It indicates the Z80 is ready to read the contents of the data bus into an internal register. It can be used by an external chip, whether memory or I/O, to deposit data on the data bus.
- *WR is write signal*: It indicates that the data bus holds valid data, ready to be written into the specified device.
- *RFSH is the refresh signal*: When RFSH is active, the lower seven bits of the address bus contain a refresh address for dynamic memories. The MREQ signal is then used to perform the refresh by reading the memory.

MICRO-OPERATIONS

The execution of a programme consists of the sequential execution of instructions. Each instruction is executed during an instruction cycle made up of shorter sub-cycles (*e.g.*, fetch, indirect, execute, interrupt).

The performance of each sub-cycle involves one or more shorter operations, that is, micro-operations. Micro-operations are the functional, or atomic, operations of a processor. In this section, we will examine micro-operations to gain an understanding of how the events of any instruction cycle can be described as a sequence of such micro-operations.

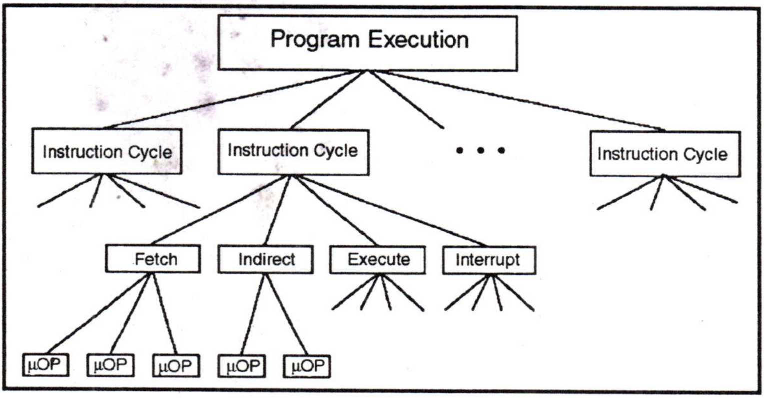

Fig. Constituent Elements of Programme Execution.

THE FETCH CYCLE

We begin by looking at the fetch cycle, which occurs at the beginning of each instruction cycle and causes an instruction to be fetched from memory.

Four reg isters are involved:

- *Memory address register (MAR)*: Is connected to the address lines of the sys tem bus. It specifies the address in memory for a read or write operation.
- *Memory buffer register (MBR)*: Is connected to the data lines of the system bus. It contains the value to be stored in memory or the last value read from memory.
- *Programme counter (PC)*: Holds the address of the next instruction to be fetched.
- *Instruction register (IR)*: Holds the last instruction fetched.

Let us look at the sequence of events for the fetch cycle from the point of view of its effect on the processor registers. An example appears in Figure below.

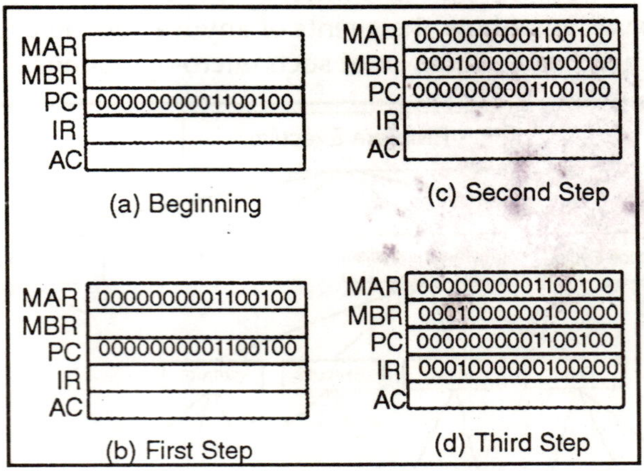

Fig. Sequence of Events, Fetch Cycle.

At the beginning of the fetch cycle, the address of the next instruction to be executed is in the programme counter (PC); in this case, the address is 1100100. The first step is to move that address to the memory address register (MAR) because this is the only register connected lo the address lines of the system bus. The second step is to bring in the instruction. The desired address (in the MAR) is placed on the address bus, the control unit issues a READ command on the control bus, and the result appears on the data bus and is copied into the memory buffer register (MBR). We also need to increment the PC by 1 to get ready for the next instruction. Because these two actions (read word from memory, add 1 to PC) do not interfere with each other, we can do them simultaneously to save time. The third step is to move the contents of the MBR to the instruction register (IR). This frees up the MBR for use during a possible indirect cycle. Thus, the simple fetch cycle actually consists of three steps and four micro-operations. Each micro-operation involves the movement of data into or out of a register. So long as these movements do not interfere with one another, several of them can take place during one step, saving lime.

Symbolically, we can write this sequence of events as follows:

- *T1*: MAR <= (PC)

- *T2*: MBR <= Memory
- PC <= (PC) + 1
- *T3*: IR <= (MBR)

where 1 is the instruction length. We need to make several comments about this sequence. We assume that a clock is available for timing purposes and that it emits regularly spaced clock pulses. Each clock pulse defines a time unit. Thus, all time units are of equal duration. Each micro-operation can be performed within the time of a single time unit. The notation (t1, t2, t3) represents successive time units.

In words, we have,

- *First time unit*: Move contents of PC to MAR.
- *Second time unit*: Move contents of memory location specified by MAR to MBR.
- Increment by 1 the contents of the PC.
- Third time unit: Move contents of MBR to IR.

Note that the second and third micro-operations both take place during the second time unit. The third micro-operation could have been grouped with the fourth with out affecting the fetch operation:

- *T1*: MAR <= (PC)
- *T2*: MBR <= Memory
- *T3*: PC <= (PC) + 1
- IR <= (MBR)

  The groupings of micro-operations must follow two simple rules:

  - The proper sequence of events must be followed. Thus (MAR <= (PC)) must precede (MBR <= Memory) because the memory read operation makes use of the address in the MAR.
  - Conflicts must be avoided. One should not attempt to read to and write from the same register in one time unit, because the results would be unpredictable. For example, the micro-operations (MBR <= Memory) and (IR <= MBR) should not occur during the same time unit.

A final point worth noting is that one of the micro-operations involves an addi tion. To avoid duplication of circuitry, this addition could be performed by the ALU. The use of the ALU may involve additional micro-operations, depending on the functionality of the ALU and the organization of the processor.

THE INDIRECT CYCLE

Once an instruction is fetched, the next step is to fetch source operands. Continuing our simple example, let us assume a one-address instruction format, with direct and indirect addressing allowed. If the instruction specifies an indirect address, then an indirect cycle must precede the execute cycle.

The data flow includes the following micro-operations:

- *T1*: MAR <= (IR (Address))
- *T2*: MBR <= Memory
- *T3*: IR(Address) <= (MBR(Address))

The address field of the instruction is transferred to the MAR. This is then used to fetch the address of the operand. Finally, the address field of the IR is updated from the MBR, so that it now contains a direct rather than an indirect address. The IR is now in the same state as if indirect addressing had not been used, and it is ready for the execute cycle. We skip that cycle for a moment, to consider the interrupt cycle.

THE INTERRUPT CYCLE

At the completion of the execute cycle, a test is made to determine whether any enabled interrupts have occurred. If so, the interrupt cycle occurs. The nature of this cycle varies greatly from one machine to another.

We present a very simple sequence of events, we have,

- *T1*: MBR <= (PC)
- *T2*: MAR <= Save_Address
- PC <= Routine_Address
- *T3*: Memory <= (MBR)

In the first step, the contents of the PC are transferred to the MBR, so that they can be saved for return from the interrupt. Then the MAR is loaded with the address at which the contents of the PC are to be saved, and the PC is loaded with the address of the start of the interrupt-processing routine. These two actions may each be a single micro-operation.

However, because most processors provide multiple types and/or levels of interrupts, it may lake one or more additional micro-operations to obtain the save_address and the routine_address before they can be transferred to the MAR and PC, respectively. In any case, once this is done, the final step is to store the MBR, which contains the old value of the PC, into memory. The processor is now ready to begin the next instruction cycle.

THE EXECUTE CYCLE

The fetch, indirect, and interrupt cycles are simple and predictable. Each involves a small, fixed sequence of micro-operations and, in each ease, the same micro-opera tions are repealed each time around. This is not true of the execute cycle. For a machine with N different opcodes, there are N different sequences of micro-operations that can occur. Let us consider several hypothetical examples.

First, consider an add instruction: ADD R1, X which adds the contents of the location X to register Rl.

The following sequence of micro-operations might occur:

- *T1*: MAR <= (IR(address))
- *T2*: MBR <= Memory
- *T3*: Rl <= (Rl) + (MBR)

We begin with the IR containing the ADD instruction. In the first step, the address portion of the IR is loaded into the MAR. Then the referenced memory location is read. Finally, the contents of R1 and MBR are added by the ALU. Again, this is a simplified example. Additional micro-operations may be required to extract the register reference from the IR and perhaps to stage the ALU inputs or outputs in some intermediate registers.Let us look at two more complex examples.

A common instruction is increment and skip if zero: ISZ X

The content of location X is incremented by 1. If the result is 0, the next instruction is skipped.

A possible sequence of micro-operations is:

- *T1*: MAR <= (CR(address))
- *T2*: MBR <= Memory
- *T3*: MBR <= (MBR)-1
- *T4*: Memory <= (MBR)
- If ((MBR) = 0) then (PC <= (PC) + I)

The new feature introduced here is the conditional action. The PC is incremented if (MBR) = 0; this test and action can be implemented as one micro-operation. Note also that this micro-operation can be performed during the same time unit during which the updated value in MBR is stored back to memory. Finally, consider a subroutine call instruction.

As an example, consider a branch-and-save-address instruction:

BSA X

The address of the instruction that follows the BSA instruction is saved in location X, and execution continues al location X-l. The saved address will later be used for return. This is a straightforward technique for providing subroutine calls.

The following micro-operations suffice:

- *T1*: MAR <= (IR(address))
- MBR <= (PC)
- *T2*: PC <= (IR(address)) Memory <= (MBR)
- *T3*: PC <= (PC) + I

The address in the PC at the start of the instruction is the address of the next instruction in sequence. This is saved at the address designated in Ihe IK. The latter address is also incremented to provide the address of the instruction for the next instruction cycle.

THE INSTRUCTION CYCLE

We have seen that each phase of the instruction cycle can be decomposed into a sequence of elementary micro-operations. In our example, there is one sequence each for the fetch, indirect, and interrupt cycles, and, for the execute cycle, there is one sequence of micro-operations for each opcode. To complete the picture, we need to tie sequences of micro-operations together, and this is done in Figure below.

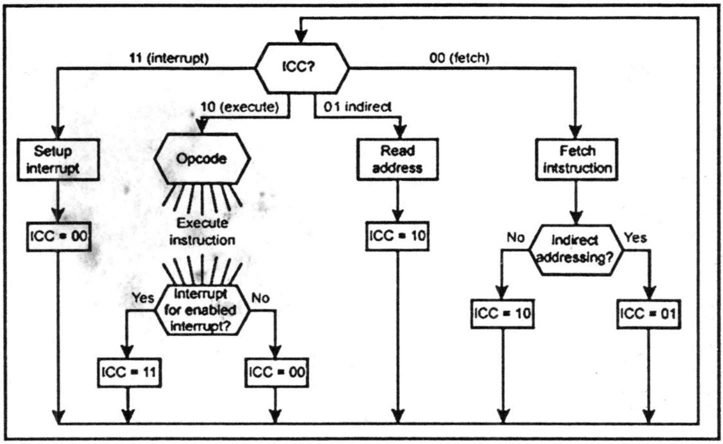

Fig. Flowchart for Instruction Cycle.

We assume a new 2-bit register called the instruction cycle code (ICC). The ICC designates the state of the processor in terms of which portion of the cycle it is in:

00: Fetch

01: Indirect

10: Execute

11: Interrupt

At the end of each of the four cycles, the ICC is set appropriately. The indirect cycle is always followed by the execute cycle. The interrupt cycle is always followed by the fetch cycle. For both the execute and fetch cycles, the next cycle depends on the state of the system.

Thus, the flowchart of Figure above defines the complete sequence of micro-operations, depending only on the instruction sequence and the interrupt pattern. Of course, this is a simplified example.

The flowchart for an actual processor would be more complex. In any case, we have reached the point in our discussion in which the operation of the processor is defined as the performance of a sequence of micro-operations. We can now consider how the control unit causes this sequence to occur.

CONTROL OF PROCESSOR

Functional Requirements

As a result of our analysis in the preceding section, we have decomposed the behaviour or functioning of the processor into elementary operations, called micro-operations. By reducing the operation of the processor to its most fundamental level, we are able to define exactly what it is that the control unit must cause to happen. Thus, we can define the functional requirements for the control unit those functions that the control unit must perform. A definition of these functional requirements is the basis for the design and implementation of the control unit.

With the information at hand, the following three-step process leads to a characterization of the control unit:

- Define the basic elements of the processor.
- Describe the micro-operations that the processor performs.
- Determine the functions that the control unit must perform to cause the micro-operations to be performed.

We have already performed steps 1 and 2. Let us summarize the results.

First, the basic functional elements of the processor are the following:

- ALU
- Registers
- Internal data paths
- External data paths
- Control unit

Some thought should convince you that this is a complete list. The ALU is the functional essence of the computer. Registers are used to stoic data internal to the processor. Some registers contain status information needed to manage instruction sequencing (*e.g.*, a programme status word). Others contain data that go to or come from the ALU, memory, and I/O modules. Internal data paths are used to move data between registers and between register and ALU. External data paths link registers to memory and I/O modules, often by means of a system bus. The control unit causes operations to happen within the processor. The execution of a programme consists of operations involving these processor elements. As we have seen, these operations consist of a sequence of micro-operations.

All micro-operations fall into one of the following categories:

- Transfer data from one register to another.
- Transfer data from a register to an external interface (*e.g.*, system bus).
- Transfer data from an external interface lo a register.
- Perform an arithmetic or logic operation, using registers for input and output.

All of the micro-operations needed to perform one instruction cycle, including all of the micro-operations to execute every instruction in the instruction set, fall into one of these categories. We can now be somewhat more explicit about the way in which the control unit functions.

The control unit performs two basic tasks:

- *Sequencing*: The control unit causes the processor lo step through a series of micro-operations in the proper sequence, based on the programme being executed.
- *Execution*: The control unit causes each micro-operation to be performed.

The preceding is a functional description of what the control unit does. The key to how the control unit operates is the use of control signals.

Control Signals

We have defined the elements that make up the processor (ALU, registers, data paths) and the micro-operations that are performed. For the control unit to perform its function, it must have inputs that allow it to determine the slate of the system and outputs that allow it to control the behaviour of the system. These are the exter nal specifications of the control unit. Internally, the control unit must have the logic required lo perform its sequencing and execution functions. Figure below is a general model of the control unit, showing all of its inputs and outputs.

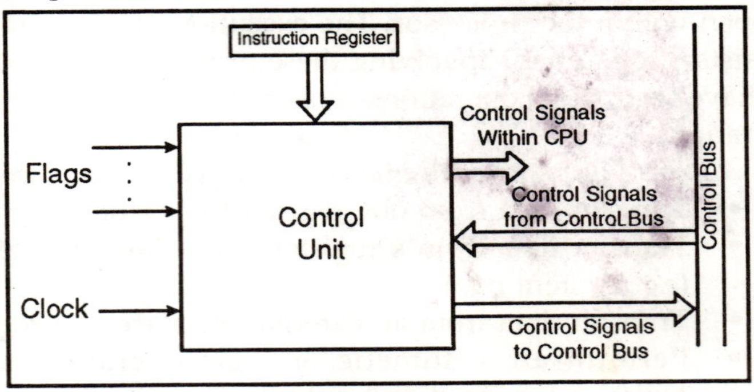

Fig. Model of Control Unit.

The inputs are as follows:

- *Clock*: This is how the control unit "keeps time." The control unit causes one micro-operation (or a set of simultaneous micro-operations) to be performed for each clock pulse. This is sometimes referred to as the processor cycle time. or the clock cycle lime.
- *Instruction register*: The opcode of the current instruction is used lo determine which micro-operations lo perform during the execute cycle.
- *Flags*: These are needed by the control unit to determine the status of the processor and the outcome of previous ALU operations. For example, for the increment-and-skip-if-zero (ISZ) instruction, the control until will increment the PC if the zero flag is set.
- *Control signals from control bus*: The control bus portion of the system bus pro-vides signals to the control unit, such as interrupt signals and acknowledgments.

The outputs are as follows:

- *Control signals within the processor*: These are two types: those that cause data to be moved from one register to another, and those that activate specific ALU functions.

- *Control signals to control bus*: These are also of two types: control signals lo memory, and control signals lo the I/O modules.

The new element that has been introduced in this figure is the control signal. Three types of control signals are used: those that activate an ALU function, those that activate a data path, and those that are signals on the external system bus or other external interface. All of these signals are ultimately applied directly as binary inputs lo individual logic gates.

Let us consider again the fetch cycle to see how the control unit maintains control. The control unit keeps track of where it is in the instruction cycle.

At a given point, it knows that the fetch cycle is to be performed next. The first step is to transfer the contents of the PC to the MAR.

The control unit does this by activating the control signal that opens the gates between the bits of the PC and the bits of the MAR. The next step is to read a word from memory into the MBR and increment the PC.

The control unit does this by sending the following control signals simultaneously:

- A control signal that opens gates, allowing the contents of the MAR onto the address bus
- A memory read control signal on the control bus
- A control signal that opens the gates, allowing the contents of the data bus to be stored in the MBR
- Control signals to logic that add 1 to the contents of the PC and store the result back to the PC

Following this, the control unit sends a control signal that opens gates between the MBR and the IR. This completes the fetch cycle except for one thing: The control unit must decide whether to perform an indirect cycle or an execute cycle next. To decide this, it examines the IR to see if an indirect memory reference is made.

The indirect and interrupt cycles work similarly. For the execute cycle, the control unit begins by examining the opcode and. on the basis of that, decides which sequence of micro-operations to perform for the execute cycle.

A Control Signals Example

To illustrate the functioning of the control unit, let us examine a simple example. Figure illustrates the example.

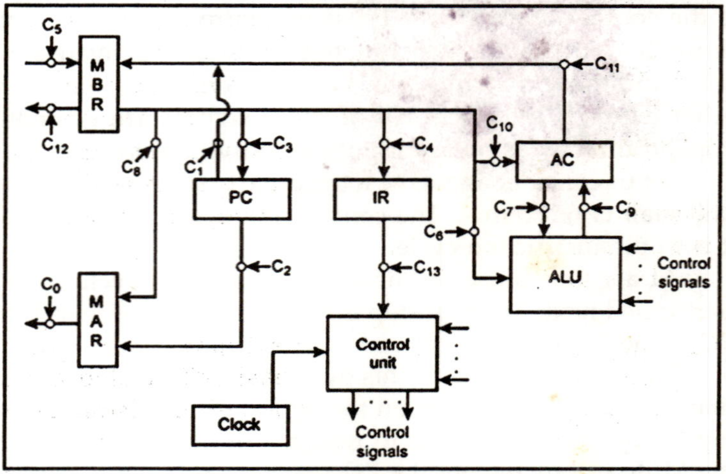

Fig. Data Paths and Control Signals.

This is a simple processor with a single accumulator. The data paths between elements are indicated. The control paths for signals emanating from the control unit are not shown, but the terminations of control signals are labeled Ci and indicated by a circle. The control unit receives inputs from the clock, the instruction register, and flags. With each clock cycle, the control unit reads all of its inputs and emits a set of control signals.

Control signals go to three separate destinations:

- *Data paths*: The control unit controls the internal How of data. For example, on instruction fetch, the contents of the memory buffer register are transferred to the instruction register. For each path to be controlled, there is a gate (indicated by a circle in the figure). A control signal from the control unit temporarily opens the gate to let data pass.
- *ALU*: The control unit controls the operation of the ALU by a set of control signals. These signals activate various logic devices and gates within the ALU.

- *System bus*: The control unit sends control signals out onto the control lines of the system bus (*e.g.*, memory READ).

The control unit must maintain knowledge of where it is in the instruction cycle. Using this knowledge, and by reading all of its inputs, the control unit emits a sequence of control signals that causes micro-operations to occur.

INTERNAL PROCESSOR ORGANIZATION

Figure below indicates the use of a variety of data paths. The complexity of this type of organization should be clear. More typically, some sort of internal bus arrangement. Using an internal processor bus, Figure can be rearranged as shown.

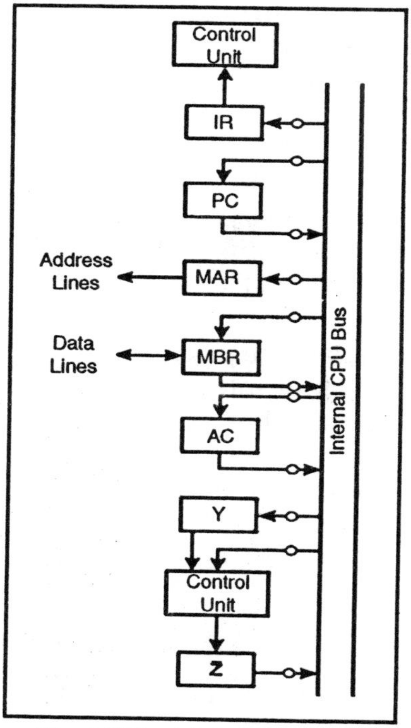

Fig. CPU with Internal Bus.

A single internal bus connects the ALU and all processor registers. Gates and control signals are provided for movement of data onto and off the bus from each register. Additional control signals control data transfer to and from the system (external) bus and the operation of the ALU.

Two new registers, labeled Y and Z have been added to the organization. These are needed for the proper operation of the ALU. When an operation involving two operands is performed, one can be obtained from the internal bus, but the other must be obtained from another source. The AC could be used for this purpose, but this limits the flexibility of the system and would not work with a processor with multiple general-purpose registers. Register Y provides temporary storage for the other input. The ALU is a combinatorial circuit with no internal storage, Thus, when control signals activate an ALU function, the input to the ALU is transformed to the output. Thus, the output of the ALU cannot be directly connected to the bus, because this output would feed back to the input. Register Z provides temporary output storage, with this arrangement, an operation to add a value from memory to the AC would have the following steps:

- *T1*: MAR <= (IR(address))
- *T2*: MBR <= Memory
- *T3*: Y <= (MBR)
- *T4*: Z <= (AC0 + (Y)
- *T5*: ac <= (z)

Other organizations are possible, but, in general, some sort of internal bus or set of internal buses is used. The use of common data paths simplifies the interconnection layout and the control of the processor. Another practical reason for the use of an internal bus is to save space. Especially for microprocessors, which may occupy only a 1/4-inch square piece of silicon, space occupied by internal connections must be minimized.

EXECUTION OF INSTRUCTION

MACHINE LEVEL EXECUTION CYCLE

After the fetch cycle has been completed, an instruction to be executed has been loaded into the control unit and the programme counter updated, and the execution cycle begins. Now, most computers store data in the memory but perform arithmetic on the contents of registers. Now, due to this, the computer functions that implement your typical programming language statement (for instance, a=b+c;), must move data from memory into registers, do the arithmetic, and then move the results back into the memory.

The actual sequence of instructions required to solve this simple arithmetic statement (a=b+c) varies from computer to computer. We will use one example that requires three instructions.

The first instruction has an opcode that specifies copying data from memory into a register in an operation called load. This instruction must indicate the memory location of the data, which we will call b, referring to second variable in our arithmetic operation.

Now, the next memory location that must be added to the number in the register and the result placed back into the register is specified by the second instruction. This instruction must also indicate the address of its data, c. The final instruction indicates that the results are to be copied from the register back into the memory in an operation called store. As with the other instructions, the address of the desired location, a, must be specified.

The table below shows what these instructions might look like in memory. In the example above, the variable b is located at the 26th decimal position in memory. Or, the address of b is 1A16. The address of c is at 1B16, and a is at 1C16. The example assumes that each instruction is two bytes. The first byte is the opcode and the second byte is an operand. Also, we assume that the instructions have been placed in memory starting at location 10016. All of this is naturally done in binary.

Memory:

Address	Contents
100:	load data
101:	1A16
102:	add data
103:	1B16
104:	store data
105:	1C16

The initial instruction fetch cycle begins with the programme pointer set to 10016 and ends with the instruction register holding the load data opcode and the programme counter incremented to 10116.During decoding of this instruction the control circuitry determines that a register is to be loaded from memory. The load opcode also specifies that the address of the data is indicated by the operand.

Before it can be copied into a register, the address of the data must be determined. The programme counter, which was updated at the end of the fetch cycle, contains the address of the operand.

The process of fetching the operand requires that the control unit do the following:

- Copy the contents of the programme counter to the memory address register.
- Issue a read request.
- Capture the operand in the memory buffer register.
- Increment the programme counter.

Remember that the data now in the MBR (Memory Buffer Register) is not the number to be placed in the register. It is, rather, the address of the number.

Using this address, the control unit can finally retrieve the data stored using the following sequence of operations:

- Send the contents of the memory buffer register back to the memory address register.
- Issue another read request.
- Capture the data in the memory buffer register.
- Tell the register to accept new data.
- Copy the data into a register.

The first instruction is officially completed once all of these steps are completed. The control unit returns to instruction fetch mode. The programme counter indicates that the next instruction is at 10216.

This address is copied to the memory address register and a read request is initiated. The instruction at 10216 (add data) is copied to the memory buffer register and ultimately into the instruction register. The fetch cycle ends with the programme counter updated to 10316.

During the execution of the add instruction, the control unit must fetch the operand and use it as an address, access the data, instruct the ALU to add the new data to the contents of the register, and store the results in the register. Fetch and execution of the add instruction causes the programme counter to be incremented to 10316 after the instruction fetch and 10416 after the operand fetch. The next instruction fetch cycle loads the store data instruction from location 10416 and increments the programme counter to 10516.

The first steps of the store instruction are similar to those already examined. The operand is accessed and sent to the memory address register. Control then causes the contents of the accumulator to be moved to the memory buffer register and then issues a write command to memory. Finally, the contents of the memory buffer register are stored at the address indicated by the memory address register. Once the store operation is complete, the control unit fetches the next instruction. What happens at that point depends on the contents of location 10616.

HARDWIRE AND MICROPROGRAMMED CONTROL

INTRODUCTION

For too many students of computer science, the level of understanding of how digital computers really execute programmes never quite makes it beyond that of "black magic." Many of them know what the basic parts of the computer are and what kinds of actions occur in each. But, in too many cases, they cannot put it all together and formulate a clear "big picture" of what is really going on inside the machine. In this article we present a simple computer architecture and describe in detail two alternative ways in which its control section may be organized.

THE BASIC COMPUTER

Every student of computer science knows that all traditional digital computers have two principal functional parts: the data path section in which processing occurs and the control section which is responsible for decoding instructions and leaving the correct sequence of control signals to make the processing happen in the data path.. Basically there are two types of control units: hard-wired controllers and micro-programmed controllers. In order to appreciate the difference and see how computers really work, we present a very simple computer. A block diagram of its data path sections is shown in Figure below:

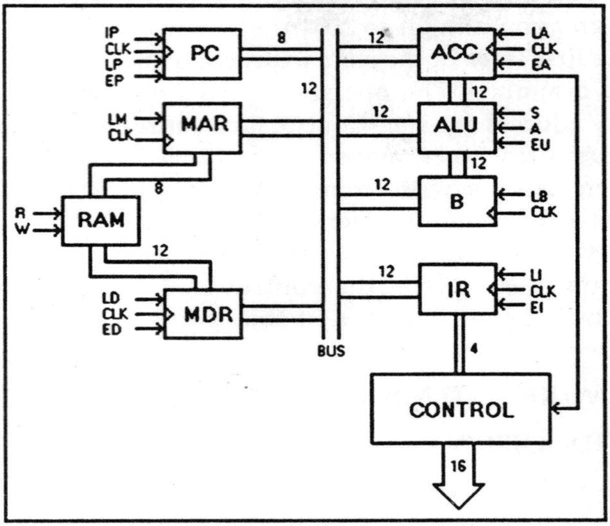

A single 12-bit-wide bus provides for exchange of information between pairs of registers within the data path section. The registers and the 256 × 12 bit RAM memory are controlled by 16 control signals. Most of the registers have Load (L) and Enabled (E) signals. An active L signal to a register causes the contents of the bus to be clocked into that register on the next rising pulse from the system clock. An active E signal enables the tristate outputs of the register, thereby making its contents available to the bus. Therefore, a register transfer from, for example, register A to register B would require active EA and LB control signals.

Processing of data is done by the Arithmetic-Logic-Unit (ALU), a circuit that is capable of adding or subtracting the 12-bit numbers contained in its two input registers: the accumulator (ACC) and register B. The operation performed by the ALU is selected by the Add (A) or Subtract (S) control signals. The accumulator also contains a single flip-flop that is set whenever its contents are negative (*i.e.,* whenever the leading bit is set—meaning a negative 2's complement number). The value of this "negative flag" provides input to the controller/sequencer, and, as we shall see, permits implementation of conditional branching instructions.

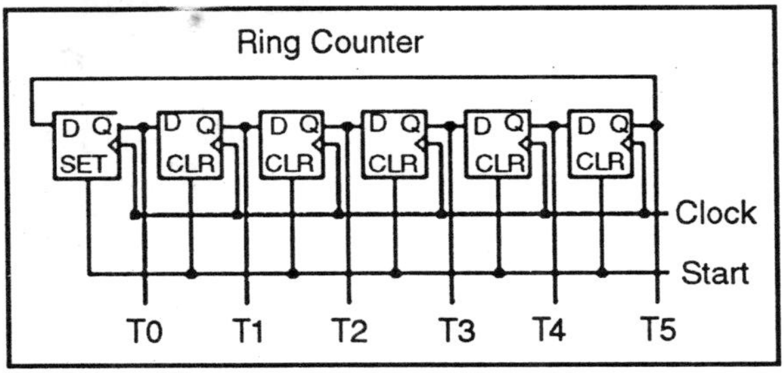

The machine's RAM memory is accessed by first placing the 8-bit address in the Memory Address Register (MAR). An active Read (R) control signal to the RAM will then cause the selected word from the RAM to appear in the Memory Data Register (MDR). An active Write (W) signal, on the other hand, will cause the word contained in the MDR to be stored in the RAM at the address specified by the MAR. Since there are no input or output ports in this simple computer, all I/O is memory mapped. In other words, several memory locations are reserved for input/output devices. Memory reads from any of those locations will cause data from the corresponding input device to appear in the MDR; memory writes to them will cause data in the MDR to be sent to the corresponding output device. A word stored in any given memory location may be data to be manipulated by the computer or a coded instruction that specifies an action to be taken.

The data path section also contains a Programme Counter (PC) whose function it is to point to the address in RAM of the next instruction to be executed. The Increment Programme Counter (IP) control signal causes the contents of the PC to increase by one. Since, as we shall see, instructions on this machine are one word long, this provides a simple mechanism for sequential instruction execution. In addition there is an Instruction Register (IR) which holds the instruction that is about to be execute and provides its opcode to the controller/ sequencer.

THE COMPUTER'S INSTRUCTION SET

An instruction on our simple computer consists of one 12-bit word. The leading four bits form the operation code (opcode) which specifies the action to be taken, and the remaining 8 bits, when used, indicate the memory address of one of the instruction's operands. For those instructions that have two operands, the other operand is always contained within the accumulator.

Hard-Wired Control Unit

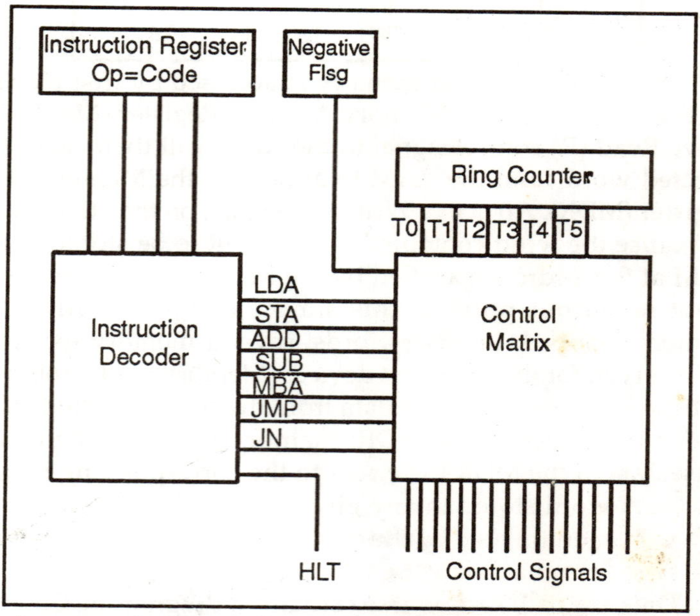

Input to the controller consists of the 4-bit opcode of the instruction currently contained in the Instruction Register and the negative flag from the accumulator. The controller's output is a set of 16 control signals that go out to the various registers and to the memory of the computer, in addition to a HLT signal that is activated whenever the leading bit of the op-code is one. The controller is composed of the following functional units: A ring counter, an instruction decoder, and a control matrix.

The ring counter provides a sequence of six consecutive active signals that cycle continuously. Synchronized by the system clock, the ring counter first activates its T0 line, then its T1 line, and so forth. After T5 is active, the sequence begins again with T0. The instruction decoder takes its four-bit input from the op-code field of the instruction register and activates one and only one of its 8 output lines. Each line corresponds to one of the instructions in the computer's instruction set. Figure shows the internal organization of this decoder.

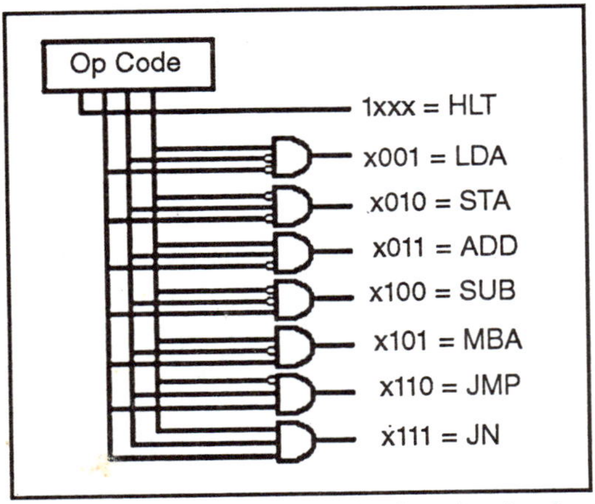

The most important part of the hard-wired controller is the control matrix. It receives input from the ring counter and the instruction decoder and provides the proper sequence of control signals. To understand how this diagram was obtained, we must look carefully at the machine's instruction set. The various control signals are placed horizontally along the top of the table. Entries into the table consist of the moments (ring counter pulses T0, T1, T2, T3, T4, or T5) at which each control signal must be active in order to have the instruction executed. For example, the Fetch operation has the EP and LM control signals active at ring count 1, and ED, LI, and IPC active at ring count 2. Therefore the first row (Fetch) of Table 2 has T0 entered below EP and LM, T1 below R, and T2 below IP, ED, and LI.

For each an AND operation is performed between any active ring counter (Ti) signals that were entered into the signal's column and the corresponding instruction contained in the far left-hand column.

If a column has more than one entry, the output of the ANDs are ORed together to produce the final control signal. For example, the LM column has the following entries: T0 (Fetch), T3 associated with the LDA instruction, and T3 associated with the STA instruction. Therefore, the logic for this signal is:

LM = T0 + T3*LDA + T3*STA

This means that control signal LM will be activated whenever any of the following conditions is satisfied:

- Ring pulse T0 (first step of an instruction fetch) is active, or
- An LDA instruction is in the IR and the ring counter is issuing pulse 3, or
- And STA instruction is in the IR and the ring counter is issuing pulse 3.

The entries in the JN (Jump Negative) row of this table require some further explanation. The LP and EI signals are active during T3 for this instruction if and only if the accumulator's negative flag has been set. Therefore the entries that appear above these signals for the JN instruction are T3*NF, meaning that the state of the negative flag must be ANDed in for the LP and EI control signals.

Figure as shown belowgives the logical equations required for each of the control signals used on our machine. These equations have been read from Table, as explained above. The circuit diagram of the control matrix is constructed directly from these equations.

- IP = T2
- W = T5*STA
- LP = T3*JMP + T3*NF*JN
- LD = T4*STA
- LA = T5*LDA + T4*ADD + T4*SUB

- EA = T4*STA + T3*MBA
- EP = T0
- S = T3*SUB
- A = T3*ADD
- LI = T2
- LM = T0 + T3*LDA + T3*STA
- ED = T2 + T5*LDA
- R = T1 + T4*LDA
- EU = T3*ADD+T3*SUB
- EI = T3*LDA + T3*STA + T3*JMP + T3*NF*JN
- LB = T3*MBA

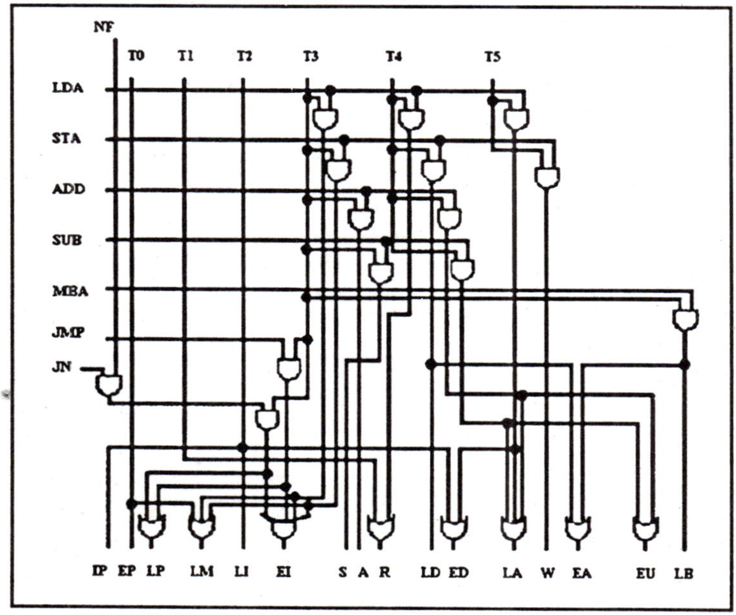

Fig. The Logical Equations Required for Each of the Hardwired Control Signals on the Basic Computer.

The machine's control matrix is designed from these equations. It should be noticed that the HLT line from the instruction decoder does not enter the control matrix, Instead this signal goes directly to circuitry (not shown) that will stop the clock and thus terminate execution.

Micro-programmed Control Unit

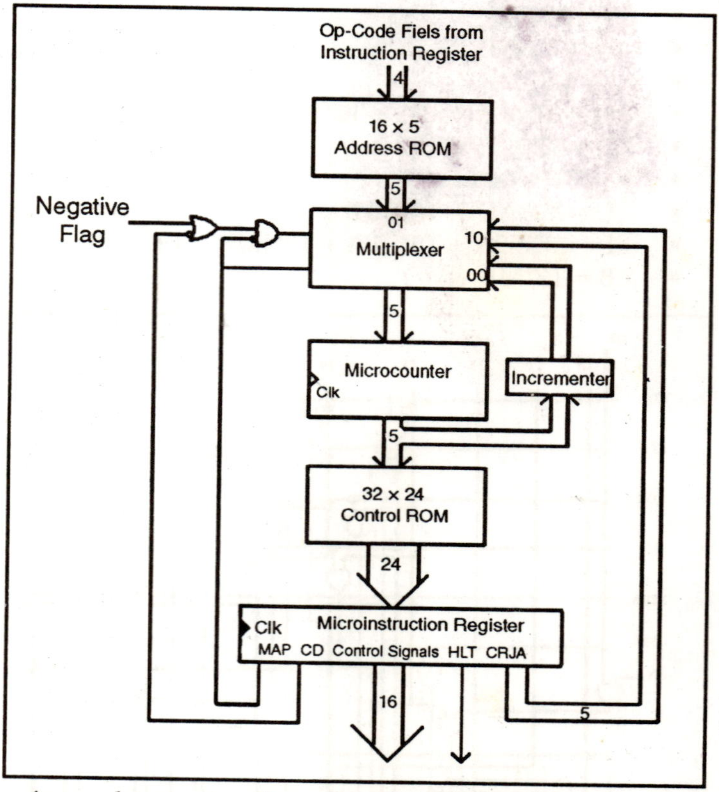

As we have seen, the controller causes instructions to be executed by issuing a specific set of control signals at each beat of the system clock. Each set of control signals issued causes one basic operation (micro-operation), such as a register transfer, to occur within the data path section of the computer. In the case of a hard-wired control unit the control matrix is responsible for sending out the required sequence of signals.

An alternative way of generating the control signals is that of micro-programmed control. In order to understand this method it is convenient to think of sets of control signals that cause specific micro-operations to occur as being "microinstructions" that could be stored in a memory. Each bit of a microinstruction might correspond to one control signal. If the bit is set it means that the control signal will be active; if cleared the signal will be inactive. Sequences of microinstructions could be stored in an internal "control" memory.

Execution of a machine language instruction could then be caused by fetching the proper sequence of microinstructions from the control memory and sending them out to the data path section of the computer. A sequence of microinstructions that implements an instruction on the external computer is known as a micro-routine. The instruction set of the computer is thus determined by the set of micro-routines, the "microprogram," stored in the controller's memory. The control unit of a microprogram-controlled computer is essentially a computer within a computer.

The heart of the controller is the control 32 × 24 ROM memory in which upt to 32 24-bit long microinstructions can be stored. Each is composed of two main fields: a 16-bit wide control signal field and an 8-bit wide next-address field. Each bit in the control signal field corresponds to one of the control signals discussed above. The next-address field contains bits that determine the address of the next microinstruction to be fetched from the control ROM. We shall see the details of how these bits work shortly.

Words selected from the control ROM feed the microinstruction register. This 24-bit wide register is analogous to the outer machine's instruction register. Specifically, the leading 16 bits (the control-signal field) of the microinstruction register are connected to the control-signal lines that go to the various components of the external machine's data path section.

Addresses provided to the control ROM come from a micro-counter register, which is analogous to the external machine's programme counter.

The micro-counter, in turn, receives its input from a multiplexer which selects from:

- The output of an address ROM,
- A current-address incrementer, or

- The address stored in the next-address field of the current microinstruction. The logic that selects one of these three alternatives will be explained shortly.

The controller's address ROM is fed by the outer computer's instruction register. The address ROM maps the op-code of the instruction currently contained in the op-code field of the instruction register to the starting address of the corresponding microroutine in the control ROM. Address zero of the address ROM contains the control-ROM address of the fetch routine; each other addresses in the address-ROM corresponds to one of the op-codes of the computer's instruction set. Table 3 shows the contents of the address ROM for the instruction set of our simple computer. To see how the address ROM works, let us assume that an ADD instruction has been fetched into the outer computer's instruction register. Since the op-code of the ADD instruction is 3, the number stored at location 3 of the address ROM (a 9) is the starting address in the control ROM of the microroutine that implements the ADD instruction.

The 5-bit CRJA (Control ROM Jump Address) sub-field holds a microinstruction address. Thus, the address of the next microinstruction may be obtained from the current microinstruction. This permits branching to other sections within the microprogram. The combination of the MAP bit, the CD (condition) bit, and the negative flag from the accumulator of the external machine provide input to the logic that feeds the select lines of the multiplexer and thereby determine how the address of the next microinstruction will be obtained.

If the MAP bit is one, the logic attached to the multiplexer's select lines produces a 01 which selects the address ROM. Therefore, the address of the micro-routine corresponding to the instruction in the outer machine's instruction register will be channeled to the control ROM. It should be clear that the MAP bit must be set in the last microinstruction of the "fetch" micro-routine, since it is at that moment that we want the newly-fetched instruction to be executed.

If the MAP bit is zero and the CD bit is zero, (unconditional branch), the multiplexer logic produces a 10, which selects the CRJA field of the current instruction. Therefore, the next instruction will come from the address contained in the current instruction's next-address field. With MAP=0 and CD=1 (conditional branch), the logic that feeds the multiplexer will produce either a 00 or a 10, depending on the value of the negative flag.

If the flag is set, it is a 10, which selects the jump address contained in the current microinstruction. If the negative flag is cleared, the select lines to the multiplexer receive a 00, which causes the incrementer to be selected. The next microinstruction will come from the next address in sequence.

It should be noticed that with this scheme, if we are not doing branching, the CRJA field should contain the address of the next microinstruction and the CD bit should be cleared. This will cause "branch to the next microinstruction" to occur. The one exception to this rule is the case of the last microinstruction within a micro-routine. Normally we would then want to branch back to the "fetch" micro-routine. Since this routine starts at control-ROM location 00000, that address should be contained in the CRJA field and CD should be 0.

The HLT bit is used to terminate execution. If it is set, the clock that synchronizes activities within the entire machine is stopped. Notice that the micro-counter is triggered by a rising clock edge, and the microinstruction register by a falling edge. Thus, we see that on each positive edge, the micro-counter receives the address of the microinstruction and presents it to the control ROM, which has until the next negative edge to output the addressed control word to the microinstruction register.

Since all operation in the data path section are positive-edge triggered, there is adequate time for the signals specified in the control word contained in the microinstruction register to go out to all sections of the external machine. The sequence of latching the address of microinstruction i+1 into the micro-counter while microinstruction i executes (positive edge) and then presenting the control word of microinstruction i+1 to the microinstruction register (negative edge) continues until a set HLT bit stops the clock.

Table 4 shows a microprogram which, when loaded into the control ROM, will implement the instruction set of the computer we have been describing. For each microinstruction, the control ROM address has been expressed in hexadecimal, and the contents in binary.

The order of the bits in the control signal field is the same as that shown in table 2: IP, LP, EP, LM, R, W, LD, ED, LI, EI, LA, EA, A, S, EU, LB, reading from left to right. The last four columns of table 4 express the status of the CD, MAP, and HLT bits, and the Control ROM Jump Address, expressed in hexadecimal. In order to clarify how the microprogram works, a description is now given of the "fetch" and JN (jump on negative) micro-routines.

The "fetch" micro-routine occupies control ROM addresses 0, 1, and 2. The active EP and LM control-signal bits in its first microinstruction cause a register transfer from the programme counter to the memory address register to occur. The MAR will now contain the address in RAM of the next instruction. Since CD and MAP are both zero (unconditional branch), the next microinstruction will come from the address stored in the CRJA field (01) — the next consecutive location. The microinstruction stored at that location has only the R bit active. Thus, the word stored in the memory location being accessed by the MAR (presumably the next instruction) will be gated to the Memory Data Register (MDR). The zeroes in CD and MAP again cause the microinstruction to be fetched from the address specified in the CRJA field, (02).

Active control signal bits for that microinstruction are ED, LI, and IP. The first two transfer the word in the MDR to the Instruction Register, and the last increments the programme counter. The new instruction is safely in the IR, and the PC is pointing to the next instruction in sequence. We have completed an instruction fetch. Since the MAP field in the last microinstruction of this "fetch" micro-routine is equal to 1, the address of the next microinstruction is determined by the address ROM, which, in turn, depends upon the opcode of

- the instruction that has just been loaded into the instruction register

When the JN instruction is executed, control is supposed to be transferred to the address specified by the least significant eight bits of the number contained in the instruction register if the negative flag is set. If the negative flag is not set, execution should continue with the next instruction in sequence. Let us see how the micro-routine stored at control-ROM locations 0F, 10, and 11 implement this conditional jump. In the first microinstruction, none of the control signal bits is set. Thus, nothing will occur in the data path section of the computer.

However, the fact that the CD bit is set means that if the negative flag is set, the next microinstruction will be fetched from the control-ROM address specified in the CRJA field (11 in this case). The microinstruction stored at that location has the EI and LP control signal bits set. Thus, the contents of the instruction register (the least significant eight bits) will be transferred to the programme counter.

The zeroes stored in the CD and MAP bits cause the next microinstruction to be fetched from the address contained in the CRJA field—a 00 in this case. This is the start of the"fetch" micro-routine. Thus we see that if the negative flag is set, the JN micro-routine places the jump address in the programme counter and transfer to the fetch routine. When that fetch is performed, control will have been transferred to the jump address.

If, on the other hand, the negative flag is NOT SET when the JN micro-routine executes, then the set CD bit in its first microinstruction causes the current address stored in the micro-counter to be incremented. Thus, the next microinstruction would be fetched from location 10. That microinstruction also has no active control signals bits, but with CD=0 and CRJA=00, the next microinstruction will be the first one in the "fetch" routine.

MICRO-PROGRAMMED COMPUTERS

It should be mentioned that most computers today are

micro-programmed. The reason is basically one of flexibility. Once the control unit of a hard-wired computer is designed and built, it is virtually impossible to alter its architecture and instruction set.

In the case of a micro-programmed computer, however, we can change the computer's instruction set simply by altering the microprogram stored in its control memory. In fact, taking our basic computer as an example, we notice that its four-bit op-code permits up to 16 instructions. Therefore, we could add seven more instructions to the instruction set by simply expanding its microprogram. To do this with the hard-wired version of our computer would require a complete redesign of the controller circuit hardware.

Another advantage to using micro-programmed control is the fact that the task of designing the computer in the first place is simplified. The process of specifying the architecture and instruction set is now one of software (micro-programming) as opposed to hardware design. Nevertheless, for certain applications hard-wired computers are still used. If speed is a consideration, hard-wiring may be required since it is faster to have the hardware issue the required control signals than to have a "programme" do it.

HARDWIRED CONTROL

Hardwired control is a control mechanism to generate control signals by using appropriate finite state machine (FSM). Micro programmed control is a control mechanism to generate control signals by using a memory called control storage (CS), which contains the control signals. Although micro programmed control seems to be advantageous to CISC machines, since CISC requires systematic development of sophisticated control signals, there is no intrinsic difference between these 2 control mechanism.

The pair of "microinstruction-register" and "control storage address register" can be regarded as a "state register" for the hardwired control. Note that the control storage can be regarded as a kind of combinational logic circuit. We can assign any 0, 1 values to each output corresponding to each address, which can be regarded as the input for a combinational logic circuit. This is a truth table.

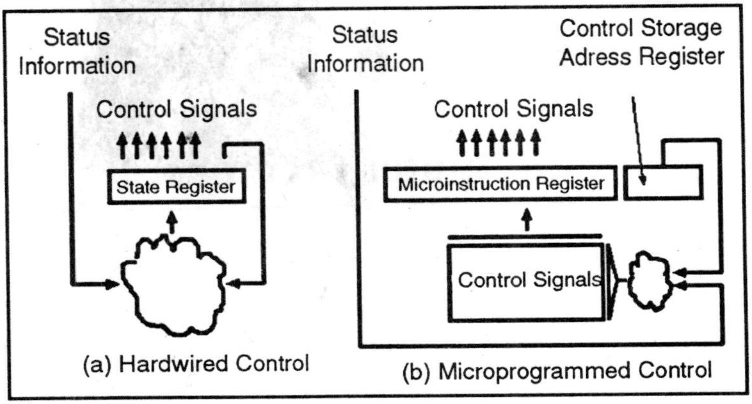

CISC also can be implemented by using hardwired control:

In the above sense, the microprogrammed control is not always necessary to implement CISC machines. Hardwired control also can be used for implementing sophisticated CISC machines. The bases of this opinion are as follows:

- The same field configuration (state assignment) can be used for both of these two types of control. This is clear because of the above identification.
- We can use any large FSM,which has horizontal microcode like state assignment, since the delay for the hardwired control logic (FSM) does not matter at all so long as it is less than or equal to the delay for the data-path, which includes adders, shifters and so on, since the control logic circuit works in parallel with the data-path.
- The horizontal microcode like state assignment has became very easy to be implemented because of the spread of the hardware description language(HDL)s. In Verilog HDL, 'define statements enable us to get perfect net-list for the large FSM in a very short time by using appropriate logic synthesizer.

6

Computer Memory

CONCEPT

MEMORY SYSTEM

Computer memory is used to store two things: i) instructions to execute a programme and ii) data. When the computer is doing any job, the data that have to be processed are stored in the primary memory. This data may come from an input device like keyboard or from a secondary storage device like a floppy disk.

As programme or the set of instructions is kept in primary memory, the computer is able to follow instantly the set of instructions. For example, when you book ticket from railway reservation counter, the computer has to follow the same steps: take the request, check the availability of seats, calculate fare, wait for money to be paid, store the reservation and get the ticket printed out. The programme containing these steps is kept in memory of the computer and is followed for each request.

But inside the computer, the steps followed are quite different from what we see on the monitor or screen. In computer's memory both programmes and data are stored in the binary form. You have already been introduced with decimal number system, that is the numbers 1 to 9 and 0. The binary system has only two values 0 and 1. These are called *bits*. As human beings we all understand decimal system but the computer can only understand binary system. It is because a large number of integrated circuits inside the computer can be considered as switches, which can be made ON, or OFF. If a switch is ON it is considered 1 and if it is OFF it is 0. A number of switches in different states will give you a message like this: 110101....10. So the computer takes input in the form of 0 and 1 and gives output in the form 0 and 1 only. Is it not absurd if the computer gives outputs as 0's and 1's only? But you do not have to worry about. Every number in binary system can be converted to decimal system and vice versa; for example, 1010 meaning decimal 10. Therefore it is the computer that takes information or data in decimal form from you, convert it in to binary form, process it producing output in binary form and again convert the output to decimal form.

The primary memory as you know in the computer is in the form of IC's (Integrated Circuits). These circuits are called Random Access Memory (RAM). Each of RAM's locations stores one *byte* of information. (One *byte* is equal to *8 bits*). A bit is an acronym for *binary digit,* which stands for one binary piece of information. This can be either 0 or 1. You will know more about RAM later. The Primary or internal storage section is made up of several small storage locations (ICs) called cells. Each of these cells can store a fixed number of bits called *word length.*

Each cell has a unique number assigned to it called the address of the cell and it is used to identify the cells. The address starts at 0 and goes up to (N-1). You should know that the memory is like a large cabinet containing as many drawers as there are addresses on memory. Each drawer contains a word and the address is written on outside of the drawer.

CAPACITY OF PRIMARY MEMORY

The capacity is defined in terms of byte or words. Thus 64 kilobyte (KB) memory is capable of storing 64 × 1024 = 32,768 bytes. (1 kilobyte is 1024 bytes). A memory size ranges from few kilobytes in small systems to several thousand kilobytes in large mainframe and super computer. In your personal computer you will find memory capacity in the range of 64 KB, 4 MB, 8 MB and even 16 MB (MB = Million bytes).

Random Access Memory (RAM)

RAM is perhaps the most important of the input/output devices. When we talk about computer memory, we are mainly talking about RAM. In this class, when we think about the banks of light switches that can be manipulated, we are thinking of RAM memory. The term Random Access is pretty unfortunate. There is nothing random about how memory is accessed.

The programme running will determine what is in memory. (of course, the programme itself is in memory too!) RAM can be read from by the CPU. This means that the CPU can 'look' at any address in RAM and get the contents of that address. It can also be written to by the CPU, meaning that the CPU can change the value of memory cells on the fly.

One VERY important aspect of RAM memory is that it requires power. RAM can only hold values while power is going through it. If the power is interrupted, the RAM will lose ALL the values in it. This is why it is so important to save your work frequently when working on a computer. RAM memory is volatile. When the room you are working on is hit by a tsunami and the power goes out of your computer, you lose everything that was in RAM.

The amount of RAM in your computer is obviously a pretty important factor. The more memory you have, the more 'room' there is in your computer for information and programmes. Modern programmes have gotten HUGE, and the kinds of information you can work with have gotten much larger. Some early home computers had 4 or 16 K of RAM. The original IBM PC had 640 K of RAM. In its day, this was thought of as an extravagant amount of memory that would never be fully used. Modern computers with less than 16 Megabytes (16,000 K) are considered a bit lame. (pun completely intended.) Older computers can be quite happy with much less RAM, but they will not be able to run the newer programmes.

If you are buying or upgrading a computer, you should seriously consider as much RAM as you can afford. There is probably no more cost-effective upgrade than RAM.

If you find that you need more memory, It is relatively cheap and easy to do a memory upgrade. Note that not all types of RAM are interchangeable. Look in the book that came with your computer for specifically which type of RAM you need when you are ready to upgrade.

Read Only Memory (ROM)

There is another memory in computer, which is called Read Only Memory (ROM). Again it is the ICs inside the PC that form the ROM. The storage of programme and data in the ROM is permanent. The ROM stores some standard processing programmes supplied by the manufacturers to operate the personal computer. The ROM can only be read by the CPU but it cannot be changed. The basic input/output programme is stored in the ROM that examines and initializes various equipment attached to the PC when the switch is made ON. The memories, which do not loose their content on failure of power supply, are known as non-volatile memories. ROM is non-volatile memory.

Memory is like the banks of switches we have been thinking about that simply contain 1/0 binary patterns. Read Only Memory (abbreviated ROM) is a special kind of memory that cannot be changed. The most basic instructions for the CPU are built in to the ROM at the factory. To the end user, there really is very little to worry about regarding ROM. The amount of ROM in your computer doesn't really matter to you. All your programmes and information will go into another kind of memory that we will learn about soon.

PROM

There is another type of primary memory in computer, which is called Programmable Read Only Memory (PROM). You know that it is not possible to modify or erase programmes stored in ROM, but it is possible for you to store your programme in PROM chip. Once the programmes are written it cannot be changed and remain intact even if power is switched off. Therefore programmes or instructions written in PROM or ROM cannot be erased or changed.

EPROM

This stands for Erasable Programmable Read Only Memory, which over come the problem of PROM and ROM. EPROM chip can be programmed time and again by erasing the information stored earlier in it. Information stored in EPROM exposing the chip for some time ultraviolet light and it erases chip is reprogrammed using a special programming facility. When the EPROM is in use information can only be read.

Cache Memory

The speed of CPU is extremely high compared to the access time of main memory. Therefore the performance of CPU decreases due to the slow speed of main memory. To decrease the mismatch in operating speed, a small memory chip is attached between CPU and Main memory whose access time is very close to the processing speed of CPU.

It is called CACHE memory. CACHE memories are accessed much faster than conventional RAM. It is used to store programmes or data currently being executed or temporary data frequently used by the CPU. So each memory makes main memory to be faster and larger than it really is. It is also very expensive to have bigger size of cache memory and its size is normally kept small.

Registers

The CPU processes data and instructions with high speed, there is also movement of data between various units of computer. It is necessary to transfer the processed data with high speed. So the computer uses a number of special memory units called *registers*.

They are not part of the main memory but they store data or information temporarily and pass it on as directed by the control unit.

HIERARCHICAL MEMORY STRUCTURE

We have three levels of partition based on which we base our hierarchy.

- Registers internal to the CPU for temporary data storage-these are small in number but are really very fast and are costliest.
- External storage for data and programmes-these are relatively large in number, fast and a little cheaper.
- External permanent storage-these are much larger cheaper and really slower as compared to rest of the two.

Since we need to send data from the magnetic disks to the disk cache and then to the main memory and finally to the cache which is located near to the CPU and also to the registers inside the CPU.

The memory references made by the processor, for both instructions and data, tend to cluster together as the ones for the instruction loops and subroutines cluster together and the ones for data array and tables cluster together.

These clusters are kept in high speed memory to reduce the average delay in accessing data. The clusters being referenced will change as the memory management module of the OS will deal with it.

Characteristics of the Hierarchy

The basic characteristics of the memory hierarchy are:

- This consists of distinct levels of memory components as the primary, secondary or tertiary memory units.
- Each level characterizes itself by its size, access time and cost per bit which help in differentiating the elements in a hierarchical fashion.
- Each higher level in the hierarchy consists of modules of larger capacity, slower access time and lower cost per bit as depicted in the figure.

INTERNAL MEMORY/MAIN MEMORY/RAM

RAM: Random Access Memory

It is a semiconductor memory which is both readable and writable. RAM is volatile in nature and thus is mainly temporary in nature. RAM can be categorized in static and dynamic form.

- *Dynamic RAM*: Storage cell is essentially a transistor which acts as a capacitor. The charge in it dissipates over time and thus often flips to zero and thus needs to be refreshed periodically. The construction is simple and hence is less expensive. An extra refresh circuitary is essential. The main drawback is that it is slower. The address lines are active when bits are read or written.

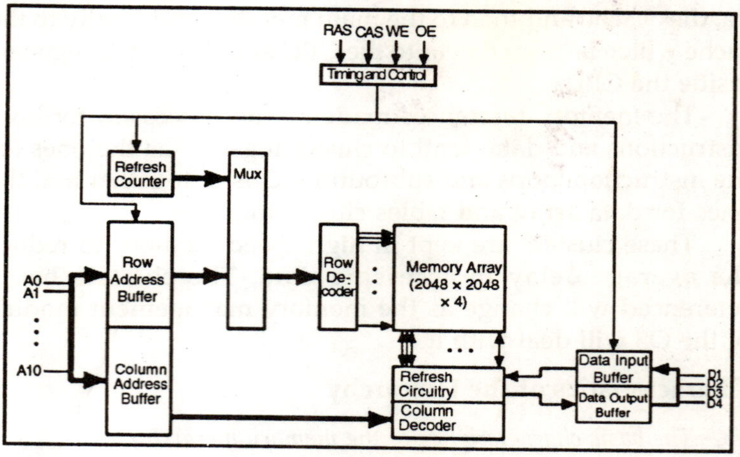

Fig. 16 Mb DRAM using (4M × 4).

- *Static RAM*: These are basically an array of flip-flop storage cells those use five to ten times more transistors than similar dynamic cell. So the packaging density is ten times lower. This RAM is although faster than a dynamic cell.

ROM: Read only Memory

It is semiconductor memory which is only readable. It is used for permanent storage and is non-volatile in nature. It is mainly used to store the library routines, system programmes(BIOS), function tables etc. The data is stored as a hard wired system during fabrication at the chip manufacturer's point. These are generally purchased in groups of 10K or more but are very expensive for small runs.

Proms

Programmable read only memory is used when the data is written once by the user employing a PROM programming device. It is useful for small production runs.

Eprom

Erasable programmable read only memory has a similar programming as that of a PROM. This is generally erased by exposing to UV light.

Eeprom

Electrically erasable programmable read only memory is generally written to many times while remaining in a system. This doesnt have to be erased first. Each individual bytes can be programmed. The writting requires several hundred microsecond per byte. This is generally used in systems for development, personalization and other tasks requiring unique information to be stored.

Flash memory -This is similar to an EEPROM in using electrical erasing of data. The erasing is really fast and is done in blocks. The density is higher than EEPROM.

Cache Memory

It is the most critical component of the memory hierarchy. Cache means a safe place for hiding or storing things. The idea behind using a cache as the first level of the memory hierarchy is to keep the information expected to be used more frequently by the CPU in the cache. Thus in cache, a small portion of the main memory is actively stored. Thus when the processor sought for a memory reference, it tries to find in the cache.

Compared to the main memory, cache is relatively small. It operates near to the speed of the processor. It is although very expensive as compared to the main memory. If we assume that an access to main memory causes a block of K words to be transfered to the cache.

The block transferred from the main memory is stored in the cache as a single unit called a slot, line or a page. Once it is copied to the cache, individual words within a line can be accessed by the CPU. Due to the high speed involved in the cache, management of the data transfer and storage in the cache is done in hardware and hence the OS has no dealings with it.

Every line of data in the cache must be tagged in some way to identify what main memory block it is and thus the line of data and its tag are stored in the cache.

Factors for Designing of the Cache

- Mapping function between the main memory and the cache.
- Line replacement algorithm used.
- Various write policies (Write back, write update, write through)
- Block size.
- Number and type of caches.

Mapping Functions used in Cache

Direct Mapping

Each main memory block is assigned to a specific line in the cache. We use the function as given below-

i=j modulo C
i-line number assigned
j-main memory block
C-number of lines in cache.

This treats main memory address as 3 distinct fields namely tag identifier, Line number identifier and Word identifier(offset).

Advantages with this techniques are:

- It is easy to implement
- Relatively inexpensive to implement
- Easy to determine where a main memory reference can be found in cache.

Disadvantages are:

- Each main memory block is mapped to a specific line
- Hit ratio can be low if the blocks are swapped in and out constantly

Associative Mapping

This technique lets a block to be stored in any cache line that is not in use. Thus it must examine each line in the cache to find the right block and line numbers(ids) have no meaning in the cache. The cache is implemented in two parts namely, the lines themselves in SRAM and the tag storage in associative memory. The associative memory search is performed for overall tags to find the desired line.

Advantages are:

- Fast
- Flexible

Disadvantages are:

- Implementation is costly

Set Associative Mapping

This is an implementation which takes up the best of both the previous implementations. This implementation divides cache into a number of sets(v), each set holding a number of lines(k). A main memory block can be stored in any one of the k lines in a set such that set number = j modulo v. If a set can hold X lines, the cache is referred to as an X-way set associative cache.

EXTERNAL MEMORY

Magnetic Disks

A hard drive is a special disk that is usually mounted permanently inside your computer's cabinet. You rarely see the hard drive, and almost never take it out. Hard drives are made of different material than floppies, and they are physically hard (although if you touched the actual hard surface, you would destroy it!) They spin much more quickly than floppies, and require much more precision. They are sealed inside a special case, and that is sealed inside the computer case. A hard drive has a much larger capacity than a floppy, and is much faster at saving and retrieving information. Modern computers frequently have hard drives with 500 MB or more of capacity. As this capacity grows, people are beginning to measure it in terms of gigabytes. Software programmes are always becoming larger and taking more room on hard drives. It never takes long to completely fill up the capacity of a drive.

SECONDARY STORAGE

These high-speed storage devices are very expensive and hence the cost per bit of storage is also very high. Again the storage capacity of the main memory is also very limited. Often it is necessary to store hundreds of millions of bytes of data for the CPU to process. Therefore additional memory is required in all the computer systems. This memory is called *auxiliary memory* or *secondary storage.*

In this type of memory the cost per bit of storage is low. However, the operating speed is slower than that of the primary storage. Huge volume of data are stored here on permanent basis and transferred to the primary storage as and when required. Most widely used secondary storage devices are *magnetic tapes* and*magnetic disk.*

Magnetic Tape

Magnetic tapes are used for large computers like mainframe computers where large volume of data is stored for a longer time. In PC also you can use tapes in the form of cassettes. The cost of storing data in tapes is inexpensive. Tapes consist of magnetic materials that store data permanently. It can be 12.5 mm to 25 mm wide plastic film-type and 500 meter to 1200 meter long which is coated with magnetic material. The deck is connected to the central processor and information is fed into or read from the tape through the processor. It similar to cassette tape recorder.

Advantages of magnetic tape:

- *Compact*: A 10-inch diameter reel of tape is 2400 feet long and is able to hold 800, 1600 or 6250 characters in each inch of its length. The maximum capacity of such tape is 180 million characters. Thus data are stored much more compactly on tape.

- *Economical*: The cost of storing characters is very less as compared to other storage devices.
- *Fast*: Copying of data is easier and fast.
- *Long term storage and re-usability*: Magnetic tapes can be used for long term storage and a tape can be used repeatedly with out loss of data.

Magnetic Disk

You might have seen the gramophone record, which is circular like a disk and coated with magnetic material. Magnetic disks used in computer are made on the same principle. It rotates with very high speed inside the computer drive. Data is stored on both the surface of the disk.

Magnetic disks are most popular for *direct access* storage device. Each disk consists of a number of invisible *concentric circles* called *tracks*. Information is recorded on tracks of a disk surface in the form of tiny magnetic spots.

The presence of a magnetic spot represents *one bit* and its absence represents zero bit. The information stored in a disk can be read many times without affecting the stored data. So the reading operation is non-destructive. But if you want to write a new data, then the existing data is erased from the disk and new data is recorded.

Disk drives are special devices that allow us to make copies of parts of RAM and store them magnetically. If RAM memory is electronic, think of disk drives as a special kind of magnetic memory. When you save something to a disk, the electronic impulses in RAM are copied and stored to the disk as a series of magnetic impulses. All a disk drive does is translate electronic impulses and magnetic impulses back and forth.

Disk drives are handy because magnetic impulses are more permanent than electronic ones. The disk drive does not require electricity to keep values in memory, so if you store something to a disk, the information will be there when the tidal wave knocks the power out to your computer. (Assuming, of course, that the disk stayed dry and clean) Disks are sometimes thought of as secondary storage for this reason.

Floppy Disk

It is similar to magnetic disk discussed above. They are 5.25 inch or 3.5 inch in diameter. They come in single or double density and recorded on one or both surface of the diskette. The capacity of a 5.25-inch floppy is 1.2 mega bytes whereas for 3.5 inch floppy it is 1.44 mega bytes. It is cheaper than any other storage devices and is portable. The floppy is a low cost device particularly suitable for personal computer system.

A floppy drive is a machine that is designed to read floppy disks. Floppy disks are the removable devices that you stick in slots in the front of the machine. Floppy disks come in hard plastic cases to make them a little more sturdy and easier to handle, but inside the plastic case, there is an actual disk. It is made of a plastic-like substance called mylar which really is floppy. Floppy disks come in two main sizes; 5 1/4 inch, and 3 1/2 inch. The 5 1/4 disks are becoming obsolete, but you still see them from time to time. The 3 1/2 inch disks, although physically smaller, can usually hold more information!

There are different flavours of floppy disks. In a modern computer, the only kind of floppy you need to purchase is High Density 1.44 MB.

Optical Disk

With every new application and software there is greater demand for memory capacity. It is the necessity to store large volume of data that has led to the development of optical disk storage medium.

Optical disks can be divided into the following categories:

- *Compact disk/Read only memory (CD-ROM)*: CD-ROM disks are made of reflective metals. CD-ROM is written during the process of manufacturing by high power *laser beam*. Here the storage density is very high, storage cost is very low and access time is relatively fast. Each disk is approximately 4 1/2 inches in diameter and can hold over 600 MB of data. As the CD-ROM can be *read only* we cannot write or make changes into the data contained in it.
- *Write once, read many (WORM)*: The inconvenience

that we can not write any thing in to a CD-ROM is avoided in WORM. A WORM allows the user to write data permanently on to the disk. Once the data is written it can never be erased without physically damaging the disk. Here data can be recorded from keyboard, video scanner, OCR equipment and other devices. The advantage of WORM is that it can store vast amount of data amounting to gigabytes (10^9bytes). Any document in a WORM can be accessed very fast, say less than 30 seconds.

- *Erasable Optical disk*: These are optical disks where data can be written, erased and re-written. This also applies a laser beam to write and re-write the data. These disks may be used as alternatives to traditional disks. Erasable optical disks are based on a technology known as *magnetic optical* (MO). To write a data bit on to the erasable optical disk the MO drive's laser beam heats a tiny, precisely defined point on the disk's surface and magnetises it.

Bibliography

Adams, James L.: *Conceptual Blockbusting: A Guide to Better Ideas*, NewJersey: Prentice Hall Publishing.2006.

Anderson, David R.: *An Introduction to Management Science*, New York: McGraw Hill, 2004.

Andrews, Dorine C.: *Business Reengineering*, NewJersey: Yourdon Press, 2001.

Babbie, E.: *The Practice of Social Research*, New York: John Wiley & Sons, 2007.

Bair, James H.: *The Office Systems Cycle*, Orlando: The Dryden Press, 2004.

Barcus, Sam W.: *Handbook of Management Consulting Services*, New York: McGraw-Hill, 2005.

Barton, F.: *A Primer on Simulation and Gaming*, New Jersey: Prentice Hall, 1997.

Buschmann, F.: *A System of Patterns: Pattern Oriented Software Architecture*, New York: John Wiley & Sons, 2007.

Coad, P.: *Object Oriented Analysis*, New York: Yourdon Press, 2004.

Donald, A.: *Organizational Learning: A Theory of Action Perspective*, NewJersey: Addison-Wesley Publishing, 2003.

John, M.: *Scenario-Based Design: Envisioning Work and Technology in System Development*, New York: John Wiley & Sons, 2005.

McInnis, R.: *Scott, Social Science Research Handbook*, New York: Barnes & Noble, 1999.

Perrow, C.: *Complex Organizations: A Critical Essay*, New York: McGraw-Hill, 2006.

Pidd, M.: *Computer Simulation in Management Science*, England: John Wiley & Sons, 2000.

Renaud, Paul E.: *Introduction to Client/Server Systems*, New York: John Wiley & Sons, 2004.

Richardson, George P.: *Introduction to System Dynamics Modeling with Dynamo*, Portland: Productivity Press, 2006.

Russell, L.: *The Art of Problem Solving*, New York: John Wiley & Sons, 2002.

Stephen, M.: *Essential Systems Analysis*, Englewood, Prentice Hall, 1998.

Stevens, R.: *Systems Engineering: Coping with Complexity*, London: Prentice Hall, 2001.

Turabin, K.: *A Manual for Writers of Term Papers*, Chicago: University of Chicago Press, 2002.

Wood, J.: *Joint Application Development*, New York: John Wiley and Sons, 2008.

Yourdon, E.: *Modern Structured Analysis*, Englewood: Yourdon Press, 2003.

Zikmund, W.: *Business Research Methods*, Orlando: The Dryden Press, 2004.

Index

A

Accelerated 12, 33
Accomplish 1, 4, 46, 144, 183
Acquisitions 33
Adders 125, 127, 130, 132, 164, 253
Algorithm 2, 3, 136, 137, 138, 139, 140, 141, 144, 148, 149, 262
Analogue 117, 118, 119

C

Cache 11, 258, 259, 261, 262, 263
Capabilities 15, 30, 42, 52, 70, 91, 103, 112, 117, 126, 178, 182, 213, 242, 267
Catalogs 105
Categorized 5, 76, 101, 117, 259
Certain 8, 14, 21, 49, 58, 70, 73, 87, 97, 104, 140, 141, 150, 178, 180, 252, 267
Consideration 163, 252
Cordless 26

D

DARPA 95, 96, 97, 98, 101, 102, 103
Dashboard 22
Defragment 22
Delays 70, 125, 126, 127, 128, 129, 130, 131
Description 8, 85, 152, 184, 191, 206, 231, 250, 253
Discussion 106, 146, 171, 177, 229
Distinguish 10, 173, 194, 197
Domain 66, 98, 99, 100, 102, 103, 104
Dozens 23

E

Effectively 6, 7, 39, 140
Efficient 4, 34, 47, 64, 79, 104, 112, 113, 152, 165, 192, 211
Embroidery 47, 48
EPROM 258
Eprom 261

F

Fanout 126
Fetch 158, 164, 165, 166, 171, 172, 173, 175, 176, 177, 186, 189, 201, 202, 203, 204, 212, 214, 215, 216, 218, 222, 223, 224,

225, 226, 227, 228, 229, 233, 234, 236, 238, 239, 243, 244, 248, 249, 250, 251
Fetching 172, 202, 203, 238, 247
Fingerprints 8
Forums 106
Fractions 122, 134

H

Hierarchy 7, 74, 87, 88, 258, 259, 261
Hybrid 5, 89

I

Implemented 2, 38, 127, 130, 138, 163, 174, 177, 199, 201, 215, 228, 253, 263
Inefficiencies 34
Infrared 27
Integrated 1, 2, 14, 45, 54, 67, 73, 107, 113, 118, 254, 255
Interrupt 161, 209, 210, 221, 222, 226, 227, 228, 229, 232, 233

J

Joystick 24, 25, 26

M

Macintoshes 28, 30
Mainframe 5, 62, 182, 255, 264
Manipulation 157, 159, 160, 201
Measuring 127
Microcode 176, 177, 178, 179, 180, 181, 253
Microinstruction 177, 178, 179, 247, 248, 249, 250, 251, 252
Modelling 2
Modules 12, 13, 15, 47, 67, 130, 195, 196, 207, 230, 231, 233, 259
Mortgage 41, 42, 47
Multiplying 132, 133, 134

N

Nanocode 181

P

Parallel 3, 4, 7, 10, 11, 12, 13, 16, 27, 100, 150, 151, 152, 162, 167, 168, 169, 179, 185, 253
Parallelism 2, 3
Peripherals 8, 11, 15, 16, 85
Persuasion 30
Pipelining 2, 162, 165
Prescribed 31
Propagate 129, 130, 131, 132, 153

Q

Quotes 22

R

Rambus 15
Relevant 34, 86, 110, 116, 195

S

Simulation 31, 127, 180
Simulator 25, 125
Simultaneously 5, 21, 101, 150, 151, 152, 162, 168, 179, 198,

202, 208, 224, 233
Slots 4, 10, 12, 14, 266
Sophisticated 36, 70, 169, 252, 253
Staggering 2
Symbolic 154, 213

T

Terminology 50, 118, 211
Topologies 70, 75, 76, 80, 86, 87, 88, 89

U

Unambiguous 140, 141
Unplugged 8

W

Widgets 22